IN THE
LEGIONS OF
NAPOLEON

THE NAPOLEONIC LIBRARY

Other books in the series include:

1815: THE RETURN OF NAPOLEON
Paul Britten Austin

ON THE FIELDS OF GLORY
The Battlefields of the 1815 Campaign
Andrew Uffindell and Michael Corum

LIFE IN NAPOLEON'S ARMY
The Memoirs of Captain Elzéar Blaze
Introduction by Philip Haythornthwaite

THE MEMOIRS OF BARON VON MÜFFLING
A Prussian Officer in the Napoleonic Wars
Baron von Müffling

WATERLOO LECTURES
A Study of the Campaign of 1815
Colonel Charles Chesney

WATERLOO LETTERS
A Collection of Accounts From Survivors of the
Campaign of 1815
Edited by Major-General H. T. Siborne

www.frontline-books.com/napoleoniclibrary

IN THE LEGIONS OF NAPOLEON

THE MEMOIRS OF A POLISH OFFICER IN SPAIN AND RUSSIA 1808–1813

Heinrich von Brandt

Translated and Edited by Jonathan North

Frontline Books

In the Legions of Napoleon

A Greenhill Book
First published in 1999 by Greenhill Books, Lionel Leventhal Limited
www.greenhillbooks.com

This edition published in 2017 by

Frontline Books
an imprint of Pen & Sword Books Ltd,
47 Church Street, Barnsley, S. Yorkshire, S70 2AS
For more information on our books, please visit
www.frontline-books.com, email info@frontline-books.com
or write to us at the above address.

Copyright © Jonathan North, 1999
ISBN: 978-1-47388-289-8

Publishing History
*Heinrich von Brandt's memoirs were originally published in German as Aus dem
leben des G.I.H von Brandt (Berlin, 1868, 3 volumes). In 1877, an abridged edition,
edited by Baron Ernouf and focusing on the Napoleonic Wars, was published in French
as Souvenirs d'un officier polonaise (Paris, Charpentier, 1877). In the Legions of
Napoleon is a translation of the French edition.*

CIP data records for this title are available from the British Library

Typeset by Tom Knott
Printed and bound by CPI Group (UK) Ltd, Croydon, CR0 4YY

CONTENTS

ILLUSTRATIONS

Illustrations, pages 129–44

Maps

ACKNOWLEDGEMENTS

Heinrich von Brandt's memoirs first caught my eye some fifteen years ago when I read Raymond Rudorff's powerful evocation of the sieges of Saragossa – *War to the Death*. Rudorff worked a number of extracts from eyewitness accounts into his narrative, and he included some of Brandt's relation of the second siege. I wanted to read more, but I was unsuccessful in my efforts to track down an actual copy of the memoirs until, years later, I chanced to be in the London Library, a superb repository with a particularly fine collection of Napoleonic memoirs. There I was delighted to find Brandt's book tucked away on a dusty shelf.

Most accounts from the French perspective available in English – Marbot's, Blaze's, Parquin's, Bourgogne's and Coignet's, for example – were translated quite some time ago and very little had been attempted in the last fifty years – resulting in the same memoirs being reproduced time and time again. It was a desire to add to what is available, and to provide a new and different voice on key events which, combined with the intrinsic value of his own particular memoirs, prompted me to attempt a translation of Brandt.

This proved not to be without its problems. I was fortunate enough to have access to a nineteenth-century French-English dictionary but nevertheless had great difficulty with some of Brandt's puns (there are several sly examples in the text), soldierly cursing (some of it in Spanish for local colour) and obscure references. On matters of military terminology, radically different from that in use today, I received tremendous help from Colonel John Elting, who read the first draft of my translation and made a number of helpful suggestions and corrections.

When it came to discovering more about some of the personalities mentioned in the text, Terry Senior proved a particular help, providing biographical data on several of the less well-known French generals – Laval, for example – and commanders. I must also thank Edward Ryan and Digby Smith, both of whom kindly forwarded material on the Vistula Legion and its officers.

The library of the Polish Institute in London contains a wealth of information on Polish military history and was most useful, and, again, the

London Library proved a tremendous help concerning details of both the Peninsular War and the 1812 campaign.

Peter Harrington and Bob Kenny at the Anne S.K. Brown Military Collection, Rhode Island, were tremendously kind in locating and providing illustrations.

Particular thanks are due to Lionel Leventhal and the team at Greenhill Books for their support and professionalism.

I am also grateful to my parents for their enthusiasm; to Jennie, for her support, assistance with the maps and illustrations, and patience; and to Alexander for his continual advice.

Jonathan North, 1999

FOREWORD

The Revolutionary and Napoleonic Wars, which ravaged Europe between 1792 and 1815, witnessed two campaigns of particular horror and destruction and Heinrich von Brandt participated in both. In the Peninsular War, the French armies were sapped and worn down in a long and remorseless struggle of attrition. In Napoleon's famous 1812 invasion of Russia, a massive force, assembled from all parts of Europe, crossed the Niemen, pushed deep into Russia and, in the space of six short months, was utterly destroyed.

In 1808 Napoleon sent his armies into Spain to bring both that errant country and Portugal to heel and add them to his coterie of obedient satellites. This act was the beginning of a terrible, savage war, based on popular and almost universal resistance to Napoleonic rule. Spanish regular armies proved brave but ineffective and their attempts at conventional warfare met with scant success – although they showed remarkable tenacity defending their cities during the conflict's numerous sieges. The Spanish struggle therefore assumed a new and more desperate character and degenerated into a guerrilla war of ambushes, assassinations, sieges, raids, punitive expeditions and reprisals, which wore down the young conscripts making up the majority of Napoleon's Peninsular armies.

Brandt was involved in this tragic war for four years. Based in Aragon – in some respects the best governed and administered province in occupied Spain – Brandt participated in the widespread repression in which French armies waged a total war against bands of guerrillas and a nation in arms. Brandt records his own bitter war in Spain; his tour of duty ran from the summer of 1808 to January 1812, punctuated by just two days' leave in Bayonne.

The vast majority of Brandt's Spanish war was spent fighting guerrilla bands, which involved guarding convoys, performing garrison duty in hostile territory and punitive raids and expeditions into the mountains. Official records bear ample testimony of the savagery, even in Aragon. Counter-atrocity followed atrocity, towns were sacked and pillaged, crops were burnt, hostages shot and villages put to the sword in an endless cycle of hate and terror.

Something of the scale of the resistance to the invading French can be measured by the mere number of bands the French had to fight in Aragon alone. Thus the names of Villacampa, the two Minas, Gayan, Renovales, Perena, Pedrosa, Cruchaga, Baget, Sarasa, Hernandez, Comoran, Chapalangarra, Pesaduro, Malcarado, Duran, Benedicto, Caravajal, Cadet, Solano, Obispo, Montijo, Theobaldo and Villastar, in addition to the regular armies arrayed against the French Army of Aragon, give some indication of the forces involved – and these were just the organised bands. Brandt likens life in the French armies in Spain to being in the position of a man sitting on a powder keg surrounded by enemies carrying matches – which was, on occasion, literally the case.

From the vicious nature of the war, it might be expected that Brandt would have little respect for his enemies, or the Spanish population as a whole. Such sentiments are echoed in almost all French, and even many British, memoirs of the period. Yet Brandt reveals an unexpected admiration of the Spanish people for their bravery and tenacity and their soldiers for their ability to recover and return to the fray even after a defeat. He writes that at the siege of Tortosa the Spanish officers 'did their duty manfully' and respects Villacampa, O'Donnell and others for their energy, ingenuity and single-minded determination to win despite an almost complete lack of material resources.

When war with Russia loomed, Napoleon withdrew the Polish units from Spain for the impending confrontation. This included the Vistula Legion and Brandt remarks on the fact that although the troops were glad to be withdrawn from Spain, war with Russia was treated as no light matter. Such an observation was quickly justified even before the calamitous campaign began. His comments on the Russia of 1812 are intuitive, and his description of the appalling slide of the *Grande Armée* into chaos and disorganisation is amongst the best that has survived.

Attached to the Imperial Guard, Brandt's regiment was sent into Russia in June 1812 roughly 3,000 strong. Of those 3,000, only some sixty armed men returned through Kovno and back into Poland in December 1812. Brandt, wounded in the foot just outside Moscow, was lucky to be one of them for the vast majority of the *Grande Armée* never returned. Perhaps never before in history had so powerful a force of arms been reduced to such a state in so short a time.

For a man in his mid-twenties Brandt had seen much: he was only eighteen when he crossed the border into Spain in the summer of 1808 and his military career in the French Army was terminated on the field of Leipzig when he was only twenty-four. Certainly these events made great impressions on him, which were partly shaped by his unique perspective. Of German ancestry, he was born in that part of Poland which had come under Prussian rule, and he had served in the Prussian army before being recruited into a Polish regiment in French service and sent to fight in the Iberian peninsula and Russia. Like many Poles, he served Napoleon with loyalty and enthusiasm. Poles looked upon the 1812 campaign as a chance to re-establish their state – Napoleon had embarked on the campaign with the proclamation, 'The Second Polish War has begun!' – and to expand at the expense of Russia. Their attitude to the Peninsular War was less focused, but Polish troops served with distinction in every theatre in which they served, and were justifiably proud of their fighting record.

Notwithstanding the many thousands of Poles who fought in the Napoleonic Wars, there is comparatively little material that has been published in Western European languages on the Polish experience during this period, and very little indeed in English. Inevitably, Western attention has tended to concentrate on the most famous Polish unit of the conflict – the Polish Lancers of the Imperial Guard. Chlapowski, Symanowski, Grabowski and Zalusky all left accounts (of which only Chlapowski's has been translated into English) of their service in that distinguished regiment; Roman Soltyk and Baron Boris Turno, who had also served in Spain, left important accounts in French of the retreat from Moscow from the point of view of staff officers.

Brandt's account is different because it is the only one available by a Polish junior officer serving in the infantry in both Spain and Russia, and it was this which – in addition to Brandt's style, sense of humour and humanity – attracted me to his memoirs. They give a lasting impression of an individual, not a superior officer or commander-in-chief but an ordinary man, participating in one of the most destructive conflicts the world has ever seen.

Brandt is a modest figure, and all the more interesting for it. Struggling simply to survive, he is keener to find bread and meat than impress the world with glorious exploit.

19

INTRODUCTION

A History of the Vistula Legion

The Vistula Legion had its origins in the formation of regiments of Poles in northern Italy during the French Revolutionary War. 1795 had seen the final partition of Poland between the neighbouring states of Russia, Prussia and Austria, despite a gallant Polish attempt to preserve her independence and an initially successful defence of the country by Tadeusz Kosciuszko. The final partition led many of the Polish troops who had taken part in this campaign to emigrate and seek employment in foreign armies. The vast majority fled to France in the hope that they would be able to continue the struggle, in some form, against the partitioning powers.

Poles had something of a tradition when it came to serving in the French Army. As long ago as 1646 a Polish regiment, Priemski's, had taken part in the siege of Dunkirk and at the battle of Lens in 1648; Louis XIV even appointed a Prince Radziwill as colonel general of Polish troops in French service. Marshal de Saxe raised a unit of uhlans for Louis XV and a large proportion of the unit was composed of Poles, although it also made use of Hungarians, Turks, Moldavians and Croats. An infantry regiment, the Royal-Polonais, was also formed, although it again included any number of assorted foreigners, and served well until absorbed by the Royal-Suédois regiment on 18 January 1760. Even so, individual Poles continued to serve. Polish troops in the Lauzun Legion fought for the French in the American War of Independence, and Zajonczech, a future general of brigade under Napoleon, began his military career when he was commissioned as a lieutenant in the 1st French Hussar regiment in 1775.

The French Revolution marked a turning point in the fortunes of Europe and for the small number of Poles serving in France. Although the Revolutionary government briefly outlawed the enlistment of foreign nationals, a number continued to serve the nascent republic. General Joseph Miaczynski, a general in French service since 25 May 1792, even saw action at Valmy. He was to survive less than a year: being implicated in Dumouriez's defeat at Neewinden and subsequent defection in 1793, he was executed on 24 May. Another Pole, General Mieszkowski, found himself sidelined to France's dirty civil war in the Vendée. Surprised by an insurgent army under Rochjacquelin, he was utterly defeated just outside St Fugent, also in 1793.

However, these individual efforts were soon to be overshadowed by a more organised Polish contribution to the success of France's armies. After the partition of Poland, and the subsequent influx of Polish nationals, thought was given to organising units along national lines. With so many Poles, particularly officers, arriving to seek employment the idea of forming a legion, as French *émigré* troops had done under Condé, began to gather momentum. However, the implementation of such a scheme had to wait until the arrival of a sufficiently talented and dedicated individual – General Joseph Dombrowski.

Dombrowski, the son of a Polish officer in Saxon service and a German mother, arrived in France after his plan for organising a Polish corps in Prussian service had been rejected. After protracted negotiations, he was finally made a general in the French army and transferred to Italy in October 1796 where he would serve as a focal point for Polish troops, so much so that, despite the Directory's initial lack of enthusiasm, a Polish Legion was formed in Milan in January 1797, in the pay of the provisional government of Lombardy but fed and equipped by the French. The Legion, commanded by Dombrowski and supported within the French Army's hierarchy by Jourdan, Championnet and Bernadotte, consisted of some 1,200 infantry and drew most of its strength from Poles deserting from the Austrian army or captured in the series of Austrian defeats in that theatre. By June 1797 the Legion had grown to an astonishing 6,600 men and costs were being shared between the French and the newly-created Italian republics. The Legion was expanded in the autumn of 1797 to include a cavalry regiment.

In 1798 the Polish troops in Italy were perhaps at their peak, but they were to suffer severely during the fighting against the Second Coalition. With Napoleon in Egypt, accompanied by a number of Poles including Zajonczech, Solkowski and Lazowski, the French found themselves under considerable pressure from Allied offensives designed to win back all that had been lost since 1796. The French forces in Italy were a prime target, and the Poles suffered heavy casualties at Trebbia, Novi and the siege of Mantua. Nevertheless, they made an excellent impression and were considered a first class and reliable fighting force.

Poles were also active in other theatres. In northern Europe another Polish legion was raised in September 1799, and designated the Legion of the Danube (it was originally to be called the Legion of the Rhine, but was given a more ambitious title after careful consideration). This unit, consisting of infantry, cavalry (who received lances in August 1800) and artillery, was commanded by General Karol Kniaziewicz – an officer who had distinguished himself under Championnet in Naples the year before. The Legion of the Danube fought well at Hohenlinden, defeating repeated attacks by Riesch's Austrians on the left of the Austro-Bavarian army.

In Italy, with Napoleon's second Italian campaign and triumph at Marengo, the Polish Legion once again took its place in the victorious ranks of the French. It particularly distinguished itself at the difficult and costly blockade of Peschiera, which ended with an Austrian capitulation.

After the Peace of Lunneville, the Polish units faced another period of uncertainty and reform. The Legion of the Danube was brought down to Italy and used to garrison Florence in May 1801, although Kniaziewicz, displeased with apparent French complacency over Poland, resigned and retired to the Ukraine. In December of 1801 the Poles were reorganised and reclassified as three Demi-Brigades, the Legion of the Danube forming the 3rd Demi-Brigade while those who had served in Italy formed the first two.

This was a difficult time for the Poles. Peace sapped the strength of the regiments and desertion was rampant. The 2nd Demi-Brigade was politically suspect and its officers were thought of as Jacobins and intriguers, agitating for an independent Poland. These factors, combined with the political unpopularity of using French troops in the West Indies, determined that when an expedition to San Domingo was organised, the Poles would be included along with a number of other foreign units in French pay.

Two of the three Polish Demi-Brigades, totalling some 5,000 men, were despatched to San Domingo, the 3rd Demi-Brigade sailing from Toulon in 1802 with the 2nd Demi-Brigade following from Genoa on 24 January 1803. Placed under the command of Ladislas Jablonowski (1769–1802), who had studied with Napoleon at Brienne, the vast majority perished there, Jablonowski among them. Succumbing to the climate and yellow fever, a third of them died within just ten days of landing on the island, and of those who survived the majority either eventually surrendered to the British or were captured on the high seas. Some subsequently enlisted in British foreign regiments, and later saw service in Canada and the Spanish Peninsula. Only a handful – such as a certain Debowski, who managed to evade capture and take a merchant ship to New Orleans – returned to France and from there were sent on to join their comrades in Italy.

The number and morale of those who had remained in Italy, at Modena, were also much reduced. As the 1st Demi-Brigade and the cavalry regiment, they had been in the service of the Republic of Italy since December 1801. Renamed the Polish Infantry Regiment in 1804, they were built back up to strength with drafts of Austrian prisoners – not only Poles but also Germans, Belgians and Illyrians – and, in 1805 formed part of the army of the newly founded Kingdom of Italy (which comprised much of present day northern Italy). Later the same year they were despatched to Naples under the orders of Massena.

The calamitous campaign which ensued almost proved fatal to the original Polish Legion. The regiment performed badly and was whittled away by disease and fatigue. Broken down into detachments, the majority were assigned outpost duty or the role of defending the French lines of communication from bands of guerrillas. The first troops to oppose General John Stuart's landing in Calabria consisted of some 300 Poles, fifty of whom were taken prisoner.

In the only set-piece battle of the campaign – the battle of Maida on 4 July 1806 – 937 Poles formed part of Digonet's brigade. These Poles faced Acland's attack against the centre of the French line. They broke and fled when the British assault pushed home, despite the French commander, Reynier, riding into their midst to personally try and rally them. Five officers and 250 men from the Polish Legion were captured, twenty-six of whom turned up at the Valleyfield Prisoner of War Camp near Edinburgh in October 1811, where they were entered on the lists as being 'stout, fine looking men'.

This disastrous performance was compounded in subsequent minor actions: 370 Poles surrendered to the British at Monteleone, 100 more at Tropea and 250, charged with guarding the French hospital at Cotrone, capitulated after a brief siege. Such a record could only reflect badly on the Poles, and for a while they floundered in southern Italy as part of the Neapolitan army established by the newly created King of Naples, Joseph Bonaparte.

Joseph was replaced as king by Marshal Joachim Murat on 1 August 1808 and was sent to Spain, where he was again to serve as Napoleon's puppet. During his time in Naples, ever concerned for his personal safety, he had taken 1,192 men from the Polish Legion and incorporated them into his Royal Guard. When Murat appeared, Joseph took this Guard with him to serve as the basis for his new Royal Guard in Spain, much to Murat's chagrin.

The rest of the Poles had been recalled to the north in 1807, as Napoleon's conquest of Prussia seemed to herald great changes for Poland. For a time they served as part of the army of the newly-formed Kingdom of Westphalia, receiving drafts of Prussian prisoners to bring the unit up to strength. It was still a rather confusing time, large numbers of Poles being drafted into the French Army (into the short lived Legion of the North, for example) in what was, from the Polish point of view, a haphazard manner. For example, in December 1806, at Mainz, the Irish Legion received 800 Poles into its ranks (203 of them were still there in 1813, when the Irish Legion, now called the 3rd Foreign Regiment, marched off to take part in the Bautzen campaign). This distribution of Poles in the imperial armies was to continue throughout the Napoleonic Wars – in June 1810 the kingdom of Holland had 335 Poles in its armies, and in 1812 there were fifty Poles in Joseph Napoleon's Spanish army, serving in the Regiment Royal Etrangère.

Despite a desire amongst the officers of the Legion that, as the Polish campaign of 1807 opened, all Polish troops should be gathered into a liberating army, the recruitment of reinforcements for the Polish Legion continued to do well. So well, in fact, that 400 non-Poles (mostly Austrians) in its ranks were transferred out and given to the kingdom of Holland.

As the regiment – now known officially as the Polacco-Italien Legion – had experienced officers, it was inevitable that some should be drafted out of the unit and into the infantry regiments then in the process of being formed in the Grand Duchy of Warsaw. Such veteran officers were a valuable resource, and their transfer was detrimental to the efficiency of the Legion.

Finally, after this period of apparent indecision, on 31 March 1808 the Polacco-Italien Legion was renamed the Vistula Legion, placed in French pay, and was reorganised into three infantry regiments and a regiment of lancers. Recruits continued to arrive, and found to their evident joy that Poles in French service had better pay and conditions than those in the service of the Grand Duchy. Consequently as the regiments were built up to strength they became almost exclusively Polish, with just a sprinkling of Germans and a few French officers. A depot was organised in Sedan and the two battalion regiments were despatched there in May 1808. When Chlapowski saw them at Bayonne in 1808 he declared that the infantry were 'very fine regiments'. The officers it is true were excellent, but the men were very young and had never been under fire. This proved a significant factor in the very heavy losses they were to suffer in the first six months of the Spanish campaign.

On 8 June 1808 the Vistula Legion became part of Grandjean's division of III Corps, then serving in northern Spain. Four long years of bitter fighting followed. The Vistula Legion was present at the first siege of Saragossa and lost heavily in the unsuccessful attempt to subdue the city. At the second siege, so well described in Brandt's memoirs, it was again present and suffered heavily in house-to-house fighting. This epic struggle, which was crowned with success only in February 1809, when Marshal Lannes received the city's surrender, cost the lives of about one-third of the Vistula Legion.

The Legion also took part in such pitched battles as Tudela, Maria, Belchite and Sagonte, but much of its operational life was dominated by the war against the guerrillas and all that entailed: 'Unhappy the

Emperor's Foreign Troops who are employed upon every disagreeable and unprofitable duty!' Punitive expeditions, forced marches, lonely garrison duty in hostile territory, escort duties and ambushes dominate the pages of Brandt's memoirs relating to Spain. Such hazardous service sapped the strength of the Legion and brought little reward. Brandt stated that in 1812 there was not one man in his company who had not been wounded in Spain.

In 1809 Napoleon attempted to form a further Polish legion from Austrian prisoners of war. There proved to be insufficient recruits, but an additional infantry regiment (the 4th) and, later, a lancer regiment, were raised and added to the existing Legion. Both units were quickly sent to Spain. The 4th Regiment served in both Spain and Portugal and con-tributed to a small victory over the British (under General Packenham) at Aldea in September 1811.

In June 1811 the Legion was reduced to infantry status as its lancer regiments – the original lancer regiment and the 2nd formed in 1811 – were converted into the 7th and 8th Chevaux-légers-lanciers of the French Army. The lancers had always served separately rather than as an integral part of the Legion. The first and original regiment ('fine savage-looking dogs' according to one British officer) gained their most notable success at Albuera in 1811, where they decimated Colborne's brigade, and they were everywhere respected and feared. They stayed in Spain until early 1813 and then were moved to the German front. The second regiment had also served in Spain but in 1812 was withdrawn and sent to Russia, where it gave good service in Corbineau's brigade of II Corps.

In 1812, with war against Russia looming, most of the Poles serving in Spain were withdrawn to refit in France. A number of reforms were put in hand for the coming struggle, with the intention of building the Vistula Legion up to divisional strength. This was to be achieved by the addition of a third battalion of raw recruits to each of its first three regiments. The theoretical strength of the Legion was thus set at about 10,000 men, but it never reached this figure and the third battalions proved disappointing. On 6 March 1812 a company of artillery was also formed and added to the infantry regiments. On 10 April the Legion left its depot at Sedan and began the long march to Moscow.

The 4th Regiment remained in the Iberian peninsula until September 1812 and was later posted to Posen. It never actually entered Russia. In January 1813 it had an effective strength of 1,800 men (never having formed a third battalion) and was still in Poland, ready to meet the remains of the retreating *Grande Armée*.

As the French advanced into Russia the first three infantry regiments of the Vistula Legion – some 7,000 effectives under General Claparède – found themselves attached to the Young Guard. The regiments' third battalions were left at Gjatsk, as the advance was taking an unhealthy toll on young soldiers not yet accustomed to active service, but the rest went as far as Moscow and, indeed, further. The advance into Russia was costly, as can be seen by the strength given for the 2nd Regiment on 1 August 1812 (28 officers and 1,256 men) as compared to the return for the same regiment just two weeks later (30 officers and 883 men).

The Legion took an active part in the battle of Borodino, supporting the final assault on the Grand Redoubt and the bitter fighting in the closing moments of the battle. It then participated in the advance through Moscow and the various battles that took place in October 1812, before being caught up in the chaos of the retreat. However, the Legion seems to have maintained some order as it was detailed to guard the Imperial Treasury and the trophies between Smolensk and the Beresina.

At the crossing of that fatal river the Legion was attached to Ney's III Corps and was one of the units involved in the brilliant French counterattack, in conjunction with Doumerc's cavalry charge, against Admiral Tchichagov's Russians. However, this battle destroyed what little was left of the Legion, only a shattered remnant making its way back to Poland. Records show that on 4 February the 1st Regiment could muster 152 men, the 2nd 151, and the 3rd 154 men. The 1st Regiment's colonel, Kousinowski, had been killed at the Beresina and the 3rd's at Krasnoi in November. Combined with the 4th regiment, some 1,800 strong, elements of these troops proved themselves useful in providing garrisons, such as that of Torgau, along the Elbe.

The Legion itself, and most of the survivors of the Russian campaign (Brandt included), went into the two-battalion strong Vistula Regiment, formed on 18 June 1813 and commanded by Malasewski, the colonel of the 2nd Regiment, until his death at Leipzig. Mikolaj Kosinski, a former major in the 2nd Regiment of the Vistula Legion, then took command. The regiment served at Wittenberg, Freyberg and Leipzig, and was largely destroyed at the last in the bitter rear-guard fighting of 19 October. Sufficient Polish infantry yet remained for the unit to be reformed and refitted at the depot at Sedan, and it subsequently saw action at Soissons, at Arcis-sur-Aube, where Napoleon sought refuge in its square, and at St Dizier.

The emperor's abdication saw the return to Poland of the vast majority of these men – indeed, Article 19 of the Treaty of Fontainebleau specifically allowed Poles in French service to retain their arms and baggage and return to Poland as free men. Some, however, found their way to Naples and joined Murat, while others sought favour with the Bourbons. Most, however, returned to Poland and either settled back into civilian life or sought employment in Russian, Prussian or Austrian service.

For those Poles who had been taken prisoner by the Allies, release was often slow in coming. The twenty-six Poles at Valleyfield were only taken to Leith on 16 September 1814, some six months after the end of hostilities, and shipped back to Poland. Some had been luckier – the Polish elements of the garrison of Torgau were simply disarmed and sent home upon surrender.

Following Napoleon's return from exile in 1815 some Poles, including men from the original Vistula regiments, formed themselves into an infantry regiment – under, at first, Colonel Golaszewski, a former major of the 4th Regiment, then Colonel Schutz – and a provisional 7th Lancer Regiment, without horses. Too late to be ready for Waterloo, these provisional units fought briefly in the defence of the Sèvres bridge on 3 July. When Napoleon's second abdication brought hostilities to a close both regiments were disbanded (6 September 1815), most of the Poles who had fought in these units then transferring into the Bourbon Legion of Hohenlohe, the immediate ancestor of France's legendary Foreign Legion.

BIOGRAPHIES OF LEADING PERSONALITIES

BLAKE, GENERAL JOACHIM (1759–1827). A Spanish general of Irish descent, Blake began the Peninsular War as a colonel of the three-battalion regiment The Volunteers of the Crown. His rapid promotion to the command of armies put considerable pressure on his military abilities and he was repeatedly defeated by the French in 1808 and 1809, most notably at Espinosa. However, from 1809 to 1812 he proved himself a reasonably capable commander of small regular forces in a war of hit-and-run raids and was a considerable thorn in the side of the French until captured in 1812.

BRANDT, HEINRICH AUGUST VON (1789–1868). Born in Mansfelde, Brandt first enlisted in the Prussian Army on 15 October 1806, becoming an ensign in the 2nd West Prussian Reservebataillon. After quitting Prussian service, he began service with the French Army in April 1808. During his career under Napoleon he was decorated with the Legion of Honour and, on 26 November 1810, with the Polish Virtuti Militari (3rd Class). He served the French until 16 October 1813 when, at the battle of Leipzig, he was very badly wounded whilst serving on Poniatowski's staff and was subsequently captured in hospital by the Russians when Leipzig was overrun. He was well treated and, after a brief period as prisoner of war in Bohemia, followed by parole in Posen, once more resumed Prussian service at the close of the Napoleonic Wars.

In 1816 he was a captain in the 33rd Infantry Regiment. A long period at this rank followed until transfer to the Military Academy in Berlin, where he wrote the book *Über Spanien* on Mina and the Spanish guerrillas. This was translated into English in 1825 by an anonymous British officer. Finally Brandt was promoted and given a staff appointment, serving as Gneisenau's chief of staff in the Prussian forces based around Posen during the 1830 Polish insurrection. After this a posting to the Prussian General Staff followed, with promotion to the rank of major general only coming in 1848. Further staff duties occupied his time until 1857 when he retired on a pension of 3,450 Thaler a year. He died on 23 January 1868, leaving a wife (Augusta Louise Charlotte Bettauer, whom he had married in 1818) and a son (Heinrich Friederich von Brandt, born in 1823).

CHLOPICKI, GENERAL JOSEF GREGORZ (1771–1854). This Polish officer fought under Kosciuszko in 1794 and then under the French in Italy in Dombrowski's Polish Legion. He fought in Spain and distinguished himself at Epila, both sieges of Saragossa and subsequently, in independent command after being promoted to general of brigade on 18 July 1809, in counter-insurgency operations. He served in Russia in 1812, was wounded at Borodino, and again a few days later at Mojaisk, but survived the retreat. However, he only briefly served the French in 1813, before resigning during the armistice, and only resumed military duties, for the Russians, in 1815 and then only until 1818. He played a major part in the 1830 Polish insurrection and was badly wounded at the battle of Grochow in February 1831.

CLAPARÈDE, GENERAL MICHEL-MARIE (1770–1842). Although he appears in Brandt's memoirs as an unpopular and unpleasant commander, and one of little talent, it was generally said that Claparède was 'a valued officer and generally liked throughout the army'. He had fought in the West Indies in 1802–3 and then under Lannes in the 1805 campaign. Claparède also saw service in Spain, commanding a division in the Army of Portugal in 1811. He commanded the Vistula Legion in Russia in 1812 and was wounded at the crossing of the Beresina. After convalescence in France he served in XIV Corps in 1813 under St Cyr and was captured at Dresden in November 1813.

HABERT, GENERAL PIERRE JOSEPH (1773–1825). A captain in 1792, Habert was a career soldier who served in the armies of the French Revolution and at one point was commander of the Irish Legion. He was captured by the British in 1798, whilst on board a French frigate, and remained a prisoner until his exchange in 1800.

He commanded the 105th Line in 1805 in Austria, fought at Eylau in 1807 and was wounded in June of that year. He was promoted to brigade general in February 1808 and was sent to Spain, where he commanded a brigade under Grandjean at the second siege of Saragossa, distinguishing himself in the street fighting. He met disaster at the Cinca crossing, losing over 1,000 men to the guerrillas – an episode described in Brandt's memoirs.

Habert served under Suchet from 1809, became general of division in June 1811 and was present at the fall of Tarragona and Valencia. In November 1813 he was made governor of Barcelona and only surrendered the city on 28 May 1814, two months after Napoleon's abdication. In 1815 he fought at Ligny and at Wavre, being wounded in the stomach in the house-to-house fighting. He was not recalled by the Bourbons after the Restoration, and went into retirement.

JUNOT, GENERAL JEAN ANDOCHE, DUC D'ABRANTES (1771–1813). One of the most enigmatic of Napoleon's leading commanders, Junot never attained the rank of marshal and yet was rather more than just a general of division. After serving as Napoleon's aide-de-camp in Italy he had a dramatic career and served as the emperor's aide at Austerlitz. He was sent to Portugal in 1807, was defeated by Wellesley at Vimiero and repatriated to France with his army after the Convention of Cintra. He was sub-sequently again sent to the Iberian peninsula and commanded III Corps at Saragossa and then, after a brief transfer to Germany, served under Massena in Portugal.

He also served in Russia, taking over the Westphalian corps from Jerome Bonaparte, and was heavily censored, both at the time and subsequently, for his lethargy and his poor performance at Valutina. In 1813 he was temporarily governor of the Illyrian provinces but was seen to be mentally unstable and unfit for office. After being recalled he committed suicide in July 1813.

KOUSINOWSKI, COLONEL MIKOLAJ ALEXANDRE (1766–1812). Kousinowski first enlisted as a captain in the 6th Battalion of the Italian Legion in Italy in October 1797. He served in Naples in 1805 and 1806, and was wounded in the right arm at Mangona in July 1806. In Spain he served as colonel of Brandt's regiment, the 2nd Regiment of the Vistula Legion, being wounded at Tudela. He became commander of the Vistula Legion in June 1811 and also a baron of the empire. He acted as colonel to the 1st Regiment of the Vistula Legion for the Russian campaign and was badly wounded leading his regiment in support of Oudinot's corps at the crossing of the Beresina. He disappeared in the aftermath of the battle. According to contemporaries, he was chivalrous, intelligent and honest.

LACOSTE, GENERAL ANDRÉ BRUNO DE FEVROL (1775–1809). A French engineer officer. Born into an aristocratic family, Lacoste had a military upbringing (his father was lieutenant-colonel in an infantry regiment). He first enlisted in 1793, saw service in Germany and, in 1798, took part in Napoleon's Egyptian campaign, being wounded in the assault on Jaffa. Between 1806 and 1808 he was present at the sieges of Gaeta, in southern Italy, Danzig and Stralsund, and at the battle of Friedland, where he was wounded. In 1808 he married, spent five days with his wife, and was despatched to Spain, serving at the first siege of Saragossa. As a reward for his services he was promoted to General of Brigade on 28 August 1808. When the struggle for Saragossa was renewed later that year, Lacoste assumed command of the siege operations and championed the slow pro-cess of sapping and mining the city into surrender rather than storming it.

31

However, on 1 February 1809, whilst posted at the St Augustin monastery, he was struck in the forehead by a Spanish sniper's bullet and died the next day.

LANNES, MARSHAL JEAN, DUC DE MONTEBELLO (1769–1809). Born in the same year as Napoleon and highly respected by him, Lannes was a first-rate commander and leader of men. Until being sent to Spain in 1808, his career was largely under the eyes of Napoleon and he fought in Italy, Egypt, in Austria in 1805, Prussia in 1806 and Poland in 1807.

In Spain in 1808 he defeated the Spanish at Tudela, but was then put temporarily out of action by a severe fall from his horse. He took over the siege of Saragossa in December 1808 and received its surrender in February 1809. He was recalled to Germany in 1809 and had his legs smashed by a cannon-ball at Aspern-Essling, dying nine days later.

LAVAL, GENERAL ANNE-GILBERT (1762–1810). Laval began his military career as a cadet in the Régiment du Conde in 1781. He became a general of brigade in 1799, fighting under Soult and at Zurich. In 1805 he served in Lagrange's division of VIII Corps and later became governor of Mecklenburg. In late 1807 he was assigned to Vedel's division and sent into Spain. He briefly served under Dupont, but, fortunately, was transferred to III Corps in May 1808. He was promoted to General of Division in April 1809, after good service at Saragossa. He continued to serve under Suchet until, at the siege of Tortosa, he was taken ill with a fever from which he died at Mora on 6 September 1810.

MALZEWSKI, COLONEL JOSEF (1782–1813). Malzewski served as a captain in various staff appointments in the 1809 campaign. He was promoted to major in an infantry regiment of the Grand Duchy of Warsaw in May 1809. On 9 March 1812 he was attached to imperial headquarters in preparation for the attack on Russia. He was promoted to colonel and took over the 2nd Regiment of the Vistula Legion on 23 August 1812. He survived the Russian campaign and commanded his regiment until July 1813, when all regiments of the Legion were reorganised into a single unit – the Vistula Regiment. Malzewski commanded this until he was killed at Leipzig on 19 October 1813.

MINA, GENERAL FRANCISCO ESPOZ Y (1784–1836). Perhaps the most famous guerrilla leader of the Peninsular War. His nephew, Xavier Mina, was also a leading guerrilla but was captured by Harispe in 1810 and imprisoned in Vincennes until 1814. Francisco Mina had a formidable reputation, gained in bitter and ruthless fighting in Navarre between 1809

32

(at first under Xavier Mina) and 1813. Mina's most notable victories over the French were as follows: Aibar, Anizcar, between Salinas and Arlaban, Erice, Irurozqui, Lerin and the plains of Lodosa, Maneru, Noatin, Peralta del Alcola, Cabo del Saso, Piedradmillera and Monjardin, Plasencia and Roncal. During the French intervention in Spain in 1823 Mina commanded an army but was defeated by the Bourbon French just outside Barcelona. He fled into exile in England.

MURAT, MARSHAL JOACHIM, KING OF NAPLES (1767–1815). This flamboyant cavalry commander was one of only two of Napoleon's marshals to become a king in his own right, thanks to his marriage to Napoleon's sister Caroline. Although a superb battlefield commander, especially in the period 1805–7, Murat was less capable off the field and has been blamed for the destruction of the French cavalry during the 1812 invasion of Russia. During the retreat from Moscow, Murat suddenly found himself placed in command of the entire army, a duty he did not relish, but passed on his duties to Eugene. In 1813 he deserted Napoleon but, although this temporarily saved his throne, he attempted to wrest control of northern Italy from the Austrians in an ambitious campaign early in 1815, suffered defeat at their hands and fled into exile. Imitating Napoleon's escape from Elba he tried to regain his Neapolitan throne from the returned Bourbons in a landing at Pizzo, but was captured by local gendarmes and shot.

O'DONNELL, GENERAL JOSEPH (1769–1834). Another Spanish general of Irish family, O'Donnell seems to have been respected by the French but never really given any command with which he could prove himself.

PALAFOX Y MELZI, GENERAL JOSÉ (1780–1847). Younger brother of the Marquis of Lazan, also a Spanish general during the Peninsular War, Palafox was the Spanish commander during the two sieges of Saragossa. He showed considerable energy, was fortunate in having good subordinates, and only surrendered when all seemed hopeless and when the strength of the city had been used up. Historians have criticised him for not doing more to hinder French siege operations and not using the troops available to him to maximum effect. Upon surrender he was taken to France and held until 1814.

PONIATOWSKI, MARSHAL JOSEF ANTON, PRINCE (1763–1813). Poniatowski, nephew of the last king of Poland, was born in Vienna. In 1807 he became Minister of War of the Grand Duchy of Warsaw and later commanded the Polish troops in the Russian campaign. There was

33

considerable friction between Poniatowski and Napoleon in Russia, but he performed well at Borodino and at the Beresina, where he was wounded. Made a marshal at Leipzig on 16 October 1813, Poniatowski was killed on 19 October trying to swim the river Elster.

ROGNIAT, GENERAL JOSEPH (1776–1840). After being present at the fall of Madrid, he was sent to serve as Lacoste's deputy at the second siege of Saragossa. Lacoste was killed in February 1809 and Rogniat replaced him at perhaps the most perilous moment. Although Brandt says he was not popular, he maintained, largely through Lacoste's methods, considerable pressure on the Spanish garrison until the surrender of the city on 20 February 1809. He was promoted general of brigade in March as a reward. He continued to serve under Suchet, was promoted general of division after his successful role in the taking of Tarragona, and was only recalled to Germany in 1813.

In 1815 he was loyal to Napoleon and served at Ligny and Waterloo, but subsequently switched his loyalty to the Bourbons. In 1819 he wrote a highly controversial history of the 1815 campaign heavily criticising Napoleon.

SUCHET, MARSHAL LOUIS GABRIEL, DUC D'ALBUFERA (1770–1826). As with so many French officers who rose to prominence in the Napoleonic Wars, Suchet served under Napoleon in his first Italian campaign, fighting at Arcola and Rivoli. He distinguished himself in 1805 and at Jena in 1806. He is, however, best known for his success in Spain, or rather eastern Spain, where he first served as a general of division in 1808. He took over command of III Corps in June 1809 when Junot was recalled for the Austrian campaign.

In July 1811 he won his marshal's baton, and a pay rise from 1,250 to 3,333 francs a month, for the capture of Tarragona. He captured Valencia early in 1812 and successfully contained both Spanish and British offensives aimed at dislodging him from Catalonia in 1813 and 1814. In 1815 he distinguished himself leading the Army of the Alps against the Austrians.

VILLACAMPA, GENERAL PEDRO (no dates). Another Spanish opponent of the French in Aragon, this general served well in many small actions and proved a capable leader in defence. His division was thoroughly shattered at Saguntum.

Part I
IN SPAIN

CHAPTER I

MY EARLY YEARS – UNIVERSITY OF KÖNIGSBERG – KANT'S FUNERAL –
THE QUEEN OF PRUSSIA IN MEMEL (1807) – MEETING MARSHAL DAVOUT
– BLÜCHER AND SCHILL – I BECOME SECOND LIEUTENANT IN THE
VISTULA LEGION – DEPARTURE FOR FRANCE – SEDAN – ARCIS SUR AUBE
– DANTON – BORDEAUX AND MONTAIGNE'S HOUSE – BAYONNE AND THE
GIRLS FROM THE ARSENAL – WHERE NAPOLEON BATHED AT BIARRITZ –
INTO SPAIN

I was born in 1789 in that part of Poland ceded to Prussia by the partition
of 1794. My family, of German origin, had settled in the small town of
Sochaczew, in the Palatinate of Mazovia,[1] and evidently took the Biblical
command of 'Go forth and multiply' quite literally, for I was one of eleven
brothers and sisters. I was born in a small village as my mother had gone
into labour in the course of some journey she was making with my father.
From this arose the idea that my life would be restless and tumultuous.
How right this turned out to be!

I studied at Königsberg Grammar School, situated in the old town. The
most vivid memory I have of those times was the funeral of the illustrious
author of the *Critique of Pure Reason* in February 1804. My classmates and
I took part in the funeral cortège. Since then I have seen the funerals of
kings and princes but have never witnessed such quiet and devoted contemplation seize hold of a crowd as when the little red- and gold-covered
coffin, containing the mortal remains of Kant,[2] passed by.

In 1805 I left school, duly furnished with a diploma, *Testimonium
maturitatis*, and entered the University of Königsberg, where three of my
brothers had preceded me. My father wanted to make a lawyer out of me
but in the opening term I was very much like all students in their first year

---

[1] Mazovia was an independent state until finally incorporated into the kingdom of
Poland in 1526. After the partition of Poland, this area became part of Prussia.
[2] Immanuel Kant (1724–1804), the celebrated German philosospher, was the son of a
Königsberg saddler and long time resident of that city.

and busied myself with everything except study. In the second term I attempted some work, but only some. The French language interested me the most, along with reading the newspapers. The genius and fortunes of the new French emperor stirred great enthusiasm in me; an enthusiasm largely shared by my fellow students. News of the ups and downs of the 1805 campaign came to us blow by blow: the capitulation at Ulm, the entry of the French into Vienna and the amazing battle of Austerlitz bewitched our youthful imagination. The violation of Prussian territory at Ansbach[3] in October of 1805 bought us to our senses and everyone believed that a confrontation between Prussia and France was not far off. News of the annexation of Hanover allayed our fears somewhat and we hoped that Prussia might yet survive this dispute with honour intact *and* with augmented territory. But storm clouds were gathering on the horizon...

I still remember with emotion, as if it were yesterday, the almost complete and general shock caused by the arrival of the news from Jena.[4] In our student meetings gazettes were read out aloud and these readings provoked endless discussions, watered and heated by considerable drinking. From about that time, students of Polish origin set themselves apart while German rhetoric was spouting all fire and flames; everyone was talking about running to arms. Three weeks after the battle of Jena an aide-de-camp of the king arrived, Lieutenant-Colonel Bronikowski,[5] charged with the raising of new troops in this part of Prussia. He was offering young men of family commissions in provisional battalions then in the process of forming. I was one of those who responded to this call and I was enrolled as an ensign in the 2nd East Prussia Battalion. They sent us off to complete our military education in the extremities of the kingdom and kept us there rather too long. Marched from cantonment to cantonment through the mud of Old Poland, we never had the opportunity of coming under fire. We arrived at Memel[6] just as peace was concluded. However, this military education did not entirely go to waste. I conscientiously read Caesar and the works of Frederick the Great and learned excellent lessons from the

---

[3] Napoleon violated Prussian neutrality when Bernadotte's corps marched through the Prussian enclave of Ansbach during the Ulm campaign. This territory was later given to Bavaria, and Prussia was given Hanover in return.

[4] Jena was the scene of Napoleon's total victory over the Prussian and Saxon armies on 14 October 1806.

[5] Bronikowski, General Mikolaj (1771–1827). Bronikowski served under Kosciuszko and was wounded in 1794. There then followed a period of retirement and administrative service under Prussia, until 1807, and then for the Duchy of Warsaw. In 1812 he served as governor of Minsk and gained notoriety by losing it, and its massive quantity of stores, to the Russians at a crucial point in the campaign.

[6] Now Klaipeda in the Baltic Republic of Lithuania.

commander of my company, an old Polish officer and a lucid and tireless instructor.

At Memel I witnessed a touching scene when I saw the young and unfortunate Queen Louise,[7] eyes reddened by tears, wandering through the muddy and badly paved streets of that little town with her children, the youngest of which was still in the arms of the child's governess. At the sight of such dignified sorrow I remembered the Persian verse which was apparently spoken by Mahomet II as he entered the palace of the last Greek emperor at the time of the conquest of Constantinople: 'The spider weaves the curtains in the palace of the Caesars and the hours are marked by the plaintive call of the owl'.

All of this, it must be said, in no way diminished my admiration for Napoleon, for he seemed to me by far superior to all the heroes of Plutarch.

As a result of the consequent shifts in territory we found ourselves Polish and my situation changed. My parents, although of German origin, now lived in a territory that had become part of the Duchy of Warsaw, the existence of which the king of Prussia had recognised at Tilsit. As a result I left Prussian service, with the permission of my father. Soon after, I was summoned to Warsaw and received a travel permit which cited, as the purpose of my travels, the necessity of fulfilling my obligations vis-à-vis the new sovereign of my country. Upon my arrival in Warsaw I was sent for by order of the governor, to whom I was introduced after being kept waiting an inordinate amount of time. Marshal Davout[8] was then at the prime of his life (thirty-eight years), and was a man of medium height with a robust complexion and lively, intelligent features despite being prematurely bald – something which tended to accentuate a look of severity.

'You've come from Memel,' he asked me, 'did you see the queen?'

'Yes, your Excellency, I saw her just before I left.'

'Did she seem sad or disturbed?'

'She was walking with her two eldest...'

'Answer my question. Did she seem sad?'

'Yes, your Excellency, she had reason to be: when you have just lost the most part of your country...'

'And whose fault is that? Who was it that pushed this poor king into this terrible adventure? Who forced him to defy the Emperor? Was she not at

---

[7] Queen Louise of Prussia (1776–1810), daughter of the Duke of Mecklenburg-Strelitz, was seen by many to have instigated war with Napoleon. She was the mother of the future emperor of Germany, Wilhelm I.

[8] Marshal Davout (1770–1823) was appointed Governor General of the Grand Duchy of Warsaw on 12 July 1807 after the treaty of Tilsit. He was created Duke of Auerstadt in April 1808 and Prince of Eckmühl in August 1809.

Jena? Did she not make warmongering speeches? Without her intrigues and the boasting of her guard officers, the king of Prussia would have remained our ally and the kingdom of Frederick the Great would not have collapsed... But be that as it may, that is no concern of yours. Return home and be faithful to your new prince.'

He dismissed me there and then. I later understood that he took this kind of tone with all young officers in the same position as myself.

I found that there had been a good number of changes in my native town. The old administration no longer existed and the new one had yet to come into being. In addition the burdens of war, in all their many forms, were weighing heavily on the country and especially on those people of German origin, many of whom took the opportunity of fleeing. In such circumstances staying in the paternal home held little for me, and besides, I'd already acquired a taste for military life. My first idea, encouraged by my family, was to re-enlist in Prussian service. My father, who was acquainted with Blücher,[9] furnished me with a letter of introduction to him and sent me off on a quest to find this general. I caught up with him at Treptow. He told me that he was overwhelmed by requests of this type and that it would be far better if I were to keep my head down, etc... Somebody then recommended I address myself to Schill:[10] he was as gracious as Blücher was coarse, but the result was the same and he could do absolutely nothing for me. I returned home in a foul temper having gone on this dangerous and wild goose chase.

A few weeks after my return an envelope postmarked Warsaw, 27 April 1808, and addressed to Monsieur Brandt, former Ensign in the Prussian Army, was delivered to me by hand by a brigadier of the Imperial Gendarmerie.[11] The letter informed me that the Marshal Duke of Auerstadt (Davout) had made me a second lieutenant in the Vistula Legion and that I was to join my unit, without delay, at the depot in Sedan.[12] There was no time for hesitation or refusal and I obeyed without, it must be said, too many qualms.

---

[9] Gebhard Leberecht von Blücher was probably the most famous Prussian of the Napoleonic Wars. Since his surrender at Rackau on 6 November 1806 he had been in a forced retirement. This was to continue, apart from a brief period as Governor of Pomerania, until 1813.

[10] Major Ferdinand von Schill had won a reputation for himself in the 1806 campaign as an organiser of partisan raids against the French. In 1809 Schill raided northern Germany whilst Napoleon was busy with the Austrians, but was surrounded at Stralsund by superior forces and was killed in the ensuing fight.

[11] A brigadier in the cavalry was the equivalent rank to a corporal.

[12] We can probably assume, therefore, that Davout had been pleased by Brandt's answers during their interview.

From Warsaw, my first port of call, I continued to Kürstin and from there, a few days later, I was sent on with around 500, mostly Polish, recruits to France. We traversed Germany, via Wittenberg and Mayence, and spent our nights sleeping in villages where, for the most part, the welcome was distinctly cold. Things improved a little as we passed the frontier into France, but I still heard abuse levelled against my recruits, who still wore their hair long and wore peasant clothes, and heard them branded as orientals, barbarians and other such pleasantries. But how the scene changed when we reached Sedan! There hundreds of soldiers, well armed and equipped, were waiting for the order to rejoin their respective regiments. We underwent a complete transformation and waited with impatience for the order that would take us to a country from which most of us would never return. We were going to Spain.

As we passed through France, one of the most pleasant halts was at Arcis-sur-Aube, where I was billeted on a relative of Danton[13] in a house that famous tribune frequented with his good friends Lacroix[14] and Fabre d'Egalantine.[15] In fact he had spent quite a long time here just before his arrest. His relative had still not forgiven the 'monster' Robespierre for the death of that good-natured and fascinating man.

In many small villages we were hailed as triumphant victors with acclamations, bouquets and all the rest. In reality only the major and two other officers had ever been under fire; but the people took us to be the victors of Jena or of Friedland[16] and we were fêted accordingly.

At Bordeaux, where we spent a couple of days waiting to receive an issue of equipment, Montaigne's[17] old house, with its little tower, caught my attention. I knew, from having read the works of the famous sceptic in the original, that he had once written, 'There is nothing more pleasant than military life'. This remark only goes to show that Montaigne had never served in the army.

My excellent host acted as my guide with considerable goodwill. He had known all the influential people of Bordeaux during the Revolutionary era:

---

[13] George Jacques Danton (1759–1794), French revolutionary leader, achieved prominence as president of the Jacobin Club but lost the factional power struggle to Robespierre and was executed on 5 April 1794.

[14] Jean François Delacroix (1753–1794) was a lawyer and deputy and was arrested in March 1794 in a campaign against Danton and his supporters.

[15] Fabre d'Egalantine (1755–1794) was an author, playwrite and Dantonist deputy. He was executed on the same day as Danton in the early phase of the Terror.

[16] Friedland, on 14 June 1807, saw the defeat by Napoleon of the Russian armies. This led to the Peace of Tilsit in July of that year.

[17] Michel Montaigne (1533–1592), the famous sceptical philosopher, was once mayor of Bordeaux.

41

the Vergniauds, the Gensonnes, the Ducos, etc, and he talked of them with enthusiasm. Lamartine's *History of the Girondins* would have so pleased this fine man, had he lived to see its publication.

Whilst visiting the ancient curiosities of Bordeaux, I did not neglect the more modern ones either even if I did study them with an altogether different kind of interest. The pretty girls of the city were charming in the costumes then in vogue; the little cloaks, blouses in bright colours, the coquettish little muslin bonnet holding back a flowing mass of black hair...

The march through the *landes*, upon leaving Bordeaux, was less tiring than we had feared. This region, at turns marshy and covered with pine trees, reminded our Poles of their own country. The dirtiness of the inhabitants and their tendency to drink in excess completed the illusion. We headed for Bayonne, via Roquefort and Dax.

Whilst crossing France we rarely caught sight of a man in uniform. At Bayonne just the opposite was true and we saw little else. In the Saint-Esprit suburb of the town, where we halted to arrange our billets, soldiers were all over the place. Hotels, restaurants, cafés were full of them and it required considerable energy to procure a steak or a cup of coffee.

The day after our arrival I was ordered to take a detachment and collect an issue of ammunition. I ran into the workers of the arsenal at breakfast and I really felt myself in seventh heaven! There were more than one hundred of them, pretty, witty, revealingly dressed, talkative and vivacious young women. From the point of view of discipline, they considerably delayed the issue of ammunition as these young ladies found my young soldiers to their taste and were not slow in showing it.

I was shown the place where, not long ago, the Prince of Asturias[18] and the Infantas had been lodged whilst Napoleon decided, or thought he was deciding, the fate of the Bourbons.[19] Only Don Carlos[20] had shown some strength of character and refused to sign the deposition placed before him, saying that he preferred death to dishonour.

A party of our men had been sent to Biarritz and I was delegated the task of taking them their supply of sixty cartridges a man. I used the opportunity to have a look at the famous *chambres d'amour*, of which the poets sang. The Emperor had bathed at this beach and I was told that he had

---

[18] The Prince of Asturias was the eldest son of King Charles IV of Spain, the future Ferdinand VII.

[19] The conference at Bayonne marked the, temporary, end of Bourbon rule in Spain. Napoleon induced the Spanish royal family to surrender their throne. Joseph Bonaparte, then king of Naples, was finally persuaded to replace them.

[20] Don Carlos, the second son of Charles IV, would lead the Carlist revolt in 1833 against his niece Isabella.

always been accompanied by an aquatic patrol to prevent a surprise attack by the English. For the whole of the time Napoleon was in the water, a detachment of Guard cavalry waded into the surf and patrolled in the water.

After a few days of rest we left Bayonne and marched across the Basque country towards Saint Jean Pied-de-Port, the last French town. Here there was a depot for the sick and wounded men of the division we were about to join. Their talk was not the most encouraging but we had little time to listen to them. The next day, at the crack of dawn, we marched out making our way up rocky escarpments which were completely devoid of greenery except for some sickly looking boxwood. Soon we reached the legendary pass of Roncesvalles[21] and I thought I would learn something of the famous hero from some of the local people. It turned out that they knew even less about him than I had learnt at school.

---

[21] Roncesvalles was the scene of the legendary battle in 778 between Roland, the ideal Christian knight, and the Moors. In actual fact, Roland, who was killed in the fighting, had been ambushed by Basque mountaineers.

CHAPTER II

~

As soon as we had crossed the frontier we began to take all military precautions adopted when in the presence of the enemy such as a vanguard,
rearguard and sending out scouts. I had acquired a rather misplaced idea of
the Spanish people from certain novels that now fitted ill with the reality of
1808. In vain I sought out the eyes of the honest hidalgo, sword at his side,
treading solemnly behind the plough. In the villages no mysterious strum-
mings of a guitar, no señora's voice reached my ears. The doors of houses
and shop fronts were all closed up. The people kept their distance casting
ferocious glances at us. *Non saber* – I don't understand, I don't know – were
the only words we could get from them. In place of señoras only a few old
hags of frightening ugliness dared venture out into the streets.

At Oubiri, the first staging post on Spanish territory, the order arrived
from Pamplona to requisition carts and mules from the neighbouring
villages to transport our munitions, but the peasants had learnt of this
almost before we had and both quadrupeds and bipeds had vanished into
the mountains. I was sent to lodge, along with six soldiers, with one of the
village notables, a certain Don Juan de la Torre. The house was grand and
sombre, with coats of arms on the balcony. We banged loudly on the door,
without success. Finally a window was flung open and a voice demanded to
know what we wanted. I answered by showing my billet ticket. The window
closed and after several minutes we heard the scraping of bolts. The door
finally opened and I saw a large man appear dressed like Figaro: velvet
waistcoat, breeches the same, silk stockings and a hair net. He signalled that

we might follow him and led us into an enormous room furnished by a couple of more or less dilapidated stools. Figaro, who was obviously the owner, then turned and wandered off muttering, in a tone one would use to wish someone to the devil (which he probably did), the stock phrase, 'My entire house is at your disposal'. He left us some old and disgusting snuff which my men then used as seasoning for their soup.

However, this gentleman was not completely devoid of courtesy and he returned to see us later in the evening and try out a little conversation. It was not easy going as he knew neither French nor German and the most literate of his guests (myself) had not yet had time to open the Spanish Grammar purchased at Bayonne. Fortunately it turned out that Señor Juan de la Torre, the youngest son of his noble family, had once studied for the priesthood and still remembered a few Latin phrases. The death of an elder brother had jettisoned the young bachelor into secular life, as it would just not do to let the great name of Torre perish! In due course he had inherited the patrimonial manor, which had been held by his family for three centuries. He gave me the details in Latin and, thanks to my comparatively recent studies of the classics, I could maintain a passable conversation which was part-theological and part-political and in which Napoleon was distinguished by the grand title of *Supremus dux Franco-Gallorum*. He learnt with great surprise that on the banks of the Vistula one could see Catholics and Protestants living side by side in the same house and even getting married.

We arrived at Pamplona at 11 o'clock in the evening, after a four days' march. Those of us who were not immediately on duty were lodged with the inhabitants of the city, as were the staff officers. However, it was obvious that the inhabitants had agreed to this with such bad grace that it was as difficult to install oneself in their houses as it had been easy to take the citadel a few months previously.

This is how that particular part of recent history was now being recounted: French troops were already occupying the town and each morning a detachment of unarmed soldiers was sent to the citadel to collect bread. On that particular day the men had their sabres hidden in their sacks. They threw themselves upon the Spanish sentries and disarmed them. At the same time a large number of other soldiers, who had seemed to be innocently throwing snowballs at each other, rushed into the fortress and captured it.

Our arrival at Pamplona coincided with Napoleon's great project of reconquering Spain, after the disastrous consequences of Bailen,[22] and

---

[22] General Dupont's surrender to the Spanish at Bailen on 21 July 1808 was an inglorious episode in French imperial ambitions in Spain. The French were forced to fall back to the Ebro, abandoning Madrid and the first siege of Saragossa.

avenging the lost honour of French arms. On 11 November, Blake's Army of Estremadura had been smashed by Victor. Napoleon intended to strike another such blow against Castaños[23] and Palafox (armies of Andalucia and Aragon). Lannes would attack them frontally and Ney[24] would cut their escape route to Madrid. Lannes' forces, with which he would win the famous battle of Tudela on 23 November, comprised Moncey's[25] Corps (III), a division of VI Corps and a few brigades of cavalry. We were destined to become part of III Corps, and were directed to pick up the depots at Milagro and then, after a halt of a few hours, march on Lodosa and effect a juncture with the main body. My regiment, the 2nd of the Vistula, was part of the 1st Brigade (Habert) of the 1st Division. Chlopicki, destined to become commander-in-chief of the Polish Army in 1831, commanded the Legion. He was one of the bravest of officers and a severe and puritanical disciplinarian.

Tudela was a tremendous boost for French morale as the Spanish army was composed of Castaños' Andalucians, the victors of Bailen, and the Aragonese of Palafox, full of pride after their first successful defence of Saragossa. They fled in complete disorder, some in the direction of Calatayud. Unfortunately, Ney had not arrived in time to cut off their retreat and they escaped. Others made off towards Saragossa where they first began to arrive, so they say, at 9 o'clock in the evening even though the battlefield was fifty-four miles from that town.

The battle had raged sometimes this way, sometimes that, from morning to night but none of our troops had been engaged for more than two hours at any one time. Habert's brigade had taken part in an attack on the heights but my battalion had been placed in reserve at a considerable distance from the enemy and where only the noise of the cannon and the shrill whistling of cannon-balls overhead could make us believe that we were on a field of battle.

That part of the enemy which fled towards Saragossa was pursued as far as Alagon, where we ourselves could not remain for want of food. This whole stretch of road was littered with corpses, mostly volunteers without uniforms, as the cavalry had shown them no quarter. These corpses would remain unburied for some weeks and this negligence was to cost us dear.

The shock in Saragossa was all the greater as the people had been led to

---

[23] Francisco Castaños (1756–1852) was named Duke of Bailen for his victory over Dupont at Bailen.

[24] Marshal Michel Ney (1769–1815) arrived in Spain on 30 August 1808 and assumed command of VI Corps.

[25] Marshal Moncey (1754–1842) was a veteran of the Revolutionary Wars, and had first fought in the Iberian peninsula in the 1794 campaign and was to do so again in the 1823 French intervention.

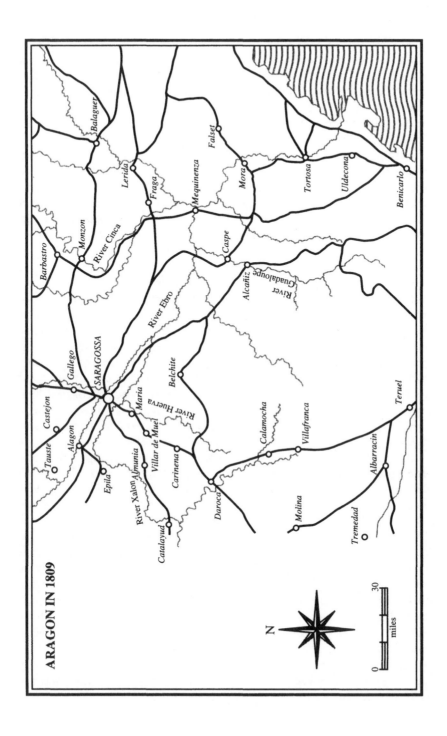

ARAGON IN 1809

Balaguer
Lerida
Fraga
Falset
Mequinenza
Mora
Tortosa
Uldecona
Benicarlo
Monzon
Barbastro
River Cinca
Caspe
Alcañiz
River Guadaloupe
SARAGOSSA
Gallego
River Ebro
Belchite
Teruel
Castejon
Maria
Tauste
Alagon
Villar de Muel
Calamocha
Villafranca
Albarracin
Epila
River Xalon Almunia
Carinena
Daroca
Molina
River Huerva
Catalayud
Tremedad

N

0   30   miles

expect a complete and utter victory over the French. Most of the inhabitants of the surrounding towns and villages, fearing French revenge, now sought sanctuary in the city with their families. In the first days after the battle more than 100,000 refugees, including many women and children, swelled the population of the town. Had we marched directly at the city without delay from Alagon, which our vanguard occupied on 27 November, we might well have taken the city without much loss of blood. Unfortunately, Lannes, who was ill, had left Moncey in charge and he had neither the requisite dash nor initiative. Besides, many of the troops who had fought at Tudela had been sent off in pursuit of Castaños, towards Calatayud, as Ney had still not appeared. Moncey retreated on the pretext that there was nothing for the troops to live off, but the true reason was that he feared to engage the enemy with three divisions, all the troops at his disposal. Twenty-four hours later Ney arrived and joined forces with Moncey. Realising too late that he had let Castaños escape, he thought he might yet avert imperial wrath by taking Saragossa.

We immediately received the order to advance. On 30 November the vanguard came into sight of Saragossa and the soldiers cheered loudly. The victory at Tudela and contact with the veterans of VI Corps and its cavalry had raised the morale of the young troops of III Corps. We did not doubt that it would be possible, or even easy, to take the town in a sudden rush with the united forces of the two marshals. Judge our disappointment, then, when on the next day we received the order to retreat back to Alagon! Ney, smarting under Napoleon's rebuke for his lack of activity before Tudela, had turned his corps around and hurried off in pursuit of Castaños and indeed committed a third error by taking *all* his troops away with him.

At Alagon we camped in conditions of absolute squalor. Apart from the little town of Tudela, the entire region around was devastated. The inhabitants had fled, the weather was atrocious – freezing northerly gales alternated with torrential downpours without respite. We camped on the bare earth, straw being an unheard of luxury in this country. The soldiers cut down the olive trees and tore off the doors and windows of the deserted houses in order to feed their bivouac fires. The rations issued also left something to be desired. The bread ration was often replaced partly or entirely by rice or beans. As for the meat, one sheep was allocated to every thirty men but the insides of the animal were always missing and the meat reached us in such an advanced state of putrefaction that it was utterly repugnant. At first there was wine in abundance but it was so quickly squandered that it soon became impossible to procure for love or money.

Our military duties were also rigorous, with constant patrolling and the sounding of the reveille at four in the morning. In addition sickness was rife in the new regiments and their young soldiers.

The siege artillery finally arrived on 16 December, as well as Gazan's and Suchet's divisions of Mortier's corps, and we marched once more upon Saragossa.

The soldiers, discouraged by having had to retreat on two previous occasions, were saying aloud that we should expect to have to do the same this time too. They were, however, quite mistaken.

On 21 December our forces mounted an assault on Monte Torero, which we had taken in the first siege without suffering casualties.[26] Whilst our batteries opened up on a position known as Buena Vista, recently constructed on the heights, Grandjean's division made a feint attack whilst part of Habert's brigade, to which my regiment belonged, turned the position. The main clash occurred in an underground tunnel through which the Tudela canal passes. This cavernous place, which the Spanish had barricaded, well deserved its name of 'abyss of the dead' (*Baranco de la Muerte*). Our voltigeurs[27] kept up a well-nourished fire and the defenders lost a large number of dead and wounded without really having had the chance to return our fire, and abandoned the position. Master of the place, Habert now debouched onto the left bank of the Huerva between the city and Monte Torero, which the enemy speedily evacuated to avoid being cut off.

Monte Torero, which serves as Saragossa's port, is situated on the banks of a canal and dominates the whole of the city. On the top of the hill there is a large convent, with two exquisite bell-towers. We lodged in the customs house until these buildings were destroyed by Spanish cannon fire. When we had first seen Saragossa, some weeks previously, the slopes of Monte Torero had been covered with villas and vineyards and offered a most agreeable sight. Now, however, the houses had been destroyed and the trees cut down: no vestige of the beautiful avenues that once made up this suburb remained. Such is the cruel necessity of war.

That evening, around the bivouac fires, we heard how Gazan's attack on the right bank had failed, despite his division being composed of veteran troops. It was also said that Suchet's troops, charged with the taking of the heights on the right bank, had been tardy in the attack and had thus allowed the defenders to make their escape. Despite this, on the next day the city was entirely invested on both banks. Our division was astride the road to Valencia and had advanced posts stretching as far as the Ebro. Immediately

---

[26] Monte Torero had fallen to the French in the first siege when it had been evacuated by a Colonel Vincente Falco, who was promptly imprisoned by the furious inhabitants on his return to the city.

[27] Each line infantry battalion included an élite company of light infantry to serve as skirmishers. These voltigeurs were usually chosen from amongst the regiment's nimblest and most agile soldiers.

before us lay one of the principal and most forward points of defence of the city, the monastery of San José.

On 22 and 23 December we attempted to flush out the enemy's light troops from some olive groves, a veritable forest that stood between us and the monastery. Fortunately there were in our regiment young men from Narev – a region renowned for its game and for its hunters. They killed some of the defenders and found that the Spanish troops were evidently refugees from the surrounding districts and still carried their money on their persons. Perhaps for this reason, our men quickly acquired a taste for the little war in the groves, and it was to their great regret when the enemy retreated out of reach.

CHAPTER III

MISSION TO ALAGON – AN IMPROVISED TENT – SERIOUS ILLNESS –
HOSPITAL, TYPHUS AND THE SPANISH GRAVEDIGGERS – A TERRIBLE
DREAM – RECOVERY AND RETURN TO CAMP – A NIGHT IN THE
TRENCHES – MARSHAL LANNES – THE *CANTINIÈRE*'S TABLE

On the evening of 24 December the colonel ordered me to proceed to
Alagon to collect those soldiers of the Vistula Legion who had straggled
due to sickness or exhaustion. With these men I was to form the escort for
a convoy of rations and clothes. This mission was not very appealing but as
I was the most junior officer in the regiment it fell to my lot. Nonetheless,
I left full of foreboding...

Alagon's military commandant was an old cavalry captain called Bruno,
who had tried hard to instil a little order and discipline into the stragglers
of various units, and had failed completely. 'Here you are entering chaos,'
he told me. However, with the help of a good sergeant just arrived from the
hospital at Saint-Jean-Pied-de-Port, I managed to round up some twenty
men from my regiment. We established ourselves for the night in a deserted
house and got a good fire going, fed from beams and floorboards 'borrowed'
from a neighbouring house. In place of straw we lay on some old hemp.
That evening, as he went his rounds, the commandant found us established
in true military style with a sentry posted at the door of our cottage and we
tucking into our leathery mutton. He complimented me on our disposition
and our *improvised tent*.

We had to leave Alagon the next day, but I almost stayed there perma-
nently. For some time I had felt not at all well. That night, in the icy
cold, I got considerably worse. In the morning I was seized by a violent
fever, complicated by dysentery, and had to be carried to a military hospital,
which was more like a den of thieves than a place of healing. The hospital
was located in a filthy monastery whose monks had fled to Saragossa
and were no doubt inflicting the wounds we were coming here to die of.
Typhus was rampant as all the area around had been infected by the

stench of the corpses left so long unburied after the battle of Tudela.[28]

For the first few days, whilst I was still conscious, I could follow the details of the burial of the many sick who succumbed. They were thrown from the windows stark naked and they fell, one on top of the other, with a muffled thud just as though they were sacks of corn. Then they were piled onto carts and taken away to the huge pits that were being dug unceasingly only one hundred yards away. The Spanish who had been charged with this duty undertook it with a diabolical glee. They pointed out to me the countless mounds of earth that marked the completed and covered graves and made signs which indicated there would be no lack of future work.

Such a sight was not of the kind to hasten my recovery. Consciousness soon began to slip away and I fell into a kind of stupor for some hours.

An incredible feeling of cold brought me round one night. I could hear cries and gasping in the shadows all around and smelt a terrible and suffocating smell. In the first light of morning I found myself on a stinking stretcher, not knowing where I was and surrounded by the dead and dying. Filled with horror, I made a determined effort to get up and flee this dreadful place, but my strength failed me and I passed out once again.

As I regained consciousness I found that I was in my bed and assumed it all must have been a terrible nightmare. But my adventure was all too real, for apparently in the middle of a bout of fever I had got up and wandered into the ward of the ordinary soldiers. Fortunately, I had been recognised and returned by one of our divisional surgeons who was serving in the hospital. This surgeon, who died in the 1812 retreat, seemed to be a brutal and clumsy individual and the men called him 'the butcher', yet he cared for me with some devotion and, after God, it was to him and Captain Bruno that I owe my life. I was ill for about a month until my youth and the strength of my constitution triumphed over the fevers. Yet the hollow thump of corpses falling from the windows of a cursed hospital were to haunt my dreams for many years to come.

At the time of my departure the Spanish gravediggers assured me that the number of corpses had already passed two thousand and I do not believe they were exaggerating. The commandant, it is true, was an excellent man, full of energy, and the chief surgeon had an excellent reputation. But as they were overloaded with duties they were forced to rely on less scrupulous and unsupervised subordinates for a host of essential details. I often recalled, in my military career, the German proverb which says that 'the subordinate is really the master'.

---

[28] Typhus is, in fact, carried by fleas, lice and mites. A Spanish monastery would seem to have made an excellent breeding ground for such parasites.

On 19 January 1809 I returned to my regiment after an absence of twenty-five days. During that interval the siege had made considerable progress, particularly in our sector. We had been masters of the San José monastery for some eight days now. The superior officers were lodged in the ruins of the country houses and manor houses whilst the junior officers and men, in order to maintain pressure on the besieged, had dug into the earth and formed oblong pits about four feet deep and covered with branches. If it rained there was trouble and we would soon be floundering in these bogs of our own creation. Keeping watch, mounting guard, patrolling and scouting were exhausting and the number of duties increased as the siege progressed. At dusk all the even-numbered companies would stand to arms. They were then relieved by the uneven-numbered companies, who, in their turn, were relieved by the grenadier and voltigeur companies. At three in the morning everyone was awake.

On the night of 21–22 January I had my first experience of guard duty in the trenches in command of twenty-five men of the battalion. To our right was a section of the 14th Line Regiment, commanded by an experienced sergeant who soon struck up a conversation. He was an old hand and had served in Italy, Austria and Poland and had gone through many sieges. He gave me and my men sound advice on how to conduct trench warfare. He showed them how to position the gabions according to different circumstances; how to construct defences so as to both keep the enemy under surveillance and fire the odd pot-shot; and how to guard against a surprise attack, as this was, he said, potentially the most uncomfortable situation to be in.

That particular night our sappers were driving parallels through the Huerva ravine in order to gain a footing on the far side. The besieged could hear the work and fired in their, and our, direction. Fortunately the mist rendered their fire ineffective. But as soon as the day broke we had to suffer a fierce enfilading fire pouring out of the convent of Santa Engracia to our left. Most of the sappers were killed or wounded and many of our gabions were knocked about by roundshot and bullets whistling overhead. Even so, none of my men were hit. As I was returning to camp, the brave sergeant of the 14th Line pointed out to me a dangerous black spot where the cover was inadequate and where it was vital to pass quickly or duck. It was just as well that I followed his advice as a few hours later another officer was mortally wounded at that exact spot.

On 23 January, in the evening, we learnt that Lannes, finally recovered,[29] was about to arrive and take over command. This news was met with

---

[29] Marshal Lannes had been seriously injured after his horse fell on an icy road and trapped him underneath.

genuine satisfaction and everyone predicted things would now move forward at a far more energetic pace.

That same evening at a particularly exposed point – I was now a connoisseur of trenches – I came across Lacoste, the General of Engineers, in deep conversation with a man in an unadorned green coat and not wearing a sword. The two of them were studying the city through their telescopes without paying the slightest attention to the bullets and roundshot that were raining all around. The man with Lacoste was none other than the marshal himself. He eventually seemed to realise the danger they had placed themselves in and said out loud, 'They've seen us, come on'. I could contemplate at leisure the handsome but severe Lannes, who I had briefly caught sight of in the distance, and shrouded in smoke, at Tudela.

Throughout 26 January our artillery kept up a heavy barrage on the city. The defenders returned an ineffective fire which did us little harm. That evening we learnt that we had achieved some success on the far bank of the Ebro. First news of this was brought, as was often the case, by the *cantinière* as we sat down to dinner. This usually consisted of a soup made of rancid butter followed by a still worse wine with sugar.

The *cantinière* had put together a kind of trestle table made of, so we were soon to learn, stones borrowed from a neighbouring cemetery. As was our habit of an evening we had gathered around a fire made of wood from olive trees, when one of us spotted a fragmentary inscription on one of the stones and managed to decipher the words *Percussus morbo decessit qui intus jacet*. How strange mankind is! Many officers got up and left – these men who braved death every hour showed some disgust at having to eat their dinner off a tombstone.

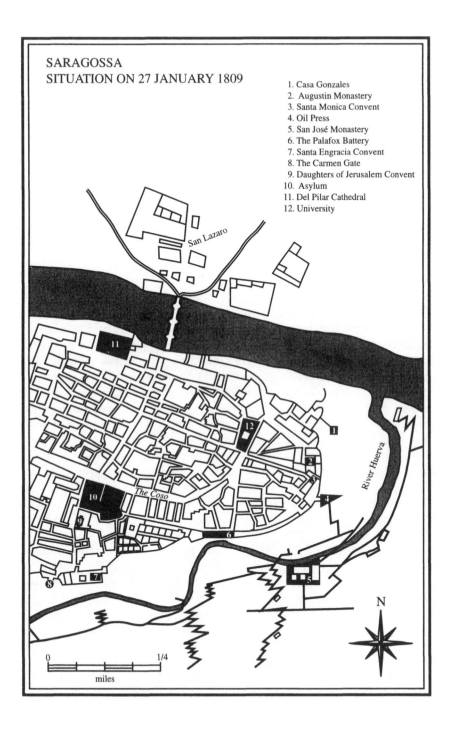

SARAGOSSA
SITUATION ON 27 JANUARY 1809

1. Casa Gonzales
2. Augustin Monastery
3. Santa Monica Convent
4. Oil Press
5. San José Monastery
6. The Palafox Battery
7. Santa Engracia Convent
8. The Carmen Gate
9. Daughters of Jerusalem Convent
10. Asylum
11. Del Pilar Cathedral
12. University

San Lazaro

River Huerva

The Coso

N

0   1/4
miles

CHAPTER IV

∼

The main assault, made on 27 January, was one of the bloodiest days of the siege. Since dawn our batteries had concentrated their fire on widening the breaches. At nine o'clock those units designated for the assault moved forward. The column meant to break into the garden of the Santa Monica convent was four hundred men strong and composed of the 14th Line and part of the 2nd Regiment of the Vistula Legion. A second and smaller column had to storm a breach to the left of this and close to one of the principal batteries of the besieged – that which bore the name of their illustrious leader, Palafox. A third column, formed by a battalion, my own, of the 2nd Regiment of the Vistula Legion, was directed to the right of the Santa Monica convent and San Augustin monastery, towards the Casa Gonzales – a stone building jutting out from this last convent towards the Ebro and linked to the defences by a covered way. These three attacks on the right had to coincide with the assault on the centre against the Santa Engracia convent.

Of all the attacks on the right only one achieved even partial success – that on the breach by the Palafox battery. The breach in the wall of the garden of the Santa Monica convent proved higher than first thought and our voltigeurs only succeeded in clambering up the rubble and establishing themselves in the debris below the breach but could move no further forward. Next, the assault on the Casa Gonzales, in which I took part, failed completely. We only just managed to get into the building, for there too the breach was almost impractical, but were met by such a heavy fire coming from the upper storey and every corner of the place that we fell back rather quickly. Major Beyer, in command, was seriously wounded and the captain

56

of my company, a certain Matkowski from Krakow, had a leg shattered by a roundshot and fell into enemy hands.

Fortunately the main attack in the centre was a complete success, led, as it was, by Colonel Chlopicki. Our troops took not only the Santa Engracia convent but the neighbouring Capuchin nunnery. The loss of this critical position forced the Spanish to abandon their line and fall back. That same evening we were able to enter the Casa Gonzalez as it too had been abandoned. We found the bodies of eleven of our comrades, all horribly mutilated. Matkowski was not there; he had been taken to hospital, where we were to find him after the siege. He was in a terrible condition with not long left to live and failed to recognise anyone. I long regretted the death of this officer as he had always shown me the greatest kindness.

The war of the ramparts was now replaced by the far more terrible war in the streets and houses. News of French victories at Ucles, Alcañiz and Licinena made no impression on the courage of the besieged as they chose not to believe such stories and remembered nothing but Bailen.

On 28 and 29 January we continued to attempt a practicable breach on our side of the Santa Monica convent, in which the enemy was still holding out. On 30 January one company of the 14th Line finally managed to secure a part of the convent's garden and take the church, maintaining its position in the face of fierce counter-attacks. A grenadier captain of the 14th, called Hardy, whom I knew quite well, was mortally wounded in this action. As they carried him back on a stretcher, I went up to him and tried to encourage him with a few words about a speedy recovery. 'Oh, no my young friend,' he said, 'I feel death in my bones. But why must I die at the hands of these brigands and not at Eylau or Friedland where we fought with men of the same calibre as ourselves?' The hand he offered me was stone cold and this brave and dignified man died on the following day.

There were many Catholics in our ranks yet their knowledge of hagiography was somewhat limited and none could say who this Saint Monica was who seemed to wish us so much ill! After the occupation of the University buildings, when the soldiers were bringing out armfuls of books from the library to kindle their fires, an officer noticed that one of these books was a life of Santa Monica. Many years later, when I saw Ary Scheffer's exquisite painting of Saint Augustin and his mother, Saint Monica, I was reminded of the two religious houses in Saragossa placed under their protection.

On 1 February the news of the death of General Lacoste caused considerable dismay, even amongst the ordinary soldiers. He was a man of talent and had the knack of knowing how to be simultaneously obeyed and liked. His successor was Colonel Rogniat who was so critical of Napoleon after the Emperor's fall from power. Rogniat, although quite capable, was not as highly regarded as Lacoste had been, and indeed there was nothing pleasant about his personality and he was found to be conceited, if not downright scornful, with his subordinates.

The more we advanced the more dogged resistance became. We knew that in order not to be killed, or to diminish that risk, we would have to take each and every one of these houses converted into redoubts and where death lurked in the cellars, behind doors and shutters – in fact, everywhere. When we broke into a house we had to make an immediate and thorough inspection from the cellar to the rooftop. Experience taught us that sudden and determined resistance could well be a trick. Often as we were securing one floor we would be shot at from point blank range from the floor above through loopholes in the floorboards. All the nooks and crannies of these old-fashioned houses aided such deadly ambushes. We also had to maintain a good watch on the rooftops. With their light sandals, the Aragonese could move with the ease of and as silently as a cat and were thus able to make surprise incursions well behind the front line. It was indeed aerial combat. We would be sitting peacefully around a fire, in a house occupied for some days, when suddenly shots would come through some window just as though they had come from the sky itself.

With these latest and most terrible developments our sappers and miners were superb. You could see them everywhere – they were there at the most opportune times, when the danger was greatest, or their help essential, at the head of attacking columns, in the cellars where the enemy were about to blow a mine, when a door needed blowing in or a breach effected. Sometimes we would burst into a house only to be met by a loopholed wall bristling with muskets. Then, suddenly, there would be an explosion and the whole obstacle would tumble down like a pack of cards. There were especial difficulties in making progress through the foundations of the great convents and churches and here the stones were seemingly allied to the determined resistance of the besieged.

The Spanish stopped at nothing to slow our advance down. Even when they were at last forced to abandon a building, they would scatter resin soaked faggots everywhere and set them alight. The ensuing fires would not destroy the stone buildings but served to give the besieged time to prepare their defences in neighbouring houses.

Even so, Grandjean's and Musnier's divisions were making some progress on the right. Their effective strength, however, was now reduced to about 10,000 men – a strength diminishing daily. Not surprising when every day one-third of the effectives were employed in the siege, another third were held in reserve and the rest, who should have been recuperating, were guarding the camp and the rear areas; and all this besides the constant alarms and the enemy's counter-attacks. These were especially strong around the asylum, which had been converted into a hospital, and we faced enormous difficulties here. The Spanish commanders knew as well as we the importance of this key position, which commanded the main street in Saragossa – the Coso.

Something horrible happened on 7 February. The Spanish had finally abandoned the asylum, laying mines as they went. The attackers burst in, without meeting any resistance, only to be met by a sight sure to dishearten even the bravest of men. The beds and the floorboards were strewn with the dead and the wounded, who there had been no time to evacuate. There had, however, evidently been enough time to light a fire, and the flames were already racing towards us consuming everything in their path! I was in charge of a detachment of twenty men, covering the left of the column, and we were making our way through the adjacent courtyards and corridors off the main building, when the sapper sergeant, who was serving as our guide, made a wrong turning and took us right into the heart of the conflagration. We suddenly found ourselves shrouded in thick, choking smoke and inhaled the nauseating smell of burnt flesh. There was a moment of panic but fortunately I brushed against a window, obscured by this hellish smoke, broke it and once more found fresh air and daylight. We took stock of our situation and after many detours, we came out of that cursed place safe and sound.

The next day our entire division took part in the assault on the Coso. Above the continual bickering of musketry the groans of much larger explosions could be heard – sometimes the booming of cannon and sometimes a mine going off. I was busy in the Coso with a detachment of some fifty men, setting up a barricade. Grenadiers, posted above us in the windows of neighbouring houses, covered this work, which was designed to protect a communications trench which ran from one side of the street to the other. Suddenly our ears were almost shattered by the familiar whistling and roaring noise of an exploding mine. A neighbouring house collapsed and unmasked a Spanish battery which blasted us with grape at point blank range. Miraculously, only three men were hit but the rest ran for it as quick as they could. Both those working on the barricade and their guards had fled to the rear leaving myself and the grenadier captain, a man called Boll and a native of Volhynia,[30] quite alone. He set off, marching as calmly as if on parade, towards the breach through which our men had disappeared. Reaching it he turned to me and said, with considerable sangfroid, 'this is an odious duty; however, the officer of highest rank always goes last'. He came through after me and rallied his grenadiers, chastising them for having abandoned their post without orders. Boll, who was a close friend of

---

[30] A region in the western Ukraine.

the colonel, very obligingly commended my steadiness on this occasion to the colonel.

The day ended badly for us. The Spanish found a means of bringing up a cannon and flushed us out from around the Coso with considerable loss. However, this setback did not seriously affect the morale of the soldiers as they were now no longer alone in the struggle as had been the case in the first weeks of the siege. The fighting henceforth raged at all points – as much on the right flank as on the left and on the other side of the river. From a battery set at the mouth of the Huerva the progress of the soldiers of Gazan's division could be followed. We thought them very lucky to be able to fight in the fresh air whilst we were condemned to this horrible war of streets, houses and passageways.

Over the following days we took, with some loss, a few positions on the Coso. On 12 February the first attack on the University buildings failed due to the fact that the miners had not been able to place their galleries close enough under the walls, the result being that the explosion failed to make a breach and our columns were exposed to a galling fire from which they fell back with the loss of about forty men. Again the casualties fell on the Poles – they were always given the most dangerous missions.

One of the last clashes, and one of the most bloody, was that for the Calle de los Arcades; and it was now our turn to put some cannon to use. Here I witnessed one of the most memorable examples of the tenacity of the besieged. One of the houses still being fought over, on the corner of the Coso and the Calle de los Arcades, was shot at from such close quarters that the roundshot passed right through the building and out of the other side. Nevertheless, the defenders simply abandoned one storey and took refuge on the next floor up and kept up such a galling fire that we were unable to advance any further that day.

The 18th was decisive. As Gazan's division seized the suburbs on the left bank, killing or taking all the defenders, we also made good progress along the Coso and neighbouring streets. At around three o'clock a 1,500-pound mine was blown and, as it was better placed than the last, caused a large breach in the wall of the main University building. Three companies of my regiment and two of the 14th Line launched a desperate assault. This time we managed to seize this important position for the cost of a dozen men. At the same time the house on the corner of the Calle de los Arcades, assaulted for the sixth time, finally surrendered, its resistance exhausted. Captain Boll directed this attack in person. He had a particular habit of wearing full dress uniform when assigned to any dangerous position and today he was dressed to the nines. 'Days of battle,' he joked, 'are our holidays.'

This time we had made real progress and capitulation now seemed to be a question of hours rather than of days. Even so, hostilities continued throughout 19 January. In the evening a Spanish emissary presented himself at our outposts, yet the Spanish proposals were entirely inadmissible. The next day Marshal Lannes personally supervised the digging of mine galleries under the Coso. One company of the 3rd Regiment of the Vistula received the order to make their way under a house next to the bridge over the Ebro and thereby cut behind positions still manned by the defenders. The company lost the most part of its men in this dangerous manoeuvre but completed their mission. We were still seriously concerned as to the fate of these brave men when we were officially notified of the cessation of hostilities. Many officers believed that these negotiations were another Spanish trick and we therefore spent another night under arms. On the next day, however, all doubts were cast aside. We were indeed masters of the city – just as well for the besiegers as for the besieged.

CHAPTER V

APPEARANCE OF OUR ENEMIES – PALAFOX – PILLAGE – INTO THE
CITY CENTRE – CHURCH OF EL PILAR – THE CALLE DE TOLEDO –
A MONASTERY'S REFECTORY

It was all over by the evening of 20 February and yet on the morning of the
next day the Spanish sentries were still at their posts, aiming at the too
curious and snarling *atras!* (get back) at them.

Finally, at noon, we made our way in full dress over blocked canals and
a landscape of olive tree stumps towards the Puerta del Portillo, where the
garrison would come to pile their arms. Each one of us made it a point of
honour to eradicate every trace of the hardship we had suffered. Greatcoats
burnt with powder and torn by bullets were carefully rolled up and
strapped on top of knapsacks; muskets carefully polished shone in the sun.
Lannes, less talkative than usual, appeared with his staff and passed slowly
along in front of the troops, saluting the flags and saying nothing to us but
'Dress the ranks there'.

After about an hour the vanguard of the famous defenders of Saragossa
began to appear. A certain number of young men, aged between sixteen and
eighteen, without uniforms and wearing grey cloaks and red cockades, lined
up in front of us, nonchalantly smoking their cigarettes. Not long after we
witnessed the arrival of the rest of the army: a strange collection composed
of humanity of all shades and conditions. A few were in uniform but most
were dressed like peasants. This turnout was therefore a curious collection
of national costume from all corners of the Peninsula – from Aragon,
Castile, Navarre, Valencia, Catalonia and Andalucia. The officers, mounted
on mules or asses, were distinguishable from the soldiers only by their
tricorns and long cloaks. These people were all smoking and chattering and
looked with complete indifference on their imminent captivity. Not all of
them, however, were so resigned and we soon saw the arrival of more people
whom our soldiers were driving before them with blows from sticks; these
had been turfed out of houses where they had hoped to escape our notice.

Eventually General Morlot, charged with escorting the prisoners, set his troops in motion and the whole of this garrison, some eight or ten thousand strong, filed past us. Most of them were of such non-military bearing that our men were saying aloud that we should never have had so much trouble in beating such a rabble.

I was told that Palafox was found almost dead in the Casa de los Gigantes. A few days later I saw him as they were taking him to the carriage, drawn by four mules, that was to take him to France.[31] An aide-de-camp of the marshal helped him along, his hat in his hand, and our troops gave him military honours. He seemed indifferent to such a show and totally absorbed in his grief or by the unhappy situation of his country. What surprised me the most was that not a single Spaniard paid him the slightest attention.

Entry into Saragossa was still officially forbidden to the soldiers, and guards had been posted on all the gates. But unofficial ways into town were well known. From the very first day the *trips into town* began and no one came back empty-handed. By the evening of the 21st there was a profusion of wine and superb cuts of bacon, and such like, cooking in pots throughout the camp.

On the 22nd I was ordered into the city to collect our wine ration. There was such a commotion at the issuing station that I would have had to wait several hours before receiving the wine. One of my comrades, forced to wait like myself, suggested we explore the neighbouring streets and kill some time.

We went first to the famous Church of the Pilar, which was quite close by. We had to make our way along the riverbank in order to avoid the barricades and the still smoking ruins.

The square in front of the church was one of those scenes impossible to forget. It was clogged with praying women and children, coffins, and the dead for whom there were no coffins. In some places there were as many as twenty corpses piled on top of each other. One coffin lay open and an old man dressed in a superb white uniform with red facings was contained within. Near him, her hair dishevelled, was his wife or daughter – a young and beautiful woman – praying fervently. From time to time she would lift her head and look anxiously at the church, quite unaware of the officiating priest.

Inside the church the priests, present in numbers and at all the altars, found that they could not fulfil all of their many tasks. The doleful con-

---

[31] Palafox was a political prisoner, according to Napoleon, and was imprisoned for the remainder of the war in Vincennes fortress. Serafino d'Albuerquerque, a Spaniard in French service, was the arresting officer.

gregation crowded under the portals and filled the aisles – the floor of the
nave had vanished under kneeling figures in black whose sobs intermingled
with the psalms. I caught sight too of some French soldiers kneeling by the
main altar. The smoke of the countless candles drifted up to the vaulted
roof, which had been riddled by our shells.

Still more sinister was the Calle de Toledo. Here the population had
sought refuge from our bombardment. Under the arches, and in indescrib-
able confusion, there lay children, old people, the dying and the dead, all
kinds of furniture and emaciated domestic animals. There was a mound of
corpses, many stark naked, piled in the middle of the street; here and there
fires were burning around which these poor people were attempting to cook
their food. Above all it was the children, thin and with the bright eyes of
fever, that were painful to behold. Shadowy figures, wrapped in their giant
cloaks, talked energetically and fell silent when we drew near, pretending
not to look at us.

I have, since then, been present at many scenes of slaughter. I have seen
the Great Redoubt at Borodino, one of the most infamous horrors of war.
Yet nowhere have I felt the same emotion as I did at that moment and
perhaps the sight of suffering is far more poignant than that of death.

The appearance of the rest of the city was no less depressing. Between
San José and Santa Engracia and as far as the Coso, all the streets were
blocked by barricades and rubble. Access was only possible through the less
damaged buildings, occupied by our soldiers. In order to find a way about
this labyrinth of ruins guides were posted at regular intervals and the
numbers of the regiments, battalions and companies had been scrawled on
the walls in charcoal. In the same way our soldiers amused themselves by
drawing cartoons and writing facetious comments on the walls, and these
made for some bizarre contrasts. So it was in the San José monastery, over
which we had struggled for so long, where the following couplet, so appropriate to its surroundings, could be read, etched on the refectory walls in
huge lettering:

Love and war are all balls;
One destroys hearts, the other, walls.

CHAPTER VI

SOME MILITARY PERSONALITIES – LANNES – JUNOT – LAVAL – HABERT
– THE MILITARY MASS – SOME REFLECTIONS

It is only really during sieges, especially sieges such as this (fifty-two days of digging trenches), that junior officers and soldiers are put into close contact with their superior officers. Amongst ours Lannes and Junot, above all, attracted our attention. The former often did the rounds of our positions and seemed everywhere, always asking questions or recommending some course of action. He was always confident and had an extraordinary courage that bordered on audacity. I remember when this marshal, after the fall of the Jesuits' Convent, perched himself on a rooftop and began to follow the movements of the enemy through a telescope. He soon found himself a target for sharpshooters hidden in the ruins of the convent and began to attract their shots. Lannes immediately grabbed a musket and fired back with such effect that the enemy responded with a shell which killed a captain of engineers right next to him. Lannes finally came down off the roof, and looked, to all appearances, as though nothing had happened.

Other generals, too, notably Junot, Habert and Chlopicki, tried their hand at an occasional shot at the enemy and I believe that they do not have to be prodigious marksmen as such demonstrations alone make an excellent impression on the troops when in difficult circumstances.

Junot was also a frequent visitor to our positions. He would sit himself down on some log or pile of rubble and chat at length with the officers. His conversation was eminently *soldierly* and peppered with colourful language. From about this time on it became increasingly apparent that he was not quite right in the head.

Laval, always remembered with respect in the French Army, was a tiny little man whose puny appearance contrasted markedly with his great reputation. The soldiers called him 'the miller' on account of the grey overcoat he was always seen in. He seemed somehow to be overshadowed by the general of our brigade, Habert, a giant of a man with a huge mane of jet black hair and athletic build but with no particular merit other than exceptional bravery. A typical example of this was an occasion when we were digging-in in a street leading to a crossroads which was still in the enemy's hands. We had thrown up a barricade in order to provide cover and so we could cross from one side of the street to the other without too much danger. The barricade was not very high and it was necessary to duck when passing along behind it so as to avoid the fire of the Spanish. Tall men, like Habert, really had to bend right over. Just as he was in the course of carrying out this particular manoeuvre one of the soldiers, lying flat on his belly by the barricade, made the frivolous remark, 'So, generals get scared too, do they?' Habert, furious, span around, seized the insolent offender by the arms, carried him out into the middle of the street and drew himself up to his full height. Suddenly a volley was fired at the strange pair and the soldier dropped dead, hit by five or six bullets. Incredibly, the general got away with nothing more than a bruise on his arm. He gave the soldier's corpse a good kick, called him a f— conscript and continued on his rounds. I must add that this act of brutal courage did not offend the comrades of the deceased and they agreed that the general was in the right, saying, 'He did the right thing. It was a shocking thing to say to a general.'

All historians have talked about the triumphant entry of Lannes into the city on 24 February and of the *Te Deum* sung on this occasion in the Church of the Pilar. None, to my knowledge, have mentioned a particular circumstance. At the Elevation of the Host our drummers began to beat a tattoo, as is done in French military masses, and there were distinct signs of apprehension and anxiety in the Spanish congregation. They mistook the drum roll to be the signal for a general massacre and were only reassured when they saw the marshals (Lannes and Mortier) kneel down to pray.

This siege shook the world. Political passions rose to an even greater pitch than usual. The resistance shown by the besiegers has been much praised and yet it would be only fair to recognise that from a military point of view, the merits of the attack were at least equal to those of the defence. For heroic tenacity the victors compare well with the vanquished. This is especially true for the divisions of Morlot and Grandjean which, with less than 13,000 men under arms, endured, alone, three weeks of horrific street-fighting against twice as many defenders.

My regiment remained in Saragossa until 6 March. We had all the time in the world to study the siegeworks and the defences. From this study it became apparent that certain of our dispositions had been faulty. Even so, we didn't dare express our opinions on this subject, even in a whisper, as discipline was so strict.

This siege had preoccupied the Emperor, as he had recalled the engineer general Lery in order to 'make a model and profile of the city in order to serve as a study of how to attack an open city whose inhabitants wish to defend themselves'. This scheme was indefinitely postponed by force of circumstance.

CHAPTER VII

THE CATS OF EL BORGO – GUADALUPE – A MILITARY EXECUTION –
ALCAÑIZ – MONZON AND ITS CASTLE – TRAGIC END OF A MUSIC-
LOVING MAGISTRATE – IMPROVISED ARTILLERY – A SKIRMISH – A COLD
BATH – CAPTAIN SOLNICKI'S REPORT

On 5 March I was sent with a detachment to El Borgo, a hamlet three miles
from Saragossa, where our cavalry had been stationed during the siege. All
the houses had been plundered and the inhabitants had fled. Only the
prowling cats had stayed, and one old woman, blind and stupid, who our
soldiers fed. I left this wonderful place as quickly as I could. Less than
twenty-four hours later I received the order to rejoin the brigade, which was
heading for Alcañiz, then being threatened by an enemy advance.

Later two companies, one of which was mine, were designated as the
garrison of the castle that dominated the little town of Guadalupe. The four
winds raged against this ruined fort, perched at the crest of a rocky peak.
The cold was biting – no surprise, as we only had enough wood for cooking
and any fire had to be made outside in the open because of the smoke.
We spent four grievous days in this inhospitable keep which frequently
managed to make us nostalgic about the trenches of Saragossa.

The one 'event' of our stay was to see a peasant who had been caught
bearing arms executed. From our vantage point we could see every detail
of the scene as it unfolded – the last words of this poor devil were 'Long
live Ferdinand VII!' and they came to us just as the shots rang out. I was
present at many executions in Spain but had the good fortune never to be
put in charge of one.

We finally left Guadalupe for Alcañiz, where my regiment was barracked
in an old and damp convent and many soldiers consequently came down
with fevers. The Valencians had fallen back as our troops advanced but we
soon heard that other enemy troops were mustering in the mountains close
to the source of the Cinca and the Segre, and our brigade under Habert was
ordered to disperse them. We crossed the Ebro on pontoons that seemed

well tired of life, and went into action in the Cinca valley. My company and one other were sent to hold the tiny fort at Monzon, a position of military significance but inaccessible.

The captain of the other company, called Solnicki, was a veteran and acted as commandant whilst I served as his adjutant. Solnicki was an old hand who well understood his duties but whose parents had probably not been ruined by the cost of his education. He made haste to occupy the fort and get the peasants to bring in ten days' supply of food. He went to considerable lengths in organising constant patrols through the olive groves which ringed the town and formed a kind of forest. For my part I had the good fortune to win over the local magistrate in a process that mimicked Orpheus. This person had an unfortunate passion for music. One particular day I had gone to see him on business and I found him scratching at a guitar and singing some seguidillas out of tune in the midst of his family. In the course of the conversation he asked me if I was at all musical. Now, at that time playing the guitar was very popular at our universities and I was as good a player as any other. I took hold of the instrument and gave a reasonable rendition of a *Krakowiak* and a *Lied*, to the great satisfaction of the magistrate and his two daughters – two dark-eyed brunettes. This civil servant, who until then had not been numbered among our friends, pressed me to come and see them as often as I could.

Apart from the necessity of always remaining vigilant, our stay here was heaven compared to what we had just endured. There was an abundance of good quality food – so much so that our soldiers would always say that things were 'like in Monzon' whenever they found themselves in good quarters. Required to patrol around the town, we ended up becoming familiar with the whole outlying area and this allowed us to pay the Spanish guerrilla chief Perena[32] a little nocturnal call in the mountains. He had his informers in the town and had managed to surprise us on the odd occasion. This time it was his turn to be surprised and forced to beat a hasty retreat. During this expedition I was in command of the detachment left in charge of the fort. Another detachment maintained communications with the little punitive column and was placed midway between us and them. We sent each other messages using olive tree leaves or pieces of specially shaped and sized blank paper, the meanings of which were agreed beforehand, carried by local people.

Even so, the enemy forces continued to grow around us and it seemed inevitable that we would have to abandon the place. But we managed to keep the guerrillas and their friends at bay for just a little longer thanks to a novel

---

[32] Felipe Perena was a regular army soldier turned guerrilla. He was later captured at the fall of Lerida.

expedient. Our little fort contained a small arsenal which had been imperfectly destroyed. We found it contained a dozen cannon with broken gun carriages but otherwise in working order. The gunpowder had been thrown down a well but the roundshot and the charcoal were still in the magazine. Our idea was to, at best, make use of this resource or, at worst, to make some kind of demonstration. One of our officers and a few of the soldiers had served as auxiliaries for the artillery at Saragossa and this made the task considerably easier. We managed to salvage some of the powder from the depths of the well and found it to be still serviceable. We improvised gun-carriages as well as we could from huge logs. In short, we found ourselves armed with artillery that we could use. True, we would have to be careful so as not to do ourselves more harm than we did the enemy.

The first test came against a column of the enemy debouching from the mountains and we obtained results far above our expectations. After having made everyone stand well back the gunners used long matches to fire the pieces. The explosion wrecked the gun-carriages, as expected, but we had the satisfaction of seeing the cannon-balls carry a certain distance. Although nobody was killed, the enemy, terrified by the noise of the unexpected discharge, fell into a hasty retreat.

This demonstration kept the Spanish back for a few hours but they soon came on again in ever greater numbers and completely surrounded the town. These ominous developments took a tragic turn when my relationship with the magistrate, which had begun so well, came to a sudden and terrible end. One day as I was doing my rounds, I came across a crowd gathered outside the door of this music-loving man and as I drew closer I saw the two young daughters crying over the body of their dead father. It seemed that someone had called out his name and at the moment he opened the shutters to reply he fell, mortally wounded by a shot fired at point blank range. No one knew the motive for, or perpetrator of, the murder. Some accused a smuggler who had an old score to settle with the magistrate. Others, casting sidelong glances at me, had seen me come as a visitor to the house and swore that the murder could only have been as an act of political revenge carried out upon an *Afrancesado*.[33] So it seems most likely that my music and I had played an important role in the demise of this poor man.

However, the next crisis soon overshadowed this sad episode. The clerk and the treasurer, with whom I had now to liaise for lack of a magistrate to

---

[33] *Afrancesado*: pro-French. Many of the middle classes showed themselves sympathetic to the political reforms engendered by King Joseph's administration. Amongst the leading *Afrancesados* were Goya, O'Farrill, Mariano Dominguez, de Quinto and the Bishop of Huesca. However, Suchet lamented that, 'there are hardly any of them who want to serve us'.

issue the rations, both suddenly absconded to the country. Where exactly in the country? It was not difficult to imagine. In the space of the next twenty-four hours all the other inhabitants played the same trick or went into hiding. On the next day, which was market day, not one peasant appeared in town and only a few women and children could be seen in the streets. Things were looking decidedly sinister and, indeed, on the same day (6 April) we received the order to evacuate Monzon at once and recross the Cinca. We expected we would come under attack in the course of this manoeuvre and we were not disappointed. As soon as it left the town the vanguard, which was escorting the baggage and the sick, came under attack and was pushed towards the river by superior forces. We now left the fort after having fired one parting shot with our improvised artillery. But the artillery had lost a little of its mystique and even as we were passing through the town we came under heavy fire as a parting farewell. There was a terrific skirmish as we pushed through the olive groves for the river. Given command of the rearguard, I managed to carry out this dangerous task without loss of honour but my zeal almost led to my funeral. I did not want to leave the riverbank until the last boat had cast off. Just as it did so and had begun to pull away from the bank, I misjudged my jump and instead of ending up in the ferry, I fell into the icy river – from which I was rescued with some difficulty.

It was night by the time we reached Barbastro after a long and arduous march. Here the French garrison was under arms and very worried about what might have become of us.

On the next morning Solnicki, the former commandant of Monzon, called me in to his room and I found him rather agitated. 'I have received,' he told me, 'the order to write a full report on yesterday's battle. Would you sit down there and set the ball rolling. Here is a pen, ink and paper.' I sat down, and regurgitated a brief resume of what had happened, adding the number of dead and wounded, some fifteen men. I read all this off to the captain and he pointed out that I had missed a couple of essential details. He then dictated some additions and corrections which had the effect of turning this minor skirmish into a colourful struggle of heroic proportions, and accorded full credit to its fortunate outcome to himself. 'That, my friend, is how you write a report,' he boasted and then got me to write out the report once again, scribbled his name with difficulty at the bottom of the page and rewarded me with a cup of coffee, a luxury I had been deprived of since Pamplona. Military histories are all too often written in the manner of Solnicki's report, if not all histories.

This good man, Solnicki, so good at writing reports, was killed a few months later at the siege of Tortosa.

CHAPTER VIII

~

Barbastro, which Habert's brigade occupied for close on three weeks, is no
doubt quite a pleasant place in times of peace but in times of war it is one
of great danger on account of the labyrinth of canals, olive plantations,
vineyards and other walled enclosures, which surround it. Habert, so
confident in open country, was not half the man he should have been in such
a terrain. He personally organised the positioning of the outposts, after an
all too brief reconnaissance, and his dispositions left much to be desired.
Any method in our security measures was obscured by a host of pointless
duties which wore out the soldiers without adding to their safety. There
was, above all, a lack of basic organisation. Each battalion was ordered to
provide men to guard first this place and then that and consequently never
grew familiar with its surroundings. This constant rotation, good and
effective in garrison, was deeply troubling in a terrain so suited to surprise
attack. We had sentries carried off or disarmed by invisible enemies every
night. It would have been better to assign each battalion a permanent post
and for them to report back to the commander details of any movements or
activity in their sector. Everyone would then be responsible for what went
on in their own district.

These constant setbacks undermined the morale of the troops. Frequent
retaliatory searches were made and they once arrested a poor devil who one
of the disarmed sentries thought he had recognised, but who swore right to
the end that on the night in question he had only been out taking the air.
Nonetheless he was shot with much ceremony before the bishop and the
mayor.

With each new misadventure the general would rage and take his
frustration out on the populace and even on his own soldiers. The soldiers
soon began to take this as just another example of the bad feeling so

72

prevalent in our armies in Spain. It is vital that any leader or commander remains at least impassive, if not happy, in times of difficulty.

Habert, having received the order to reoccupy the valley of the Cinca, left Barbastro on 12 May and headed for the hills via Sixena, where we arrived on the evening of 14 May after having marched through a terrible storm. Meagre streams had been transformed into raging torrents and both horses and men would lose their footing in the slippery mud. In Sixena my battalion was lodged in a convent renowned for its excellent wine. Unfortunately the soldiers of V Corps had passed through just before us and the famous cellars were now nothing but a distant memory.

On 15 May Habert marched on Alcolea, where he counted on being able to cross the Cinca. But the enemy had taken up an excellent position on the other bank and prepared to dispute the crossing. On the next day we moved down to Pomar, where we hoped the terrain would be more favourable to us. Under the protection of our artillery we set about crossing the Cinca using two barges, each one of which could ferry across the best part of a company. However, the eldest of the bargemen kept looking up at the sky and showed distinct signs of unease. The sky was clear overhead but menacingly dark over the mountains. He attempted to share his fears with the general and inform him that this river was prone to sudden and violent currents after storms in the Sierra and that he would be wise to postpone the crossing. He was rewarded for his advice by a good kicking and the insults 'blockhead' and '*carajo*'. Everything seemed to be going well and eight companies of French and Polish voltigeurs and grenadiers had been ferried to the other bank. Other troops were just embarking when a huge wave came sweeping down the Cinca and brought water, rocks and logs crashing down upon us. A real Spanish tempest. The ropes snapped like straws and the barges were swept away downstream. The soldiers on board had immense difficulty regaining dry land. Soon the whole plain was flooded by the deluge and we had to scramble for the heights. An enormous lake now separated us from our unlucky comrades who we could just see on the far bank. The general, desperate, tried in vain to get them to hear him and point out to them a direction that they might follow. His voice, powerful as it was, was drowned by the noise of the torrent. He appealed for the bravest swimmers to come forward and attempt to reach the other side. All gave up or died without having reached the half-way point. One, by a supreme effort, reached a rock swept by the waves. I saw him clinging there, then, making a sign of distress, or farewell, he let go and disappeared.

During all this the storm that had caused this disaster finally broke over our heads. The rain fell with violence and it was impossible to distinguish anything on the far bank. After a very unhappy night, the general took us back to the heights above Monzon and there attempt a passage of the river.

This is where he should have begun. But the Spanish were too strong and we lost a whole day in skirmishing as a result. Habert was grief-stricken. I caught sight of him under the arches of a ruined bridge and this otherwise energetic and cold-hearted man was crying and wringing his hands repeating, 'My poor grenadiers, my brave voltigeurs!' He could think of nothing better to do than to march back to Barbastro on the 18th, from where we had set out six days previously on this unfortunate expedition.

Forty-eight hours later I was commanding an outpost in a position where the enemy was expected to appear any moment. I caught sight of a group of cavalrymen advancing with care; it was our cuirassiers, lost since the 16th, who had managed to swim back over the cursed river. We learnt from them the terrible fate of the eight companies of infantry.[34] Their commanding officer had had the unfortunate idea of throwing them into the hills in a desperate bid to reach the French frontier that way. Intercepted by the guerrillas, attacked in front by regular troops coming from Lerida, having expended their ammunition and lacking food, these brave men, about one thousand strong, all elite troops, had had to submit and surrender after three days of marching and fighting. They were now to be sent off to the infamous isle of Cabrera. Later they were sent on to the British hulks, which were not much better. Many years later I met with a Pole who had survived this captivity, which was more deadly than any battle. He had not been released until 1814.

This unhappy event had been caused by a mixture of bad luck and misjudgement. Our first mistake had been to quit Monzon when we should have remained there in strength. Habert would not have lost his vanguard if, instead of losing precious time at attempting a passage at different points, he had concentrated his energies against Monzon and occupied the town in force, where he could have held out against the Spanish despite the flood.

We were soon pulled out of the Ebro valley. This manoeuvre confirmed that the rumours about Blake threatening Saragossa were true. If I am not mistaken, it was during this difficult march over the Sierra d'Alcubiere, between Barbastro and Villafranca, that we first learnt that Junot had been replaced by Suchet in command of III Corps.

---

[34] The troops ferried to the other side were the voltigeur companies of the 2nd Regiment of the Vistula Legion (two companies) and the 14th Line (three companies), one grenadier and two voltigeur companies of the 116th Line and one squadron of the 13th Cuirassiers. In all twenty-five officers and 717 men were captured in this unfortunate incident.

CHAPTER IX

After numerous comings and goings in the Ebro valley, Habert's brigade marched for Monte Torero on 25 May, leaving two companies of the 2nd Vistula Regiment, Solnicki's and my own, to guard the bridge at Gallego. We remained at this post for three weeks. At night we could see close by, in the hills of Perdiguera, the fires of the very Spanish partisans our patrols had been fighting running battles with for some time. Down in the plains, all seemed quiet. We saw the peasants coming and going from dawn till dusk, carrying their produce to Saragossa. The new commander-in-chief, Suchet, was far more severe on matters of discipline than his predecessor had been and any junior officer who took a few eggs from a peasant would soon find himself before a court martial.

Suchet, believing that the guerrillas were too close to Saragossa for comfort, ordered them to be attacked on the night of 7–8 June. Six battalions crossed the bridge at Gallego and moved silently into the mountains, heading for Perdiguera, the headquarters of the commander of the local guerrillas – Brigadier Perena. The Brigadier kept a poor lookout and we arrived at this small market town in broad daylight without having met either patrols or sentries. The Spanish, taken by surprise, put up only token resistance and we pursued them into the mountains as far as Licinena. We made quite a good haul of booty in this expedition. I secured an excellent mule for myself which, in spite of its nationality, served me well.

Two days later our commander-in-chief paid us an unexpected visit. He reviewed us, thoroughly examined the arms and equipment of the men and congratulated us on our good turn out. He gave Solnicki ('a soldier who deserved his respect') a warm handshake and this compliment was probably due to our report on the Monzon affair. Our previous commanders had never bothered to pay us such visits, but this one had an excellent effect on the men.

On the same day, 10 June, we were relieved of our wearisome posting at Gallego and sent on to Saragossa. For forty-eight hours I was quartered near the Pilar Church and this stay was marked by a unique incident – I was spontaneously invited to dine with a Spanish gentleman for the very first time. The home of this hospitable old man was most modest, as was the meal. There was the inevitable *Puchero*, chicken fried in oil, accompanied by various savoury pies. The evening was supervised by a respectable serving maid far advanced in years. Luckily the wine was passable and the conversation interesting. This good man was interested in the *señores franceses* and was convinced we would be surrounded by Blake and forced to surrender as Dupont had been at Bailen the year before.

After dinner we went out onto the balcony which overlooks the square. He remarked on some of our men gathered around the door of the church listening to one of their comrades reading from a large book. He asked what the significance of this scene was. The reader was a man from my company and was a native of Boryzin and a Lutheran, as were most of the population of German origin from that region. In the course of the siege he had found, in the university library, a seventeenth-century edition of Luther's translation of the Bible and from then on read out passages to his co-religionists as often as he could. This was perhaps the first time a Protestant, with Luther's Bible in his hands, had preached before the main entrance of Saragossa cathedral and we had had to wait for Napoleon to make this possible – even though his main concern had been to put his brother on the throne of Spain rather than spark a religious Reformation. The good Spaniard was dumbstruck whilst I was explaining all this to him. I think he rued ever having invited a heretic to his table.

At Monte Torero, the next day, I learnt that I had been assigned as commander of some sixty voltigeurs who had escaped the disaster on the Cinca and who were to form the cadre for new voltigeur companies. It was a position of trust, the more so as I was the youngest officer in the regiment. I owed this good fortune to the kind recommendations of captains Boll and Solnicki, two brave men who did not, alas, have much longer to live.

Everyone was now counting on a decisive confrontation. After two weeks of useless inertia, the Spanish general had finally set his troops in motion and on the morning of the 13th we too received orders to advance and march on Santa-Fé, close to Belchite, where the enemy had gathered in force. We had to pass right through Saragossa to do this. The streets were deserted and the windows and doors barred. Only here and there could we dimly make out a few curious, shadowy figures woken by the noise of our drums.

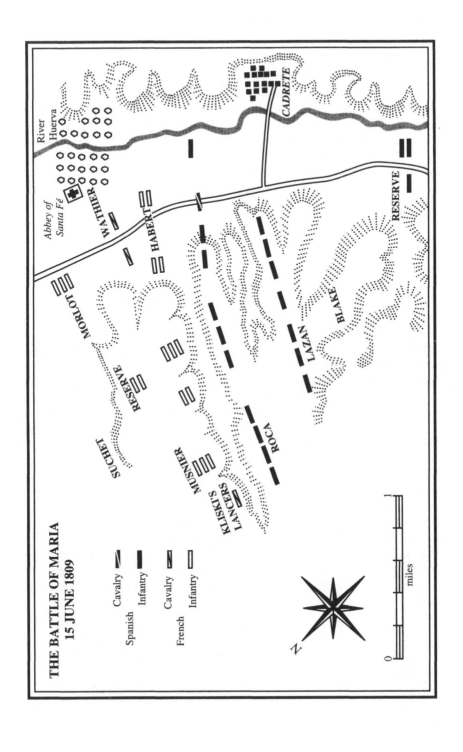

THE BATTLE OF MARIA
15 JUNE 1809

Spanish
  Cavalry
  Infantry

French
  Cavalry
  Infantry

N

0   miles   1

River
Huerva

CADRETE

Abbey of
Santa Fé

WATHIER

HABERT

MORLOT

RESERVE

SUCHET

MUSNIER

KLISKI'S
LANCERS

ROCA

LAZAN

BLAKE

RESERVE

We camped in the midst of an olive grove close to the monastery of Santa-Fé, which is remarkable for its bell. The fires of the enemy were close by and there were several false alarms during the night.

The next morning, the 14th, there was a continual bickering between our outposts and those of the Spanish, which lasted the whole day. The Spanish were showing considerable resolution and even gained ground. The struggle continued on the morning of the 15th but proved indecisive for several hours. I was posted on a slight eminence with my voltigeurs, behind some rocks, and had the good luck to repulse three successive charges of the yellow 7th Numantia dragoons right under the nose of Suchet.[35] He even sent a staff officer, Captain Desaix, to congratulate me on my 'heroic resistance'.

By noon, our ammunition was running low and indeed had almost been exhausted. A burning sun bore down on our heads and we were dying from the heat and of thirst. I distinctly remember the moment one of my comrades, Lieutenant Ratkowski, was in the process of offering me his flask when it was hit by a ball and blown clean out of his hands. He fetched it back, offered it again and said, calmly, 'drink while you can, this flask wants to make a tactical withdrawal.' Poor Ratkowski was unlucky. He was one of the bravest among us and had been wounded at Saragossa. One day he was in command of a convoy when it was attacked from all sides by superior forces and lost a few wagons. The general in charge of the division felt it necessary to blame Ratkowski's conduct in an order of the day. Ratkowski never recovered from this rebuke. He still dwelt on this insult he had received in Spain and right up to his final moments, at the crossing of the Beresina, the mental scar remained with him. 'I wish the bastard who dishonoured me had been in my place,' he said, 'he'd have seen how we were attacked!' He was one of my best friends and his memory has always made me wary of criticising subordinates in public reprimands, as it is most unjust to men of good heart.

Meanwhile, the Spanish, who were preparing to advance, were themselves attacked vigorously by a column composed of the 115th Line[36] and the 1st Regiment of the Vistula. We (the 2nd) were in reserve but were soon called forwards once more and directed to support the severely tested 115th. The weather had changed by this time and the rain was falling in torrents as the French made one final effort. Thanks to a fine charge by the cavalry of General Wathier[37] and the élan of a column of infantry led by Habert,

---

[35] Although Brandt says the Numantia Regiment, it was, in fact, the Olivenza Dragoons, who also wore yellow coats.

[36] At Maria the 115th Line was commanded by Colonel Dupeyroux.

[37] General Wathier commanded the 4th Hussars and the 13th Cuirassiers.

we wrested the battlefield from the Spanish, who withdrew, in good order, a short distance to the heights of Bottoritta. They did not relinquish this position until the night of the 16th–17th, when they retreated to Belchite.

After a long and difficult march through terrain that was alternatively rocky and marshy, we arrived, on the evening of the 16th, at the village of Puebla de Alboron, deep in the mountains. This village had been absolutely devastated and offered no resources. I do not believe victors in their camp have ever been so cold and hungry in the middle of June. Even so, morale was high after the previous days' successes and we expected better on the morrow.

The next day was indeed decisive. We drew up before Belchite at an early hour. This little town was strongly garrisoned with the main body of the enemy placed behind it on the heights. The French advanced, aiming to skirt round the town. My regiment was on the right flank – my voltigeurs and I were escorting two guns[38] and we were having difficulties keeping up with them as they started downhill. Taking up position, the cannons opened up on the enemy. By a tremendous stroke of luck, one of them hit an artillery caisson with its first shot. The caisson blew up and triggered a massive explosion as other Spanish ammunition wagons went up in turn. This disaster threw the whole Spanish line into panic and whole battalions threw away their arms and fled, thinking themselves attacked in the rear. The shout 'We have been betrayed!' went up. We would have made many more prisoners had the gate on our side of the town been less solid and the entrance somewhat wider. As we sought to break our way in, the enemy were fleeing out through the other side. One battalion, in the main square, resisted, and was ridden down by Polish lancers.[39] Most of the Spanish showed considerable agility in getting away and consequently we took few prisoners. We did take nine cannon, some twenty ammunition wagons and a vast quantity of food.

The remnants of the Spanish forces were pursued as far as Alcañiz, where we arrived on the 19th in atrocious weather. My battalion was sent back to Belchite the day after to escort the captured supplies to Saragossa. However, we had been forestalled by the commissariat and most of the provisions had already disappeared. Of the many thousands of wagons and mules taken at Belchite, only about one tenth ever reached the Saragossa magazine. The rest had been sold back to the populace at a steep price for the profit of the civilian employees who ran the commissary.

---

[38] The two guns were under the command of Lieutenant Auvray, one of Suchet's aides-de-camp.

[39] The regiment ridden down by Colonel Kliski's 1st Lancers of the Vistula Legion was the 1st Regiment of Valencia.

CHAPTER X

AT BELCHITE – A CONTRASTING HOST AND HOSTESS – THE
GUERRILLAS – STORMING OUR LADY OF AQUILA – THE DAROCA
TUNNEL – A NIGHT ATTACK – OCCUPATION OF CALATAYUD – I BECOME
COURIER FOR THE NIGHT

We spent a week at Belchite under tolerable conditions. Our soldiers were
lodged in one of the town's three convents and I, with some comrades, was
billeted close by with one of the local gentry, a certain Don José Bernardo.
This gloomy old man professed to loath the French; a feeling not shared by
his wife, who was much younger and not at all bad looking.

The good times could not last. We no longer had to fear attack from
regular troops, but their dispersal had swelled the ranks of the guerrilla
bands and we had to keep the pressure on these bands to ensure our own
survival. It was a real see-saw battle between the partisans and ourselves:
they were everywhere we were not, they disappeared upon our approach,
escaped our clutches and reappeared behind us. As most of the people of
the region were on their side, they inevitably had all the advantages. We had
to be vigilant at all hours of the day or night so as not to be taken by surprise
and risk a loss of either life or honour. Frequently some unfortunate officer
would be condemned to pass weeks, even whole months, with a detachment
of thirty or forty men in some decrepit old building that had been transformed into a blockhouse. There he would be cut off from the rest of the
world and had only himself to count on. He had to supply escorts for
couriers, constantly embark on dangerous expeditions to procure food
and even drinking water, through areas where everyone you met, or who
you were seen by without ever seeing, was an enemy or a spy. He had to
scrutinise every bend of the road, every hill and undulation of the ground
and watch every one of the numerous chapels and hermitages dotted across
the Sierra – places once intended for prayer but now devoted to ambush
and death and where the smell of gunpowder had long since replaced that
of incense. The commanders of these little outposts in the mountains were

placed in the position of a man sitting astride a keg of gunpowder surrounded by people trying to set it alight and would consider himself fortunate not to be blown sky high. If he was blown to smithereens – well, he only had himself to blame.

We soon had to leave Belchite, where we had been comparatively well off, and go and camp out on the plateau which the massed ranks of the Spanish army had occupied before the last battle. My regiment was allotted the task of guarding communications between Saragossa and Alcañiz. On 21 July we formed part of an expeditionary force, led by the commander-in-chief himself, directed against the monastery of Our Lady of Aquila, situated at the peak of a mountain that dominated the surrounding countryside. This was the headquarters of the Aragonese guerrillas. One of Suchet's aides-de-camp, a Lieutenant Rigny (who, as a general, twenty-five years later, led an ill-fated expedition into Africa), came and asked our colonel for a company of good marchers to outflank the enemy. I was placed at his disposal with my voltigeurs. But the Spanish, forewarned of our intentions, fell back at a still quicker pace. We only managed to seize some stragglers and baggage after a skirmish in which we would have found ourselves badly isolated from our supports had the enemy resumed the attack. The monastery was occupied without resistance. We put it to the torch and the glare of the conflagration could be seen for miles around and served as a warning to the inhabitants that this fort had not been as impregnable as they had been told.

Suchet returned to Saragossa at once and left us to finish off the bands. The pursuit continued until Daroca, which was one of the most important towns in Aragon. We arrived there late on the night of the 27th. We were unfortunately without guides and not one of us was familiar with the region. Just as we were coming down towards the town, which we could vaguely make out in the early morning light, the whole regiment turned a corner and found itself plunged underground. We stumbled around slipping at each step and knocking against boulders in pitch darkness. The bravest amongst us were not a little taken aback and we had no idea what had happened or, indeed, what might become of us. A few snipers would have sown complete panic. Finally we again found ourselves in fresh air, by the river Xiloca – upon which Daroca is situated. We had marched right into a tunnel which had been blasted through the rock two centuries ago with the intention of channelling flood waters away from the town. In times of drought it served the useful purpose of acting as a passageway and short cut to the town.

The enemy had not bothered to wait for us at Daroca. During my stay there I escaped, by a kind of miracle, from the greatest danger. I was ordered to occupy an old fort with my voltigeur company. As we were moving off towards this fort, the order was countermanded and we were instead sent out to reconnoitre down the Molina road. We'd only gone about a hundred yards in this new direction when a violent explosion blew the fort we were to have occupied sky high. It was a little farewell present from our Spanish friends to bid us welcome to our new station.

On 30 July we reached Paniza, where Don Ramon Gajan, one of the chief guerrillas of the area, held sway. Naturally, as we were his guests, he refused us nothing and just as naturally he did not leave us lonely for long. We were sharply attacked on the night of 3 August. Throughout this time our commander, Major Beyer, made nightly attempts to surprise the guerrillas and led us into the mountains, taking us first this way and then that without ever allowing us to light fires. We would only return to the town in the mornings, utterly exhausted. Therefore, it was a great pleasure to be able to quit Paniza on the 6th and march on Almunia, a little town of some 4–5,000 inhabitants, situated in the Jalon valley, on the road from Saragossa to Madrid. The enemy were in force a short distance off, positioned in another town the name of which, after all these years, still makes me tremble – Calatayud.

Between 9 and 14 August we were involved in a series of clashes between these two small towns, the most important of which took place some three miles from Venta del Frasno. Assailed by superior numbers, we were forced to retreat to Alumina. We were reinforced, on the same day, by three battalions of infantry, a detachment of cuirassiers and some artillery, marching up from Saragossa. Colonel Henryod, of the 14th Line, who commanded this reinforcement, immediately went into the attack and the Spanish were pushed back to Calatayud.[40] That very evening I had a strange adventure which almost finished me off for good. I was with Henryod about two miles from Calatayud, when he had the idea of despatching me as a courier with a message for the rearguard, ten miles away at Venta del Frasno, on the road to Almunia. He wanted me to return at once and inform him of its position. He also warned me to be on the lookout for guerrillas. I was an excellent *marcher*, but an inexperienced rider. I had only been on a horse once before leaving Poland and the prospect of having to cover eighteen or nineteen miles as an absolute beginner, along unfamiliar roads, in the middle of the night and at full speed, filled me with dread.

But an order is an order and I set off. All went well at first and I reached the rearguard. The return leg of my trip was more complicated and to make matters worse my new mount was playing up horribly. I was so absorbed in keeping my balance that I managed to take a wrong turning and found

---

[40] At El Frasno, the Spanish commander, Villacampa, commanded a force composed of men from the regular Spanish regiments of Soria and La Princessa – some 3,000 men – who were operating as irregulars.

myself some three miles out and in the worst possible direction. I had already passed some suspicious figures when, by good fortune, I recognised the scene of a skirmish we had fought just a few days before. I pulled on the bridle and swung the horse about, but it was only after a hard gallop that I heard the '*Halte-la! Qui vive?*' of our sentries. This sound was like heavenly music. I was so exhausted and dirty that I was bedridden for a couple of days. I made a full and timely recovery and did not miss any of the fighting.

CHAPTER XI

~

At Calatayud, my host was one of the town's notables and a great enemy of
France. There was no contact between us. He said, right at the start, that
he felt ill and had me served separately in my room. Every evening I would
see a long procession of shadowy figures appear, dressed in the obligatory
cloak and sombrero, they would file past us with eminent disdain, casting
menacing glances.

On 19 August we received official notice of the decorations awarded to
the regiment for its part in the siege of Saragossa. In all there were only
seven awards: two for men who had since died of their wounds and two for
men still in hospital! We deserved better than this but it was true that, on
the whole, they thought more of the Poles on the day of battle than they did
afterwards.

On the 24th bad news kept coming in. A company of the 14th Line,
posted at Venta del Fresno, of which I had such painful memories, had been
surprised in the night and taken prisoner. In another place, one of our
detachments, sent to Carinena to safeguard our lines of communication,
was attacked in force in a difficult position, La Puerta de San Martin. I was
sent to its succour and arrived just in time to save Krakowski from the
enemy that was closing in. This Puerta San Martin was a crossroads deep
in the mountains and was reputed to be the gathering place, before the war,
for those men involved in the honourable occupation of banditry; a profession so akin to that of the guerrilla.

I was sent back to del Frasno. Calatayud had, in the meantime, been
evacuated by our troops and had become the headquarters of Villacampa,
one of the most formidable guerrilla leaders. A new expeditionary force,
formed from the 1st and 2nd Regiments of the Vistula under Chlopicki,
who had recently been promoted to Brigade General, was sent against this

place. We took the offensive and marched out of Daroca on the 30th, heading for Calatayud in an attempt to surprise the enemy.

My battalion formed part of the vanguard. The Xiloca valley, normally swarming with people, was deserted. In the plains not a single head of cattle could be seen and in the villages the houses were either hermetically sealed or open and empty. We were met at the entrance to the town of Calatayud by a deputation of clergy and the magistrate, identifiable by his gilded staff of office. This civil servant was so terrified that he addressed himself to me, calling me 'Your Excellency'. He had taken me to be the commander-in-chief.

A few days later a blunder on the part of the general's aide-de-camp placed me in a dangerous predicament. Quite probably my campaigns would have come to an inglorious end then and there had I not had a little sang-froid and a lot of luck.

After the occupation of Calatayud I was sent, on 3 September, to Almunia with my voltigeurs and some twenty cavalrymen. As soon as I arrived there, I received fresh orders to return, at once, to Carinena, spend the night there and push on to Daroca on the next day, the 4th. There I would place myself at the disposal of the French commandant of the place. The first part of the plan passed off smoothly, despite some dangerous moments – especially at the infamous Puerta San Martin – but I was on my guard.

As we approached the pass at Retascon, which we had to pass through before the descent to Daroca, my voltigeurs pointed out a man, whose appearance had cause to make them suspicious, walking towards us. I asked him if he had news from Daroca and he replied: 'Our troops are there'. Just then my men came running back with the news that they had spotted Spanish sentries at the entrance to the defile. I soon perceived that there was a body of troops there roughly equal to my own. These were apparently the vanguard of a larger formation that had occupied the town where we had hoped to find *our* troops. Had there been a misunderstanding or some kind of disaster? Whatever the case, the situation was pretty grim. Eighteen miles (and what miles!) separated us from any assistance. If we retreated, all would certainly be lost.

Fortunately, I knew the area. I attacked the enemy, drove him into the defile and took possession of a chapel that commanded the road and which I had made good note of beforehand. This chapel was of solid construction with narrow windows and would serve admirably for our purpose. I was sure we could hold out quite a while before being rescued. At the same time I sent a detachment to the village of Retascon, below the chapel, to bring up provisions and water sufficient for several days. I also had the local authorities brought along, the priest, the magistrate and the registrar. I told them in a polite but firm voice that due to circumstances beyond my control, I was obliged to ask them to procure two reliable messengers for me and, meanwhile, hoped that they might keep me company until the messengers returned. My three civil servants seemed decent enough, but this is how such things had to be done. Acting on their information I was brought two characters of dubious appearance, to whom it was explained that the very existence of the Junta of Retascon depended entirely on their celerity. I handed them a message in duplicate for Calatayud which explained our situation in a few words and, just to be sure, was written in both French and Polish.

We stayed in position the whole of the day. The Spanish watched us from a distance; they did not attempt to attack us, at least for the moment, but blocked all avenues of escape. From our vantage point we could see their reinforcements streaming in from all sides.

Finally, at about eight in the evening, I had the pleasure of welcoming back, safe and sound, my two messengers. They had covered thirty-six miles (there and back) and brought back with them a receipt for my despatch, signed by one of my comrades. From then on, deliverance was only a question of hours and, in fact, around midnight, a strong relief column arrived, led by Chlopicki himself. He immediately demanded to see the order by which I had acted. When he saw that the order required me to advance on the *4th* to Daroca, he complimented me on the measures I had taken in so dangerous a situation, and one for which I was not responsible. It turned out that the aide-de-camp had, in neglect, written 4th instead of 5th. The advance should only have taken place on the 5th and had to coincide with an expedition ordered to expel the partisans from Daroca on the same day. That negligence almost cost me dear!

CHAPTER XII

THE SPANISH AND THE FRENCH – MIGUELA – A STRANGE EXECUTION –
TWO DOCTORS IN DANGER

The French were not as universally hated as has since been alleged. The monks and priests, who fought for *aris et focis*, were generally against us, as were the majority of the peasants and, in the towns, the very young – who were still under the influence of the clergy. In the middle classes, older people were exclusively against us, but amongst those aged between twenty and thirty there were many *Afrancesados*, who hoped that the presence of the French might speed up essential reforms in society and in the administration of their country.

Although women, especially the mature ones, bitterly rebuked the French for their lack of religion and for their insatiable appetites, generally they were of the opinion that it was the duty of the men to fight for the legitimate king, but that the women should restrict their attention to the housekeeping. This intelligent opinion held sway in the countryside and in the little villages and it was only in the important cities that the women meddled in war and politics.

On occasion, during our wanderings, we had the agreeable experience of meeting ardent francophiles, especially young brides with old husbands or *monjitas*, nuns or novices, whose mother superiors had set them at liberty on the approach of the French. They went back to living with their families but as the French were everywhere it was rather like jumping out of the frying pan and into the fire.

After my adventure in the Retascon pass I spent quite lot of time at Daroca, interrupted, it is true, by expeditions to drive back the guerrillas or safeguard cattle requisitioned by the army. This requisitioning gave rise to great abuse. The commissariat would resell the best of the herd for their own profit and the escort, in its turn, would appropriate its share for its fires and grills, but it was usual to write *died en route* for those cattle that failed to arrive.

It was, as always, the most inoffensive and hardworking sector of the population that had to endure the heaviest burdens. The guerrillas cared even less about their compatriots than we did and certain chiefs held sway over the countryside by terror alone. When they intercepted requisitioned cattle, it was in order to confiscate them for their own profit. When they themselves requisitioned something it was usually upon pain of death to comply. I have held in my hands many decrees which read thus: 'The young people of the village of ... who will not join up will be executed.'

I was billeted at Daroca, with some comrades, on an old and slightly senile magistrate whose house was occupied by a fugitive monk and a novice – these were his in-laws, and he had offered them asylum in his home. The monk, a well-built and noble man aged around thirty, was father-confessor at a convent and consequently knew more about the ways of the world than most of his profession. I won him over by translating into French some supplication of his that he wished to present to Suchet. He was keen to do us all kinds of favours, some of which were not really compatible to his religious standing, and professed a strong admiration for 'Napoleon the Great'.

The novice, Miguela, was a pretty girl of twenty who seemed pleasantly resigned to her forced re-entry into the world and studied any new face with a keen interest. She was a person of gentle character, very hospitable, who spared nothing in order to try and amuse us. After us came others to whom she behaved in the same way, although possibly to an even friendlier extent as the conduct of this young *monjita* was reported to the ecclesiastical authorities.

A year later, as I was convalescing from a serious wound, I spent some time at Saragossa and one day visited the former residence of the kings of Aragon and the courtroom of the Inquisition, the gloomy *Aljaferia*. Suddenly, I heard my name whispered in a plaintive voice that seemed to come from out of the ground and I recognised, through a vent, barred as though in a prison, the thin and emaciated figure of Miguela. The poor child was performing her penance in a few months of seclusion, away from foreign armies. I was much affected by her disgrace but I, as much as I wished, could do nothing to take her from there: my intervention would only have made things worse. All I managed to do was to utter a light reproach and recommended her to be more reserved in future, a recommendation that, coming from me, sounded rather odd and to which the poor recluse smiled despite her tears.

On 15 September we set out on a large-scale, and carefully planned, operation. We were commanded, to the joy of the ordinary soldiers, by Choplicki in person, and we began by pushing forwards into some of the steepest, highest and most barren mountains of Aragon, between

Molina[41] and la Yunta. Molina was one of the guerrilla's principal arms factories and would have to be destroyed. At la Yunta some of the inhabitants had stayed behind and the magistrate delivered an impressive plea to the general to try and excuse the absent citizens: 'It is true that certain individuals, with evil designs, had occupied some of the region and made for themselves a bad reputation. Some people had fled before us, but this was only from fear; we are ready to do anything for the troops of Napoleon the Great' etc, etc. We believed him, or we pretended to. However, as we were busy exploring the outlying area, the cuirassiers, who we had left in the town, sacked a few houses in order to amuse themselves. In any other Army Corps, such a thing would be excusable but Suchet rarely turned a blind eye to this kind of activity. Upon our return, the instigator of the pillage was court-martialled and condemned to death. I was there when the execution was carried out. The condemned man was shot and, as was normal, fell to the ground. Something strange then happened. His comrades rushed over and when they found that he really was dead ran off to find their colonel as though it was something entirely unexpected. 'Why shouldn't he be dead? A thief and good-for-nothing. Oh well, so much for that. It is a good riddance for the regiment, isn't it cuirassiers?' It transpired that the guns had only been charged with powder but the man had died of shock.

On the 19th we reached Calamocha, in the Xiloca valley, after passing along atrocious roads. For most of the journey we were required to man-handle the artillery up and down the slopes. On the 23rd, when we arrived at Calatayud, we found an order waiting for us to immediately return to Daroca. Our departure was so hurried that we managed to leave behind, as a kind of deposit, the regiment's chief medical officer and a doctor from our battalion. These two were so deeply asleep that they heard nothing. We were quite far off when we noticed their absence and we would have had to fight a battle to fetch them back as the enemy, as usual, had followed us closely. We managed to get a message to the magistrate of the town and told him there would be hell to pay if the two doctors were not returned to Daroca safe and sound and with the minimum of delay. This gave rise to a heated discussion between the military and civil authorities. The latter prevailed. A few days later we had the pleasure of seeing our two stragglers

---

[41] Molina was an important base and was later captured by the French. In 1811 General Hugo came across its garrison of forty Poles 'reduced to the most desperate circumstances'. The Poles did not have the strength to force the local population to bring in food; the population was unwilling because of the poor harvest; the garrison, beset by the guerrillas of the Empecinado, could not get messages out to the main army; and, in any case, the main French army could not spare men from its field operations to support the garrison. In October 1811 the place was evacuated and the fort blown up.

turn up and the general placed them under arrest for a week in order to teach them how to sleep a little more lightly in future.

After many other skirmishes, marches and counter-marches between Daroca, Almunia, Calamocha and Calatayud, we ended up in a kind of semi-permanant occupation of the last for the final three months of 1809. It was here that I had an adventure which has a distinct place in my memories of my youthful days.

CHAPTER XIII

MANUEL, HIS SHOP AND HIS NIECE

Sometimes we would stay in the town for five or six days running. These were good times for the soldiers, who could now recover a little from icy nights in bivouac and make the necessary repairs to their kit, especially to their shoes which had undergone trials by ordeal in the Sierras. In this lull of relative calm, my battalion was, as usual, lodged in a convent. We officers had rooms in the town, close enough to keep an eye on the men during the day and at night, unless there were... *Exceptis excipiendis!*

My rooms were next to a shop which sold pastries. In order to imagine how such an establishment appeared in the Spain of 1809, in a backwater, it must first be remembered that even in France and Germany the cafés were not what they are now. Spain was behind the rest of Europe by at least a century in regard to the comforts of life. In these old shops one could only find lemonade, chocolate and sherbet, along with some horrible pastries, at least a week old, difficult to chew on and, when they got to the stomach, true auxiliaries of the guerrillas.

Manuel, the baker of Calatayud, was a real devil of a man, bearded and with a nasty temper; in fact, more likely to do you in than pass you the sugar. Despite entertaining most of the officers of the garrison he still passed himself off as a sworn enemy of the French. He made frequent and mysterious trips out of town, entrusting the shop to an old woman of a respectable age and someone else far more precious...

I was a regular at this establishment. One day I got there somewhat earlier than usual and found myself face to face with a young lady of considerable beauty who was dressed in the habit of a novice nun. She could have stepped out of one of Velasquez's or Murillo's paintings of the Madonna, although in a place most unbecoming. She was an orphan and the niece of the ferocious lemonade seller and she was a *monjita exclaustrade*, like Miguela from Daroca, only far better guarded (at least until then). Her uncle had, reluctantly, agreed to take her in and she lived

91

the life of a recluse – when she went out it was only to church. By an amazing coincidence, on that particular day, making use of the absence of her jailer/uncle, she had come down into the still deserted shop. Despite her hasty withdrawal on my approach, I managed to notice a little surprise and confusion rather than any displeasure at my appearance.

I immediately made enquiries of Catalina, the old chaperone of mind and soul. After imploring the intervention of all the saints and of the Virgin Mary to spare her from her sufferings she finally got round to telling me what I wanted to know at the sight of a few coins. I found out that the *monjita* had been born in Madrid and that her name was Ines.

I had been in Spain long enough to be versed in the principles of this second kind of siegecraft. I bought some of the least offensive looking pastries and begged Catalina to pass them on to her mistress on my behalf. It can be imagined that I had to overcome some additional defences at this point; indignant exclamations, lamentations on the folly of man and their worldly indiscretions which always led to catastrophe, etc, etc... She finished off this little homily by reciting the popular Spanish proverb, *dadiva branta plena y entra sin barrena* – money is the best tool to force a door!

On the next day I learnt that she had not refused my little gift. Naturally I worked on the *duena* a little more and swore that I would be the happiest person alive should I be allowed to offer the same present again, this time in person. Naturally, I was required to bombard the woman once again with the same missiles in order to achieve success. 'Well,' she said, 'that is how it must be if God wills it!'

An expedition against Atoca interrupted my own little siege. During my absence the uncle came back and promptly departed again. Catalina confided in me that my own return had been awaited with impatience; someone had watched out for me from the grilled window that looked out over the square where the garrison used to parade. Finally, after renewed negotiations and new gifts, the *duena* agreed to introduce me that very night to Ines who, on her part, wished to meet the young chevalier. Throughout that day the minutes seemed like centuries and right to the very last moment I was terrified in case something unexpected might happen and we would have to call the whole thing off. At the appointed hour I got a comrade to cover for me at the barracks for an hour or two and, with a brace of pistols and a sword for any unexpected eventualities, I set off for the pastry shop.

The door was ajar. Our confidante bolted the door behind me and then led me down a long corridor at the end of which burned a poor light: it was the *duena*'s lamp. 'Here we are sir,' she whispered as she let me into a tiny, dark and humid room which, even after fifty years, I still see before me.

In my country the poorest labourers live in better conditions. The entire furniture consisted of two chairs, a table, a modest bed, a small basin below a picture of the Virgin Mary, and a jug of water. The good Catalina announced me as 'Don Enrique' and then left us alone.

There is nothing to beat such an adventure for developing skills in a foreign language. Right from the start I was at the mercy of Spanish grammar. I had prepared beforehand a little compliment, with the aid of a dictionary, which I delivered reasonably well apart from a terrible accent. 'Miss, I feel myself most fortunate to finally be able to satisfy the longings of my heart and to be able to present to you a token of the esteem which you have inspired in me.' With a trembling hand she reached out and took the little parcel that I was holding out to her, and placed it on the table. She then lowered her eyes, played with a piece of thread and blushed. I admit that I have never been so captivated. I was twenty and she seventeen at the most; we were both surrendering to the power of a first love!

'*Per l'amour de Dios!*' she finally said, 'Who would have thought?'

'Is it such a big crime,' I asked, 'to consent to receive a little token of affection?'

'But, it is the way this has all so suddenly begun...' she said with an imperceptible smile.

We talked a little longer, our conversation interspersed with long silences and gentle hand-squeezing. I showed her the weapons I was carrying in case of an unpleasant encounter. 'Jesus!' she exclaimed, 'those who live by the sword die by the sword.' I could tell she was not Spanish for nothing and, nevertheless, was rather touched that I was braving dangers in order to come and see her. I managed to get her to promise another meeting for the next day; I believe I was there a few moments longer when old Catalina called out to us that it was getting late and that it was about time we said our goodbyes. I made it back to my quarters without mishap, by keeping in the shadows of the houses.

Of course, I did not sleep a wink that night and I was the first to arrive at the pastry shop, where Catalina indicated that my beauty was still asleep. Luckily, I had my rounds to keep me busy and also made an inspection of the Xiloca valley, which took me until nine in the evening.

By eleven I was at Ines' side. I had brought back from my trip a few wild flowers which pleased her immensely. This time I was a little less shy, at least with my words. 'What would happen,' I laughed, 'should the abbess and father-confessor suddenly appear here now?'

'Jesus! How could you say such a thing!' she said and put her hand on my mouth. 'How can you have such ideas?' After a pause she continued: 'It would be worse if we were to be surprised by Uncle Manuel. He is a bad man and a ferocious enemy of the French. God would forgive me if I were to love you, Don Enrique, but Uncle never would!'

I very much hoped to come again on the next day, but man proposes and God disposes. At ten in the evening we received the order to move off at once and head for the Clares valley where a group of guerrillas had been sighted. I had the idea of pretending that I was ill, as I had seen a number of my comrades do in like circumstances; however, duty triumphed over love. I passed the home of my true love with a thumping heart and said to myself, out of consolation, that things would be even more lovely upon my return.

CHAPTER XIV

MANUEL'S NIECE

This expedition, which should not have lasted more than twenty-four hours, ate three whole days. We had some tough fighting and the noise of musketry and cannon fire reached as far as Calatayud on more than one occasion. Upon my return I found Ines pale and one could see that she had been crying and keeping a vigil. For the first time she threw herself impulsively into my arms.

I found out some not altogether surprising facts about the terrible *Tio*. 'Oh, don't talk to me about that man,' she said, 'my blood freezes when I think about him. He is hand in hand with your enemies and he wants to massacre the lot of you!' She moved closer to me as though to protect me. 'My God,' she said, 'I am so happy now! In a few days he will be here; what will become of me then?' I tried to calm her and told her I would think through our situation and would come up with a plan for our future happiness.

I was thinking of eloping. It was an easy enough thing to do and more than one comrade would help me out. But what would become of this child afterwards? She would no longer be able to stay in her country and it was impossible for me to return to France. She was seventeen and I twenty; she was Catholic, and quite religious, and I was Protestant. Well! I did not consider such things important as love had made me blind to the pitiless realities of life. On the next day I talked to Ines about my plan to elope but she interrupted me after my first few words. 'No, no', she said, 'I have a better plan, that I will tell you about another time.'

That evening she seemed no longer afraid of her uncle and no longer fearful of the future. She laughed gently at our situation and its absurdities and, with our hands intertwined, she sang the popular Spanish song:

If mother only knew
She would bar the windows
And bolt the doors

95

'So,' she added, 'how will Don Enrique manage to stay with his Ines?'

Don Enrique had a nasty shock the next day, or rather later that same day as I did not leave until two in the morning. As I went into the pastry shop to take the habitual chocolate, I found that Uncle Manuel had returned two days earlier than expected. He seemed more sullen and grumpy than ever but obviously did not suspect anything was amiss.

'It seems that it has been a while since we have seen you', I said nonchalantly.

'I have been away for a few days.'

'And what news can you tell us?'

'The country through which I passed is a complete desert and the *señores Franceses* are committing numberless horrors there. I know nothing of other news.'

Over the next few days I tried to show myself less at the pastry shop as I feared we would be discovered. However, I still went from time to time, using the quite plausible excuse that the only newspaper with news from Europe, the *Franco-Spanish Gazette of Saragossa*, was there. It is quite true that Spanish patriots, such as Manuel, would talk quite openly to the allied Polish and German officers of the cruelties and excesses of the French and quoted from illegal Spanish bulletins that were, however, easily available in towns under French occupation. Our generals even found these publications to be of some use, as they kept them informed of news from Europe some weeks before the arrival of the French papers.

Throughout this time, Aragon was slowly returning to normal. The inhabitants of the plain were once again returning to their labours and we, as we passed on our rounds, could smell the odour of soaking hemp. The communications between Calatayud and Daroca were as safe as they had been before the war, if not safer.

I set off for this latter town in order to visit my former hosts and Miguela, who was no longer in penance – quite the reverse in actual fact. She played the coquette with me but I was unmoved, being preoccupied with Ines.

One evening I took part in a ball where Miguela and her cousin, the father-confessor, were present along with myself and a grenadier captain based at Calatayud. He was quite a handsome boy who fancied himself as something of a ladies' man, despite never having conquered anything except the most *undefended of positions*. We eventually got to talking about the pretty women of Calatayud; my comrade pretended he had seen the lot and was quite familiar with them.

'Do you know of the most insufferable and, so they say, the prettiest – a certain Ines, niece of Manuel the lemonade seller?' asked Miguela.

'Señora Ines,' said my fop without hesitation. 'Yes, I have seen her at church. It is true that she is not bad, but she is nothing special.'

'But she has never been out of her house since we have been there,' I blurted out thoughtlessly.

'So, Don Enrique, you know her?' said my good friend the father-confessor, and gave me a sly look.

'Not at all, actually,' I replied, trying to make myself sound as indifferent as possible and cover my gaffe, 'but I live close by and I have heard that her uncle has never let her out since we have been there. He is the greatest enemy we have there.'

'Yes, yes,' said the father-confessor, 'Manuel is well known for his extreme patriotism and his niece no less for her beauty...' And this devil of a man, who knew all the nuns of the region much better than we did, changed the subject as though he had caught a dose of my embarrassment.

I have often asked myself whether this indiscretion of mine had anything to do with the sad end to my adventure.

A few days later I returned to Calatayud and had the satisfaction of finding that the repugnant Manuel had gone. That evening I went to see Ines, who welcomed me with extreme joy. However, I noticed that there was something troubling her. It hadn't taken much to notice that the terrible Uncle had seemed even more animated in his hatred towards us during his last stay: he had now gone to Valencia to make his report to his Spanish superiors and was surely planning something unpleasant. I tried, vainly, to reassure her.

'Do you see, dear Enrico', she said, showing me a little knife that I had given her as a present, 'this weapon that God granted you to give to me; I will use it to rejoin you if something happens to you. That wicked man knows the locality and surrounding area like the back of his hand and all of your habits. He acts as a guide to the guerrillas and I have no doubt that you will be ambushed as you were at del Frasno and Paniza.'

She was not wrong. There really was a plan to surprise us in Calatayud but it was temporarily delayed by new military developments.

I stayed longer than usual. Instead of calming her down, I ended up by being drawn under the influence of her sadness and it was as though both of us had a presentiment that we would never see each other ever again. She presented me with a ribbon on which she had embroidered, in golden letters and in exquisite style, our intertwined initials and the motto, 'Holy Mother, protect my friend!'

The poor child could not bring herself to say goodbye. For the first, and, alas, the last time, she accompanied me to the door of the house.

'Oh, I am suffocating!' she exclaimed as she tore herself from my arms. 'My heart is breaking! Come back tomorrow as early as you can. I cannot exist without you!'

It was at least three o'clock in the morning. After so many years, the slightest details of that fateful morning are still as clear to me as though they happened yesterday. It was terribly cold and both soldiers and officers were all awake and were stamping their feet to try and warm themselves.

'Did you hear that we are off on a major expedition today?' a fellow officer asked me.

'No, I did not.'

'I saw some cuirassiers yesterday and they reckoned that we were to form part of an important expedition moving off from Saragossa.'

'Oh, well,' I said with as much indifference as I could muster, 'it is a shame that I cannot come with you as I have a terrible fever and can barely stand upright.'

At that moment we heard the voice of Major Beyer calling for the company officers.

'We are leaving in an hour,' he said to us, 'and I doubt that we will be coming back. The order is to evacuate everyone.'

'And the sick?' I asked.

'The sick are to go to Daroca.'

An hour later, with a broken heart, I marched out into the open country through a thick and freezing fog...

Two weeks later, after military events that I will shortly describe, my regiment was back in Calatayud. I found Uncle's house locked and barricaded, and only the pastry shop was open, staffed by a man who I had never seen and who responded to all my questions with the usual *non saber*.

I asked the neighbours. Nobody knew, or wanted to tell me, what had happened to Manuel, Ines and Catalina.

Desperate, I found a way of forcing my way into the house that was now the sanctuary and tomb of our love. Two Germans from my company had deserted. I went to the commandant and pretended that I had reason to believe I knew where the deserters were hiding. I obtained the necessary search warrant and the consent of the local authorities. Need I say which was the first house that I searched?

I was kept waiting a long time whilst the magistrate's people located the old woman who held the keys. She finally showed up, and I went down the familiar old corridor and passed the grilled window where Ines had watched for me. We rummaged in the corners and recesses but I did not have the heart to go to the room of my beloved. Finally, just as I was leaving, I pretended to notice the door to her room for the first time and asked my guide whether anyone had lived there.

'Yes,' she said, 'that was the room of the novice Ines, Manuel's niece, the most beautiful and wisest girl in the whole region.'

'And where is she now?'

'*Non saber*, she has gone off in tears with her uncle and Catalina and nobody knows where they have gone.'

For the last time I went into our little room. It was completely empty. Nothing remained of the lowly furniture. The basin, the picture of the Virgin Mary had disappeared; not one of the dried flowers, not a pin or a nail that I could take away as a souvenir!

'But,' I said in a trembling voice, 'do they know why this young novice left in tears?'

'*Non saber*, but she was inconsolable. She fainted and had to be carried out to the wagon by her uncle and Catalina.'

I left that house for the last time and all my enquiries as to the fate of Ines were fruitless. For many days I was beside myself. Surely they cannot have just vanished. The poor child will betray him or will be betrayed herself. I wanted to abandon everything and track them down to revenge the death of Ines or to deliver her from eternal confinement.

Our sudden departure and the trials and tribulations of military life gradually whittled away at my despair. Calmer, I asked myself whether or not this severing had not been for the best and whether I should be grateful to Providence for being torn away from this little corner of reconquered paradise before having succumbed to temptation. How would she have fared among all the horrors of that infernal war? What good and happiness could have been expected from a relationship between a Protestant of twenty and a Catholic of seventeen from two nations locked together in merciless combat by the iron will of Napoleon?

Never have I seen anything as beautiful or lovely as that young girl. It was as though life had been transfixed by a heavenly vision composed of all that was good and, in the words of Guizot, 'a living creature, a work of God, when it shows its divinity, is the most beautiful of things and God is the greatest of poets'.

Today, still, that angelic figure is before me... *Et tacitum vivit sub pectore vulnus.*

More than once, at the most critical times of my life, such as shortly afterwards at Villel where I was severely wounded, or in Russia, where I escaped death by a series of miracles, I thought I heard, in the midst of feverish hallucinations, the tender voice of Ines. It seemed to me as though the novice of Calatayud was keeping safe my memory and was praying for me.

99

CHAPTER XV

THE BATTLE AT OJOS-NEGROS – ADVENTURES OF A CUIRASSIER – TRUTH ABOUT THE BATTLE OF TREMEDAD – OCCUPATION OF TERUEL – STORMING AND SACKING OF ALBARACIN – A STRANGE DISCOVERY IN A MONASTERY

Between our sudden departure from Calatayud and our return to the town of my cruel deception, we spent the days marching backwards and forwards and the nights under the stars. We also took part in some important combats such as the battle at Ojos-Negros and the taking of the Tremedad monastery. My regiment formed a flying column along with the 14th Line, the 13th Cuirassiers and a few pieces of artillery.[42] It was whilst on this last expedition that I saw, for the first time, the treacherous staff officer Van Halen who was to become infamous for his double betrayal.[43] We gave him the nickname *Utique Domine* because, as he knew French very badly, he usually tried out his awful Latin when in conversation with Chlopicki and Henryod, and this little phrase of agreement was his stock reply. We took an instant dislike to the man.

At the Ojos-Negros pass a vigorous frontal assault coupled with a turning manoeuvre through Villar del Sar forced the enemy to fall back, and our cavalry turned this withdrawal into a complete rout. Ojos-Negros is a mining area and the inhabitants rejoice in a certain affluence, and as they had all run off with the guerrillas there were considerable spoils.

---

[42] The flying column consisted of three battalions of the 14th Line, eight companies of the 2nd Regiment of the Vistula Legion, the 13th Cuirassiers, 150 Spanish auxiliaries, two cannon and a mortar, all under Colonel Henryod.

[43] Van Halen, according to Suchet, was a Spanish officer of Dutch or Belgian origin who had served King Joseph since 1808. In 1813 Van Halen's treachery led to the fall of Lerida, Mequinenza and Monzon. The last had withstood an eight-week siege before being tricked into surrendering. Interestingly, Van Halen served as Mina's chief of staff in the 1823 war.

I was witness to an event both curious and rare. During the pursuit the cavalry captured a coach that had either been abandoned or had got stranded. There was a pretty woman inside half-dead from fright. One of the cuirassiers, charged with escorting her back to camp, took her off to one side and into an isolated farm. Shortly afterwards he came out alone and guilty of a double crime that he could easily have kept hidden as we were about to continue the advance. However, this man who had succumbed to temptation now succumbed to remorse and as he came into camp he turned himself in as a prisoner and denounced himself as a robber and murderer. They first assumed that he was drunk, but he insisted and indicated the exact spot where the body of his victim could be found. This individual, a man with many years of military service behind him, was one of those that the soldiers termed a *sneak* and was court-martialled and executed.

The day after this skirmish at Ojos-Negros, the monastery at Tremedad, headquarters of Villacampa, was taken in an operation that was comparatively straightforward. This monastery was perched on an escarpment about one mile above the Molina Valley. It was a very strong position and it would have cost us dear had the Spanish shown a little more tenacity. I, for my part, occupied the village of Origuela, which was deserted save for a few dogs in the street and cats on roofs. Three cannon shots signalled the start of the combined assault carried out by the voltigeurs of the 14th and those of the Vistula Legion.[44] An open space, some thousand yards wide, lay between the village and the wooded slopes of the hill that led up to the monastery. My men bounded over this open space, drove the enemy's light infantry back through the woods and began the steep ascent up to the walls of the convent. Here they ran into the French voltigeurs who had made a similar ascent on their flank. The monastery and its outhouses were occupied without resistance but the enemy, as they fell back in retreat, set fire to a shepherd's hut in which ammunition had been stored. It made us run for cover to avoid a shower of debris. We returned to Origuela where, lacking anything else, we made a good fire out of the furniture and beams of the houses.

This is all that happened in this battle which Suchet makes into a heroic struggle in his memoirs. I was very surprised to read that 'the powder and munitions stored in this sanctuary were considerable and the explosion dreadful'. The ammunition was never in the church but in a nearby building and they made not one terrible explosion but a series of detonations that went on throughout the night. And it is not quite true to say that the fire

---

[44] This élite column was commanded by Captain Porlier of the 14th Line. It was not unusual to detach the élite companies and organise them into provisional battalions – for example, a composite grenadier battalion fought at Albuera and Barossa.

'spread to the woods that surrounded the monastery and even to the village of Origuela, where it was checked by our soldiers'. Before our departure I was required to reconnoitre all around the monastery and I saw no trace of a fire. The village itself was completely sheltered from any such danger as it was well clear of both the monastery and the woods. Suchet, who was not present, had obviously fallen into the trap of reading a report written with the same attention to detail as Solnicki's description of the battle at Monzon.

We then made a stab at Teruel, the residence of a Junta which ran away before our approach. And thus we found ourselves once more at Calatayud. My duties fortunately diverted me from any heartache. We were required to keep Villacampa in check, collect contributions, gather supplies and des-patch them to Saragossa, and patrol the Xalon Valley and the neighbouring heights incessantly. These duties frequently took us far from the town and we slept in the open air, in the middle of winter, in exposed places where there was no firewood. During the whole period between our return to Calatayud and 20 December 1809, when we finally left, I do not believe that I undressed even once.

We finally left this arduous place and headed via Calamocha to Teruel. We arrived there after three days of forced marches, covering sixty miles of terrible roads, but without having fired a shot. The commander-in-chief was at Teruel and was passing regiments in review. He was also giving dinners and I was invited to one. I owed that honour to our excellent colonel, Kousinowski, who had presented me to Suchet at the review and commended me as being one of his bravest and most intelligent officers.

On 24 December the combined voltigeur battalion (French and Polish) marched on Santa Maria de Albarracin. I was sent off on a reconnaissance into the neighbouring *sierra* at the source of the Guadalquivir River. If possible I was to disperse a band of guerrillas who had apparently occupied Frio and Fuente Garcia and had designs on one of our convoys supposed to be passing through the area. Despite combing the region I found neither men nor convoy and returned empty-handed some three days later after having spent one of the coldest nights I can remember by a little lake which my guide called the Poza de San Juan. My comrades had been luckier, and had spent less energy, at Albarracin. The bishop, the local authorities and the leading citizens had taken flight and hadn't had time to take anything with them. There was, above all, much cloth, and the soldiers had managed to lay their hands on everything they needed. I found my battalion com-mander celebrating with his officers in one of the town's larger houses. Naturally, I was invited to take my place at the feast and despite my un-happy love affair, I did just that. Camped beneath the windows, our voltigeurs were doing the same and were downing a huge quantity of steaks, grills and wines. Goodness knows where they had managed to get such a vast quantity of good things but they really wanted for nothing. As was usual the French were looking for the choicest portions and the Germans and Poles the biggest. This orgy of pillage contrasted with the usual discipline of Suchet's troops but it was said that the Junta at Albarracin was one of those that circulated proclamations calling for the murder or poisoning of the French.

As I went round the various groups, I spied a man with a long grey beard in a shabby and torn overcoat. He was devouring some food like a wild animal and seemed devoid of reason. The soldiers had got into the cellars of an abandoned monastery and broken through a barricaded door, which they had taken to be a wine cellar, behind which they had found this famished individual chained to a pillar. They had brought him up into the daylight but had not managed to get a word out of him. Some of the villagers reckoned that he had been a blacksmith who had beaten his wife to death with a hammer. He had fled to the mountains, but had been caught and brought before ecclesiastical judges. These, for extenuating circumstances, had condemned him to solitary confinement for life.

This is as maybe, but the fact is that he was found in the cellar of a monastery. At that time my imagination had been set on fire by such novels as *The Monk* which described secret crimes committed in Spanish monasteries.[45] In addition, I regarded monks with revulsion after my experiences in Calatayud. I imagined the poor Ines locked away in a cold cellar, calling out vainly for help. I therefore proposed taking this man away and hearing his evidence so that it could be inserted in the *Saragossa Gazette* and might go some way to nullifying the influence of our sworn enemies the monks. My major did not share this opinion. He thought the story about the blacksmith had been made up. He did not think it worth going to any trouble over some man who, after all, was probably a scoundrel condemned to isolation for some crime. According to him it was all some quarrel between different monastic factions and we had better not get mixed up in it.

There certainly have been some exaggerated stories of cruelty and immorality committed by Spanish religious orders. All these accusations, nevertheless, cannot be coincidental. Well do I remember that during the siege of Saragossa, one of our mines revealed a secret passageway which ran quite a distance and linked a monastery to a convent. They left it open from then on and it was apparent that this revelation made a distinct impression on the inhabitants.

---

[45] *The Monk*, written by Mathew Gregory Lewis (1775–1818) and first published in 1796, was a notorious Gothic novel about a monk who raped a young girl in a charnel house.

CHAPTER XVI

~

SOME SPANISH MULES – IN THE XILOCA VALLEY – A SURGEON'S UPS
AND DOWNS – A PRETEND DUEL AND A REAL DUEL – SLEDGES IN SPAIN
– FOOD PUT TO STRANGE USE

Our return to Albarracin via Teruel was without incident. We received a
few parting shots as a farewell, but there were no casualties apart from some
mules. These animals were wounded and we subsequently had to put them
down as they got out of hand and wrought havoc in the column. On several
occasions in this war I have found truth in the old saying about being
'stubborn as a mule'. How many times have I seen those cursed beasts
suddenly stop at the slightest pretext and remain obstinately motionless
and impervious to kindness or blows, until whatever whim it was had
passed. In the plains such behaviour was not very inconvenient, but in the
mountains it was a different thing altogether and if a mule misbehaved an
entire convoy might grind to halt and thus be exposed to considerable
danger. Such was the case one year later, during the siege of Tarragona,
when we were escorting a convoy of 6–800 mules carrying supplies for the
army. We had to be draconian with those obstinate beasts, patriots in their
own way.

From Teruel we reached Daroca and the entire division went into winter
quarters in the Xiloca Valley. I occupied Camino Real, and acted as
commandant there, with my voltigeurs. The rest of the regiment was
dispersed and detachments sent to Monreal, where the Colonel was based,
Calamocha, El Poya and Fuentes Claras. Communications were secure,
there was food in abundance and we led a merry life for the first few weeks
of 1810.

I remember a rather nasty practical joke five fellow officers played on a
surgeon of ours called Gulicz who was a good, if rather naïve and gullible,
fellow.

He was stationed at El Poya but came over to Calamocha every day in an
attempt to seduce a pretty servant working at a well provisioned hotel in the

town. This got on the nerves of the officers and they resolved to teach the doctor not to trespass on their territory.

So one evening, as Gulicz dallied over a fine dinner or something else, our officers stole out of the hotel, disguised themselves as peasants and armed themselves with pistols charged with powder. The doctor, full of thoughts of love, finally appeared meandering along the course of the river until he suddenly found himself confronted by two shadowy men who met him with the usual cry of the guerrillas, *Demonino carajo!* He span around only to find himself face to face with three other enemies who opened fire on him. Gulicz, out of his mind, fled towards the river and it was only then that the assailants realised that the joke might have gone too far. They ran after their victim, calling out to him by name. The poor doctor, running faster than ever before, leapt into the depths of the freezing river and reached the other bank in an instant. He carried on to Calamocha and lost no time in telling of his adventure. But the sentries had heard the firing and had already raised the alarm. Before long, cavalry were sweeping the valley and pickets of infantry were combing the river banks.

Meanwhile, our pseudo-Spaniards, now petrified by the consequences of their little game, had run to the commandant at El Poya and confessed; he, in turn, made his report to the colonel of the regiment. The colonel did not take the matter kindly and sentenced each of the guilty party to eight days of arrest and delivered a sharp reprimand to the doctor.

But the poor boy was not to be left in peace for long. Some more officers, accomplices of the others, determined to show him that the affair could not be allowed to stop there and that things had reached such a stage that one of the officers would have to demand satisfaction from the doctor. The pistols to be used in the duel were only charged with powder without the doctor being any the wiser. As the duel began the doctor, shaking with fear, fired first and, inevitably, 'missed' his opponent. His opponent fired back and as he did so his second threw a bullet he had been concealing in the palm of his hand at the doctor, and it hit Gulicz in the side. The doctor yelled, 'I've been killed!' and reeled back into the arms of his second. Everyone rushed to him, feigning consternation, and began to look for a wound they knew they had little chance of finding. Finally, they managed to make the doctor believe that he had had a lucky escape and that what he had felt had been the rush of air that follows in the wake of a bullet. Then, the adversaries shook hands in a friendly fashion.

It was some months later that we were at last able to inform Gulicz as to the truth of the matter, after one of the principal players in this little act had died, and to persuade Gulicz that he had, once more, been made fun of.

Oh, but those were good times! How brave, merry and confident of the future those young officers of the Vistula Legion were! They had faith in the future of their country. Their ancestors had sighed 'France is too far away to help!' at the time of the partitions. But now, after Friedland and Wagram, France was everywhere! This illusion would shortly cease to be, just as the majority of us would also soon cease to be. Of the five officers who participated in this little adventure, one would shortly be killed in Spain and three others would perish in the slaughter in Russia in 1812. Only one would survive, for better or worse, and would die in 1852 – a high-ranking officer in the Russian army!

As January drew to a close, the Franco–Polish combined battalion of voltigeurs was sent to Villafranca along with two squadrons of cuirassiers. We were the vanguard for the French and often clashed with the enemy. At Villafranca, I had all the duties of a commandant. In this capacity I was drawn into conflict with certain officers over their maltreatment of the local populace. This brought about a quarrel between me and a lieutenant called Czaki, who had just arrived from Warsaw and had the reputation of being an excellent duellist.

We fought with swords and, almost straight away, I received a cut on the side of the head; however, I was determined the fight continue. We were, however, separated, with some difficulty, and went on to face unpleasant consequences. I received a very strong reprimand from my commanding officer and was in Chlopicki's bad books for some time afterward. As it was said that I had been more wounded than was really the case, Gulicz decided he would rush over and tend me. This act of friendship cost him dear. As he journeyed over, he was this time attacked by real Spaniards and he arrived with his hat full of holes, owing his life to the speed of his horse.

Before our stay in the Xiloca valley drew to a close, much snow fell. We took advantage of this to organise sleigh rides. This was the first time we had managed to do this since arriving in Spain and it reminded us of our own country. Generals Chlopicki and Laval, along with Colonel Kousin-owski and other superior officers, also came along. We had a great time and dinner took much longer than usual. The return trip was enlivened by an adventure of General Laval's. This general, who was no longer young, disliked the cold and wore a huge fur cap on his head. On the journey back, his sleigh tipped over and spilt passengers and baggage all over the ground. Laval, in the chaos, lost his hat and began to fumble about in the darkness until he came across a big round object, which he could not really get a good feel of in his big gloves, and placed it as firmly as possible on his head, not withstanding a little resistance. When he showed up he was met by a tremendous howl of laughter as the torches revealed just what he was wearing on his head. It was an enormous pâté which had not been eaten and had been prepared by the chef and put into the sleigh, being tipped out with all the other contents when the accident occurred. This adventure caused considerable mirth for some days and Laval was the only one not to succumb to laughter.

CHAPTER XVII

OPERATIONS IN THE GUADALAVIAR VALLEY – A VISIONARY OFFICER

On 8 February we left our winter quarters and marched directly at the enemy, who was attempting to establish himself in the neighbouring district. On the 9th his forward posts were driven in by our vanguard at Torre-la-Carcel and our troops then camped out in the snow before, on the next day, pushing on as far as Teruel. The Spanish were fortifying this place but they abandoned it to us with little show of resistance.

On the 11th our combined voltigeurs made a reconnaissance in force along the heights of Guadalaviar and we got caught up in some heavy fighting against our all too numerous enemy. On the 12th we returned to the offensive and drove back some Spanish who had got as far as Villastar. Our losses were, however, quite heavy as the enemy outnumbered us and were fighting well. We were faced by the indefatigable Villacampa, who had built up a force of at least 6,000 men. We fell back to Teruel in order to await reinforcements.

Here one of the strangest incidents of my entire career occurred. I am writing my memoirs, not a novel, so I must say that the following events, although as strange as they could possibly be, are in fact the absolute truth.

On the evening of the 15th, Chlopicki invited a number of the brigade's officers to dinner. Just as he was sitting down to table he received an important message from the divisional general, Laval, which required his prompt attention. He left and did not return for some hours.

Amongst those invited was a Captain Rakowski, an imposing figure of a man, middle-aged, and sombre and taciturn in nature. He dabbled, so it was said, in the occult, and it was rumoured he had a sixth sense.

That evening he was sat a little apart from the rest of us, close to the fireplace, and seemed absorbed in deep and profound contemplation whilst the rest of us young officers frolicked about. One of us, a Lieutenant Zarski of the grenadier company, who I was friendly with, said to me, 'Come on, let's go and ask the old wizard to interpret a dream.'

I don't remember what he said to Rakowski, but I remember what Rakowski said to him: 'Young man, do not make fun of me. Before the year is out, you will learn that some things should be taken seriously. Beware of the mountains. And you Lieutenant,' he said, addressing me, 'what do you want to know?'

And I told him of a dream I had had a few days before, whilst encamped at Villastar. I dreamt I had been abandoned on the Sierra and, racked by thirst and hunger, I had swallowed snow which gripped my entire body with an icy coldness. I had had this dream two nights running.

'Yes, you really did dream that. But do not ask me to explain it to you as I do not like to predict misfortune.'

He spoke with such conviction that Zarski turned to me later and said, 'My word, he takes his role seriously.'

The day after next, in the battle at Villel, I was seriously wounded, as wounded as possible without actually being killed. Less than a year later (on 12 November 1810) poor Zarski died, his legs having been smashed by a roundshot somewhere in the mountains.

On 12 November 1810, when I learnt of his death, I happened to be in the trenches before Tortosa and right next to Rakowski. His face was unreadable when I asked him if he had foreseen these events.

'I knew,' was his reply.

The death of this visionary officer was no less strange than his life and I would like here and now to relate it.

On the second anniversary of Chlopicki's dinner there was a reunion of some of those who had survived. But this time it was in Russia, on the banks of the Beresina and on the eve of the terrible crossing of that river! I was suffering from a terrible wound suffered just after our entry into Moscow and had had to follow the retreat as a convalescent. I was under a tree, leaning on my crutches. Around me were Captains Dobrzyki and Starwolski and a little beyond them could be found Colonel Kousinowski and Major Regulski. We were in a clearing where the remnants of the Polish Legion were encamped, one of the few units that was still of some use.

We anxiously listened to the cannon fire that sealed the fate of Partonneaux's division and might finish off the entire army once and for all.

Suddenly, the old wizard, Captain Rakowski, appeared amongst us. He went up to the Major and handed him a watch and a purse containing some hundred napoleons, saying: 'My final hour approaches. I entrust you with my watch and my life savings, try to get them to my brother at the hospice for the blind at Bordeaux. Farewell, good sirs!'

And he left us and headed off to a farm and to the few men who remained of his company.

'Another example of the old man's madness,' said Regulski.

A few hours later and the majority of those brave men of the Vistula Legion were dead, killed in the heroic struggle to reopen the way to Vilna. The visionary died there too, as well as the colonel and the two captains who had camped close beside me. Only Regulski escaped, although wounded in the arm, to survive the retreat and carry out Rakowski's last wish.

I have no desire to convert those who see in this no more than coincidence. But I am bound to repeat that what I heard and saw puts me in mind of the words of Hamlet: 'There are more things in heaven and earth, than are dreamt of in your philosophy.'

I also believe that these supernatural stories and presentiments of approaching death, as related by reliable witnesses, are not rare in the annals of war. Napoleon himself cites the remarkable example of General Laharpe.[46]

---

[46] General Amédée-Emmanuel Laharpe (1754–96) died during a confused action at Codogno, in Italy, on the night of 8 May 1796. The night before he had appeared 'overwhelmed by a fatal presentiment'.

CHAPTER XVIII

THE BATTLE OF VILLEL – MY ALMOST FATAL WOUND – TAKEN TO
TERUEL – THE COMMANDER-IN-CHIEF'S VISIT – I AM DECORATED

On the morning of 16 February 1810 Chlopicki's division went into action and began moving along the long ravine below Teruel which ran in the direction of the Guadalaviar. The combined voltigeurs, sent ahead as scouts, soon met determined resistance which hindered their advance and that of the main body. The Spanish had taken up an excellent position in a slight depression at the top of a hill behind Villastar. This hid them almost completely from view. They could see us much better and kept up a galling fire at exactly that point through which we would have to debouch. The voltigeurs, going on ahead, attempted to rush the position but were forced to go to ground and disperse among the boulders to avoid being decimated by the next volley.

In such a situation, Chlopicki was never far away. He appeared suddenly amongst the Polish troops and rallied them in their mother tongue. I too found myself in the thick of the fighting with my company, which now came into action in support. I cried out to my men 'Forward' and threw myself towards the enemy and the rocks and boulders. The Spanish made the mistake of firing too early, as soon as they saw us coming at them. Before they managed to reload, the quickest of our voltigeurs, who had stayed close to me, reached the crest of the hill and opened up on the enemy hidden below. This sudden volley terrified the Spanish and they took to flight, despite the best efforts of their officers. This was very fortunate because their troops numbered some 500 men and I had only some fifty or sixty with me, as many French as Polish. The main body had not managed to keep up, and had the Spanish realised the true situation they would probably have turned right round and fallen upon us.

Just then Chlopicki arrived – a cane in hand as though out on a stroll, with an aide-de-camp as escort – he had followed us throughout the course of this little action. He warmly congratulated us on our audacity and ordered me to pursue the enemy and not allow him to rally. This was the first time he had spoken to me since that unfortunate duel. The enemy's vanguard had been totally demoralised and they abandoned a series of excellent positions to us as they fled before this handful of breathless men who were, one by one, collapsing from exhaustion. I was almost at the end of my strength and more than once I had recourse to refresh myself with the snow that could be found in the crevices between rocks and rid myself of the thirst that was torturing me, just as in the dreams I had had.

As we moved closer to Villel the enemy gradually began to show more mettle. Soon we caught sight of a few outhouses or isolated farmhouses, linked by a ditch and occupied by light infantry. Behind this first line of defence, on a little plateau, they had thrown up an earthwork and garrisoned it in some force. I spotted an officer mounted on a black horse who was going from one point to another, encouraging his men to resist. It was probably Villacampa himself. We pressed on towards the Guadalaviar and despite our small numbers managed to occupy one or two of the little outhouses and direct a withering fire on the others. Chlopicki again appeared: 'It is vital that we throw the rascals out of here or they will all get away! Reform and get at them!'

I obeyed and had my bugler, Jankowski, give the signal for this fresh assault and an angry little drummer from the centre companies of the 44th Line joined in too – goodness knows where he came from!

But this time the soldiers, worn out or fearful of the enemy's vastly superior numbers, would not advance with me and I found myself charging alone with the little drummer. As we could not take the redoubt by ourselves, we fell back. I saw that some of the men were reforming and getting themselves ready for another effort and I went forwards with them to the edge of the ditch. Here I was bowled over by a bullet which hit me in the head and I fell down as though dead.

I have only the vaguest recollection of what happened over the next few days. I remember thinking, upon hearing shots in the distance, 'How is it I can hear them still firing even though I am dead?' Later I saw the sweet figure of Ines appear before me and then, later still, thought that I had better make an attempt to get up. But despite my best efforts I was quite unable to move a muscle. Finally, it felt as though I was floating above the ground and I said to myself that it was the angels come to take me to Heaven (a presumptuous hope if ever there was one) and I lost consciousness completely. After some time I heard a voice call out, 'That one there is coming round,' and I felt something trickling down my throat. At that point I relapsed into a coma from which I was not delivered for some time. Even then, I found that my memory was completely blank, and that I could not even remember the name of my servant, and it seemed as if I would only recover the full use of my faculties gradually.

I now know what came to pass after I fell to the ground, wounded. My men saw me fall and at first fell back in disorder, leaving me in the hands of the Spanish, who relieved me of my boots, stripped off my epaulettes and my watch, which had Ines' ribbon tied to it. My sword, which I was holding at the time I was hit, was later found further along the ditch and they had evidently tried to make off with it but had lacked sufficient time. As it turned out, although I had been plundered, our troops received reinforcements, returned to the offensive and finally took the position from the enemy. A group of Spanish cavalry, cut off from their main body, valiantly broke through our lines and managed to escape into the mountains, after having raided the hospital I would later be evacuated to. One of the surgeons was seriously wounded in this affair.

After the battle the wounded were loaded onto donkeys and mules and taken to Teruel. I was stuffed into a double pannier and some soldiers' haversacks were put on the other side of the pannier to act as a counter-weight.

The most dangerous moment lay ahead and that was when one of the divisional surgeons (Courtois) thought he saw in this almost incurable wound, a wonderful opportunity to try his hand at trepanning. This time I owed my life to the intervention of two of my fellow officers who warmly insisted that the surgeon let me die in peace. I remember only that one day I felt the doctor enlarge the hole in my head and poke around inside with an instrument. This did not hurt at all as I was beyond feeling any pain. But it seems that they found out that my skull had not in fact been broken and the doctors considered this to be a good sign.[47]

When I recovered consciousness, I found out that Suchet, who had been passing through Teruel, had come to visit me in person to ask news of me and to bring me the Legion of Honour which he had requested be granted to me for my conduct at Belchite and Maria. I also had the satisfaction of seeing my name printed in an order of the day concerning the action at Villel and to read a report of the battle printed on 8 April 1810 in the *Franco-Spanish Gazette of Saragossa*. This report, as was usual, exaggerated the enemy losses. According to it the Spanish lost 'some hundred men killed and 300 drowned in the Guadalaviar, whereas we had only three men killed and twenty wounded. Amongst these is the young and intrepid Lieutenant Brandt, of the 2nd Vistula Regiment, to whom the commander-in-chief presented the Cross, etc, etc...'

---

[47] Trepanning, despite Brandt's fears, did sometimes work. John Browne was seriously wounded at Waterloo by a bullet above his ear. He was left for dead and reported killed. However, he recovered after trepanning – much to the joy, and surprise, of his family.

In November I also received the cross of the Polish 'Mérite Militaire'. I had therefore been decorated twice before my twenty-second birthday: and that really meant something in those days!

CHAPTER XIX

THE GARRISON OF TERUEL'S BRILLIANT DEFENCE AND EVENTUAL
DELIVERANCE – CAPTAIN GORDON – COLONEL PLICQUE – CAPTAIN
LEVISTON – TERUEL AND ITS AQUEDUCT – ITS MARKET

After two weeks, thanks to my strong constitution and to good care and attention, I was able to start moving around again. But I couldn't really walk without getting dizzy and my convalescence was considerably delayed by the crisis which dominated my time in Teruel and lasted two whole weeks.

The occupation of Teruel and the battle at Villel had been the preliminaries to a general advance on Valencia. This was the dangerous operation which Suchet, acting on orders from Madrid, was now endeavouring, not without some reluctance, to undertake. These orders were countermanded too late by instructions coming from Paris. The commander-in-chief, as he set out on the expedition, put a certain Colonel Plicque in charge of the defence of Teruel, depot for the sick and wounded, and the key to safeguarding the French lines of communication with Saragossa. To fulfill his task he was given just 150 or 200 men but told that this weak garrison would be augmented in the course of time by convalescents. Consequently he placed all his troops, sick as well as fit, in the Seminary of the Jesuit College, a solid building in which certain defensive measures had already been made. These measures immediately proved of use. As soon as the French left in the direction of Valencia, our indefatigable enemy, Villacampa, having quickly rallied his men, swept down on Teruel on 25 February, drove in our posts, isolated us in the Seminary and summoned us to surrender. You can guess our response; but our position was critical and became worse when the Spanish succeeded in taking the church and bell-tower adjoining our building. They managed to take these positions, it was said, due to the connivance of their friends the clergy, who had been allowed to remain in the church to perform their offices. We therefore found ourselves not only isolated but menaced on all sides, except on that side of the building protected by the Guadalaviar river. Fortunately the enemy lacked artillery and we had with us an excellent officer of

115

engineers, called Leviston, who threw up defences at those points where an attack might be expected and barricaded the windows and so on.

Meanwhile the Spanish informed us that if we were to persist in holding out, we would all be blown sky high. They had, in fact, managed to break into an adjoining house without us being able to stop them, and we could now distinctly hear them working away beneath us. From my bed I could even count the number of times the picks struck stone and it could well be imagined that this did not do much to hasten my recovery.

A vigorous sortie won us back the bell-tower but our situation seemed little improved. Another envoy arrived to tell us they were about to act on the threat delivered last time and even offered us the opportunity for one of our engineers to come and ascertain the truth that lay behind this threat. The commander accepted the offer and sent Leviston. He reported back that there was indeed a mine, primed and charged beneath us, but he was not sure if there was sufficient powder for the enemy to carry out his plan. So that part of the building which would be affected by the mine was evacuated and measures were taken to defend the rest of the building. Those wounded who were sufficiently recovered took their places in the defence and the grenadiers and voltigeurs, as was their prerogative, asked to be placed in the most exposed and dangerous positions.

On 8 March one of our officers, called Gordon, carrying correspondence from Saragossa, managed to cut his way through into the town, although most of his escort was killed or wounded and he himself was badly hurt by a blow to his left arm. But a detachment of ours made a sortie and managed to get him inside. We were only to learn later of an event that had greatly helped this audacious act. Villacampa had detached some of the blockading force and sent them against the rear of our army marching on Valencia; this detachment surprised a Polish company at Alventosa. Due to this turn in events our communications with Saragossa were restored for a few crucial hours. But Villacampa quickly retraced his steps upon hearing that some French troops had left Daroca escorting four pieces of artillery.

On the morning of the 9th we heard a cannonade coming from this direction. The encounter had taken place on a plateau not far from the confluence of the Alhambra and Guadalaviar, one hour's march from Teruel. The explosions continued one after the other and we first of all thought that we had won. But we were soon to be terribly disappointed. In the afternoon, Villacampa himself came to tell us of his double triumph over the Poles at Alventosa and over the body coming out of Daroca – which he exaggerated into a strong relief column taken prisoner along with its artillery. He then promised that Suchet's army would be smashed at Valencia and repeated his threat of blowing us all sky high should we not capitulate immediately. This new summons was rejected as the others had been; but of the three pieces of bad news he brought we had reason to believe that the first two, at least, were well founded, and that the third might soon be confirmed by the distinct and constant sound of picks and shovels beneath us. Leviston, however, insisted that the mine was not sufficiently charged otherwise the enemy would not have waited as long as they had. He was right: the Spanish did not have enough powder.

Despite this they continued their preparations for a siege; barricading the streets, loop-holing houses and pushing on noisily with their underground labours. But the hour of our deliverance at last arrived, rather inconveniently in the middle of the night of 12–13 March. Suchet had not suffered a check before Valencia but had, nevertheless, lost any hope of being successful with the limited forces at his disposal. He retraced his steps, harassed constantly by the enemy. He learnt of the blockade of Teruel and my poor friend Zarski had asked for the honour of being first to our imminent rescue. He was so full of zeal that he put a considerable distance between himself and the rest of the vanguard and, with only a handful of men, he fell upon the enemy in the main street that led to our refuge, before they knew what had hit them. How can I express the happiness we felt upon hearing the 'who goes there?' of our sentries met by 'France, the 1st Regiment of the Vistula!' It was so beautiful that we first of all thought it must be some kind of trick and that the Spanish were forcing some of those Poles they had taken at Alventosa to deceive us. But Zarski asked to be able to come forward alone and that we send out Lieutenant Brandt to recognise him.

Soon all our fears were swept away and there was general rejoicing. As we contemplated the glow given off by the campfires of the relieving army, we felt ourselves released from a long and terrible nightmare. We still had some wine and a little butter, which would have lasted us a few days, but we had run out of fresh meat and even water.

Next day, Suchet arrived. He inspected the besiegers' works and addressed a few kind words to the wounded as well as warmly congratulating Colonel Plique at length. He was less generous with poor Leviston, who had really been the life and soul of the defence.[48] This Colonel Plique was a character. For most of the siege he spent his time locked away in his office, preparing reports and cursing anyone who might come to disturb him and interrupt this important work. With the soldiers he always seemed embarrassed and hardly had a word to say to them. I do not know what would have become of us had Leviston and a few other energetic officers not been there.

Suchet, in his *Memoirs*, is highly critical of those officers commanding

---

[48] Leviston was killed on 8 January 1812 at Valencia.

the two detachments surprised by Villacampa. But he should bear in mind that all of the artillerymen who were moving up from Daroca were killed at their guns.[49]

Teruel, where all this unpleasant business had taken place, was one of the most interesting Spanish towns I chanced to see. With its nine new monasteries and its seven huge churches, it always seemed more considerable than it really was. In one of the churches, that of St Peter, they would show the relics, more or less genuine, of the lovers of Teruel, which are as famous in Spain as Romeo and Juliet are in Italy.[50]

The most remarkable thing about Teruel is its gigantic aqueduct, with 105 arches, which carries water to the town over a deep abyss. The aqueduct was in fact built in the seventeenth century but, nowadays, the people believed that it must have been built by the Moors or the Devil, which meant more or less the same thing.

The main square came as a considerable surprise on market day and was as busy as it was attractive. I have never seen such a swirling mass of coats, capes, mantillas, horses, mules, donkeys, swearing, oaths and gestures, in such an enclosed space, as though the whole of Spain had come to buy its vegetables there. When the Angelus was rung a dramatic silence would suddenly fall and buyers and sellers would kneel and cross themselves devotedly until the last bell was heard, when everyone would resume their infernal din.

---

[49] Suchet says that the detachment coming out of Daroca was 'badly led and poorly commanded.' The Polish officer at Alventosa, according to Suchet, chose 'the worst possible option' in trying to escape across country with his 170 men and should have locked himself with his troops in the old castle that dominated the town.

[50] The Lovers of Teruel were Diego Juan Martinez de Marcilla and Isabel de Segura, who lived in the thirteenth century. Their story was adapted, famously and crudely, by Boccaccio.

CHAPTER XX

THE GUERRILLAS AGAIN – PREPARATIONS FOR THE SIEGE OF TORTOSA
– MARCHING ON TORTOSA – A DANGEROUS DEFILE – INTO THE HUERTA
VALLEY – BEFORE TORTOSA – A BRILLIANT BATTLE

After my deliverance from the hands of Villacampa, I was sent to Saragossa
to complete my recovery – which I did thanks to the care and attention
lavished upon me.

On 1 May, despite my wound not having quite healed, I was deemed fit
enough to rejoin my regiment and was sent to Calamocha. My welcome was
overshadowed by preparations for a punitive raid against the guerrillas of
Comoran and d'Hernandez, who had gathered in the mountains somewhere around the source of the Panetudo river.

This expedition lasted some twelve days. We endured a host of difficulties but our efforts were crowned with the success they deserved, thanks
to a novel tactic we adopted for the occasion. After pursuing the enemy for
some days and failing, as was usual, to catch them, we pretended to give up
the chase. We retreated a short distance but then wheeled right round and
caught the guerrillas completely off guard just outside Lancosa. They were
severely punished in a bruising fight which has failed, as far as I know, to be
mentioned in any of the history books.

After my return from this expedition, I fell into an unfortunate disagree-
ment with Major M–, who had temporarily been placed in charge of the
regiment. In an inspection of my company's equipment he found that the
soldiers' shoes were in a deplorable condition and blatantly accused me of
negligence. Now this officer was known to be on very good terms with the
contractors who supplied all our equipment and clothing, and had amassed
a fortune over the years. I therefore felt justified in replying that nothing
could be done with such shoddy goods and it was no surprise that the
shoes wore out overnight. For this little outburst, I was placed under arrest.
Chlopicki, however, overruled the major and I was released.

After a few more raids and skirmishes, the 2nd Regiment of the Vistula was sent to Morella, where we arrived on 28 June. Suchet had almost recovered from the unfortunate consequences of his unsuccessful attack on Valencia and was once more keen to take the offensive. On 14 May he took Lerida, then, on 8 June, Mequinenza, and preparations were underway to seize Tortosa. This time we were in for quite a party and one which would drag on for many months.

Morella is situated in a peculiar part of the kingdom of Valencia. It is a mountainous and barren part of the world and its population is poor but warlike. The little town of Morella, tucked under the Muela de Garamba peak (a very hostile and inaccessible mountain), is defended by a medieval city wall and has, in addition, a citadel which dominates the town and the whole of the surrounding region. The Spanish troops, hotly pursued by General Montmarie, had abandoned the place without a fight and seemed prepared to abandon the entire region. This was a tremendous error on their part as it offers a vast assortment of magnificent defensive positions and the kind of terrain well suited for guerrilla warfare. Indeed, there was nothing but rocks, streams, torrents and ravines covered in thorny and twisted bushes. A leader of Mina's calibre would have made us pay dearly in such a terrain.

Laval's entire division, concentrated at Morella, moved off for Chert on 30 June. We had to advance over the very worst of the country and that which seemed most savage and inhospitable. This is especially true of a position called the San Mateo pass, which was a real Thermopylae and a handful of men could easily have stopped us dead in our tracks. For six terrible hours we wound our way through a tortuous defile, snaking between rocks and boulders. There was only sufficient room for three men to march abreast as we were flanked on either side by huge and immovable boulders. Even the soldiers could not understand why such a position had been left undefended. We finally found ourselves at the end of this interminable defile and caught sight of the Vale of Tortosa spread out before us with its fields, canals, vineyards, tropical vegetation, dazzlingly white houses, and the bell-towers of the churches peaking out from between the palm trees.

On 1 July we made camp at La Jana, amongst the orange trees and myrtle. Our men were especially pleased with the abundance and high quality of foodstuffs: hams, smoked fish, fruits and all kinds of vegetables, and, to wash it all down, as much wine as could be asked for.

There were plenty of potatoes, which were so common in this area that the locals called them *comida per los cochinos* (food fit for pigs). All that was lacking really was good forage, and this we overcame by giving the horses fruit, which they thoroughly enjoyed.

At dawn on 4 July, we began our attack on Tortosa. We were so little

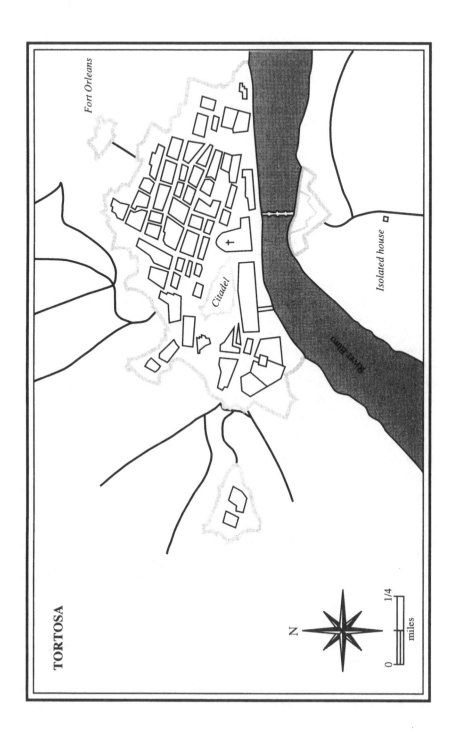

TORTOSA

Fort Orleans

Citadel

Isolated house

GUADALQUIVIR

N

0   1/4
miles

expected that the Franco-Polish voltigeurs, commanded by Colonel Mesclop, found peasants still working in the fields. Three miles from the town we came across a battalion of Walloon Guards, most of whom were sabred or taken by the cavalry.[51] We performed our duty so well and pushed home the attack so vigorously that we overtook the rest of the fugitives before they reached Tortosa.

I had got some way ahead of the combined voltigeur battalion with most of my voltigeur company and we now found ourselves but a little distance from the outer defensive works of the town – a *tête de pont* guarding the bridge over the Ebro. We had not been noticed by the city's garrison and had not yet come under fire from its defences. I even thought the city had been left undefended, things were so quiet. We walked right up to the palisades and began our preparations to climb over. I am convinced that, had the entire battalion been present at this precise moment, we could have carried the position. But things happened differently and the cry '*Los franceses!* The enemy! To arms!' went up. The Spanish artillery at last woke up and sent us our first roundshot, which passed over our heads. The river was, at this point, no more than 60 yards wide and we could easily distinguish all the panic in the town, the cries of the crowd and the frantic beating of drums. Suddenly crowds of defenders began to appear above us on the earthworks and we were assailed by a murderous fire. We had to fall back as we were entirely without cover. The houses had been demolished and the trees cut down all around the town for some distance and we had to cross a considerable expanse of open terrain before we made it to the first piece of cover we found – a two-storey house, with an enclosed garden, some 500 yards from the defences. As I had not received any orders, we established ourselves here as well as we could and awaited developments and, we hoped, support.

I posted a detachment of my men behind the garden wall and occupied the house itself with the rest. I had with me, apart from my own company, a few voltigeurs from the 44th Line who had managed to keep up with us. I had just completed my dispositions when the Spanish artillery in the old castle opened up on us with telling effect and soon the roof of the house had been destroyed and the garden wall facing the town had more holes in it than bricks.

The bombardment suddenly stopped and it became obvious we would now have to face an infantry assault. A large detachment of *Miquelets*[52]

---

[51] The Walloon Guards had been originally recruited in the Spanish Netherlands – now Belgium – but by the time of the Napoleonic Wars the guards were almost entirely composed of Spanish and German troops, with a sprinkling of assorted foreigners.
[52] *Miquelets* were Catalan irregulars named after Miquelet del Prato, a Catalan leader in the War of the Spanish Succession.

poured out from the defences. We managed to shatter their first attack but no sooner had we done so than the cursed artillery opened up on us again and rained shot and shell down upon us which destroyed the entire second floor. Under cover of this diversion, the enemy managed to break into the garden by means of the breached wall and my men were forced to pull back into the house. Our casualties were mounting. The enemy were frighteningly close to us and we could make out their every feature. Their faces seemed contorted by an implacable hatred of us. Just then an artillery salvo gave us a brief respite but it was enough for us to mount a vigorous sortie which recaptured the garden. Nevertheless, we could not advance from there. The Spanish, firmly established behind the garden wall, could not be driven off and were directing a murderous and much more accurate fire on us than I had ever experienced from Spanish troops. 'The future looks bleak,' a sergeant of the 44th said to me.

It was quite true that things were not going as well as perhaps they might. We were exposed to powerful artillery fire and surrounded by a host of furious enemies. We were totally exhausted by a forced march, followed by a remorseless struggle which we had endured for some three hours. A terrible thirst tormented us and we could do nothing about it as the well was in a particularly exposed part of the garden and quite out of bounds.

Taking advantage of a brief lull in the fighting, I assessed our position and had a brief council of war with the second lieutenant and the sergeant-major. As there were so few of us, too few to force a break-out, we unanimously decided that it would be better to defend each room to the last and die in the ruins rather than surrender. It also seemed impossible that our troops would not come, eventually, to our rescue, and I managed to persuade the soldiers likewise.

The enemy then returned to the attack but with less vigour. We shot at them through the windows and through the holes made by the roundshot until I perceived some sort of commotion in their ranks, especially those nearest to the road to Valencia. Soon they were seized by panic and they fled en masse towards the city. We attempted to pursue them, given fresh strength by the hope of our deliverance, but were brought to a halt by a furious storm of artillery and musketry coming from the earthworks by the bridge. I was bowled over and covered in earth by a roundshot ricocheting right by me. At the same time my right hand was hit by buckshot which went into the flesh so deeply that it has since been impossible to remove it. Indeed, it still gives me trouble to this day, reminding me of that first day of the siege of Tortosa.

That fierce struggle had cost me fifty-two men dead and wounded, and the colonel commanding the vanguard reproached me for having sacrificed them needlessly. For my part I believe that he deserved to take the blame for not having hurried over to relieve me sooner than he did. This opinion was shared by our commanders and especially Chlopicki, who came, a few days later, to congratulate my men on their courage and to shake me by the hand. Inevitably, to avoid a scandal, this incident was hushed up. But I look back with pride on our defence, which we conducted with honour and initiative and which was remembered for so long by all who had taken part.

CHAPTER XXI

SIEGE OF TORTOSA – HAND-TO-HAND FIGHTING IN THE TRENCHES –
A SORTIE REPULSED – I GO INTO THE TOWN TO SPEAK TO THE
GOVERNOR – ONE OF MY SOLDIERS CONSIDERS DESERTING

Between the 6th and the 12th of July we entrenched on the right bank of
the Ebro, fighting off the continual sorties of the enemy and enduring his
artillery. It was during one of these sorties that my friend Captain Boll was
killed by a parting shot from the retreating Spanish. For the next three
weeks they were to leave us in peace.

This first siege of Tortosa would last for five months, prolonged by
unfortunate circumstances which delayed the arrival of the siege train and
kept us waiting for support from the Army of Catalonia.[53] Conditions
started to deteriorate from the end of July for the besieging troops. We
were before a strong position, well provisioned with troops, we had the
Valencians on one flank and Catalans on the other, and behind us, in the
mountains, a population in arms. To compound our troubles it was
stiflingly hot, food was scarce and we had to go a considerable distance to
find water.

On the night of 1–2 August I was on outpost duty and we could distinctly
hear troops and wagons on the march on the other side of the Ebro. I sent
in my report, which was given scant attention by the staff as nothing of
significance happened on the next day and the Spanish did not fire once.
The same occurred on the next day. We later understood that this noise
signified the arrival of a strong reinforcement led by our most dangerous
opponent, the commander of the Catalan army, Henri O'Donnell.

The heat was unbearable on the afternoon of the 3rd. That day coincided
with the arrival of the Army's inspector general, and all staff officers,
captains, *fourriers*[54] and so on were called away to work with him in a house

---

[53] The Army of Catalonia was commanded by Marshal MacDonald, Duke of
Tarantum.

[54] A quartermaster, or *fourrier*, was attached to each company of line infantry.

a little distance from the camp. It is probable that the enemy took good note of this situation.

We were laid out on the grass behind our earthworks, in total relaxation. It was about four o'clock when we heard three cannon shots from the fort. The roundshot passed over our heads.

'It's a signal!' I cried out and jumped up, despite the scoffing of my incredulous comrades. I ran off towards my company. As I did so, I could see that the fighting had already broken out in the trenches. Our men were not easily taken by surprise. They had spontaneously run to arms, more or less formed up as units, and were now putting up a good fight.

As I was rallying my voltigeurs, Chlopicki arrived in his jacket, Nankin trousers and carrying the inevitable cane. He drew us up into ranks with the grenadiers on the right and the voltigeurs on the left, cried out, 'Forward with the bayonet!' and led us from the front in a counter-attack.

Whilst all this was going on a body of 300 Spanish cavalry from the Santiago regiment issued from the town, led by O'Donnell in person. They turned our defences and charged right into the village of Jesus, our head-quarters. Here they sabred some of our cavalry in the streets and killed one of the sentries posted at the general's door. Fired on by the duty company, they broke up and fled in different directions and very few of them seem to have made it back to Tortosa. If they had not lost their heads, they might have destroyed the artillery park, which was poorly guarded, and then come back and taken us in rear.

For the infantry there was some short but bloody hand-to-hand fighting which we soon won. The *Miquelets*, above all, were fighting like madmen and almost impaled themselves on our bayonets in attempting to get at our officers. I caught sight of one of them, a huge swarthy-looking man drunk on patriotism or something else, coming straight at me. He was about to make a lunge at me when one of my sergeants killed him.

After having repulsed the first attack with loss, we took the enemy in flank as they issued from the bridgehead. This manoeuvre threw their columns into disorder, despite the very best efforts of the Spanish officers, who were doing their duty manfully. Their rearguard hastily returned to the defences, but the rest were cut off and we took about 200 prisoners, including some high-ranking staff officers. My regiment had taken the brunt of the assault and had done most of the fighting. Consequently our losses were high and included poor old Solnicki, the former commandant at Monzon, struck by a ball in the chest. He was not killed outright but as they were trying to dress the wound he opened his eyes, sighed 'I feel better now' and slipped into his final sleep.

As soon as the last of the Spanish had got back into cover, their artillery poured an infernal fire onto our trenches. Five or six young fools, including myself, clambered up onto the parapet and began to tease the enemy. Soon we saw Adjutant Rechowicz walking over towards us in his measured step. He came over to us on the outside of the trench and thus exposed himself to the same kind of danger as ourselves in order to inform us that 'the general did not look kindly on such behaviour and would be glad if we desisted'. When he got back to Chlopicki, the general asked him why he had not stayed under cover. Rechowicz replied that 'an officer performing his duties always had to, according to regulations, take the shortest possible route'.

Suchet, in his *Memoirs*, attributes our success on this day to the sudden arrival of General Laval, who 'directed a column on the enemy position which menaced their retreat'. Now I saw Laval arrive on the field at the head of a few grenadier companies and he was even wounded in the fighting. But the most important phase of the combat was over in some fifteen minutes and Laval had been too far away with his staff to have participated in that part of the battle or to have had much influence on the decisive moment. The issue was already decided before he arrived and the Spanish had fallen back as soon as they were outflanked by Chlopicki's brigade.[55]

Two days later I was sent into Tortosa as an emissary and to ask for the personal effects of the men we had taken prisoner. I was very proud to have been given such an important task as I was only twenty-one. So I put on my dress uniform, my epaulettes and some taffeta over my old and new wounds. I also got Jankowski, my bugler, to smarten himself up and warned him to remain sober.

I was given the prisoners' letters and in addition a letter from General Laval to the governor of Tortosa. We moved off, taking the usual precautions, and did not spare the bugle until we were just beneath their palisades. There I could see rows and rows of muskets all pointed at us. The cry '*Alto!*' was shouted out in a most unfriendly tone. There were some very excitable people in the place and my mission was one not without danger. However, it seemed that curiosity was stronger than hate and nobody fired at us. After a pause of a few minutes I spied a middle-aged officer coming over to us and likewise accompanied by a bugler. He asked what the object of my mission was and asked if he might take the letters. I pointed out that he was formally required to conduct me to the governor. He considered this for a moment but finally I was blindfolded and, as was the custom, lead on by two officers on either side of me.

---

[55] Laval's counter-attack is given thus in Suchet's *Memoirs*: 'General Laval, at the head of the 44th Line, arrested the enemy's progress and was so well supported by General Chlopicki with the grenadiers of the Vistula Legion, that the Spanish were pushed back against their palisades and lost a considerable number of dead and prisoners.'

I went over the palisade and onto the bridge of boats, remembering to guess its length by counting my steps. On the other bank, I easily distinguished the subdued murmurings of a crowd that had gathered on seeing our party approach. I heard a voice say, 'But he is so very young!' Then two or three more shouted, in the most menacing tones, right into my ears, '*Al viage de sangue el carajo!*' This 'place of blood' is not far from the town and was the scene of a massacre of French soldiers during the siege of Tortosa by the Duke of Orleans in the War of Spanish Succession.

After having spent quite a while trying to push through this far from hospitable crowd, we turned sharply and followed a wall or a building until we started to climb some steps. Finally they removed the blindfold and I found myself before the Count of Atocha, the governor of the place, who seemed unusually pleasant. He took the letters from me and went out to an adjoining room to read them, leaving me with several officers who offered me some chocolate and iced water.

'You are having a hard time of it out there', one of them said to me in French, 'you would be better off with us.'

'We are used to privations and hardship and are looking to the future,' I replied.

'The future? You had better not think of that!'

During this brief exchange the Count came back in and entrusted to me a letter for the general. He then asked me if I was a captain and upon my replying that I was only a lieutenant, exclaimed, 'Good God! If you came over to us we'd make you a lieutenant-colonel!'

This ambush struck me dumb for a moment but I soon managed to reply and, indicating the Spanish officers, said, 'But how would these gentlemen like to serve with a deserter?' I then asked him to sign an authorisation for me to be let out at once, which he did with good grace.

As I came out into an antechamber I was not a little surprised to run into Jankowski. He was behind an overflowing tankard and he made it clear that I could leave without him as he would be staying on with the Spanish – 'the best people in the world'. Despite my warnings and his promises, he had succumbed to temptation and was now very much the worse for drink.

'What?' I said, 'after I had especially selected you from the entire regiment for this honour, you would insult the lot of us? Very well, stay and have the satisfaction of watching them kill your brothers in arms!'

My reproach sobered up this poor devil, who was quite attached to me. He threw the tankard to the ground and exclaimed, 'You can keep your bribes! I'm off with my lieutenant...'

Above left: Josef Chlopicki, commander of the Vistula Legion in Spain, pictured in the uniform of the Polish Legion in the 1790s. Chlopicki later rose to general of brigade and served with the French until 1813.

Above: Colonel Stanislav Kliski of the Vistula Legion's lancer regiment distinguished himself at the battles of Maria and Belchite in June 1809. He commanded a brigade of cavalry in the 1813 campaign.

Left: Colonel Mikolaj Kousinowski was colonel of the 2nd Regiment of the Vistula Legion – Brandt's regiment – in Spain. He was wounded at Tudela, just before the siege of Saragossa commenced. Kousinowski died at the crossing of the Beresina during the retreat from Moscow.

Opposite: Marshal Suchet was the most successful French commander of the Peninsular War.

Left: Brandt served in a brigade commanded by General Habert, pictured here, at Saragossa.

Below: Chlopicki leading the 1st Regiment of the Vistula Legion into the breach by the Santa Engracia convent, during the assault on Saragossa of 27 January. Chlopicki advised on the technical details of this painting.

Spanish resistance was bitter throughout the siege of Saragossa. The French blamed the Spanish clergy for inciting the population against them. After the surrender a number of clerics were executed by the French for this very reason, including Don Basilico, Palafox's 'spiritual advisor'.

Above: One of the ubiquitous Spanish guerrillas, this particular individual being armed with a lethal-looking blunderbuss. Brandt was wounded in the hand by a missile from such a weapon at the siege of Tortosa.

Opposite page, top: Pedro Villacampa was a Spanish partisan and regular army officer. He was an implacable, and occasionally successful, enemy of the French in eastern Spain. Brandt fought against his troops at Tremedad, and was wounded by them at Villel.

Opposite page, bottom: General Joachim Blake (sometimes rendered as 'Black' in French accounts), a Spaniard of Irish origin, commanded the main Spanish armies in eastern Spain until his defeat and surrender at Valencia in January 1812.

Right: General Mikolaj Bronikowski was appointed commander of the short-lived 2nd Vistula Legion in 1809. He then served under Suchet in Aragon. During the invasion of Russia he was governor of Minsk, but was chased out of the city in November 1812, losing the vital stores and provisions held there just as Napoleon had need of them.

Below: General Fischer was instrumental in organising the Danube Legion and rose to prominence in the army of the Grand Duchy of Warsaw. He was Poniatowski's chief of staff during the Russian campaign and was killed at the start of the battle of Winkovo on 17 October.

Left: General Claparède, a veteran of Haiti and Spain, was the unpopular commander of the Vistula Legion during the invasion of Russia. He was wounded in the hand during the battles at the Beresina crossing in November 1812.

Below: The dashing Polish prince Josef Poniatowski, minister of war of the Grand Duchy of Warsaw and commander of the Polish V Corps in 1812. He was created a marshal in 1813 but died attempting to cross the Elster river after the battle of Leipzig.

Above: Smolensk under bombardment. Both the Russians and the French deployed a vast array of artillery in the struggle for the city.

Left: Smolensk after the battle. Russian civilians evacuate the city as the French enjoy the fruits of their victory in the smoking ruins. Smolensk was destroyed to such an extent that the French, during the retreat from Moscow, could not find sufficient shelter to winter in the city.

French officers survey the site of the battle of Borodino.

The scene after the battle. More than 75,000 men became casualties. Brandt described the night after the battle: 'In the shadows around each of the flickering fires, the agonised and tormented wounded began to gather until they far outnumbered us. They could be seen everywhere like ghostly shadows moving in the half-light, creeping towards the glow of the fire.'

Opposite page: French infantry advance at the battle of Valutina, a bitter struggle fought in an attempt to destroy the Russians as they retreated from Smolensk. Brandt, briefly attached to the imperial staff, saw the aftermath of the battle and noted that 'for all this slaughter we took not one cannon or ammunition wagon'. This painting by Faber du Faur perfectly captures the confusion and drama of battle.

Napoleon looks on as his troops loot and pillage Moscow. After the hardships they had been through, it is perhaps not surprising that they gave themselves over to excess in the Russian capital.

Polish troops, moving to defend the Borisov bridge in November 1812, under attack by Russian cavalry. Despite Dombrowski's attempts to hold the vital bridge, it fell to the Russians and compelled the French to construct their own bridges over the Beresina. In this scene Major Hohendorff of the 14th Polish Line shoots and kills the colonel of the Pavlogrod Hussars.

The scene as the remnants of the French army make their way onto the Beresina bridges. The confusion, anguish and despair, as related by eyewitnesses to the event, are all too evident.

The scene on the other side of the river as those fugitives who have succeeded in crossing the Beresina make their way to Vilna through the frozen mud. The carriage in the foreground contains the injured Prince Poniatowski.

Napoleon, escorted by cavalry of the Neapolitan guard, quitting his troops at Smorgoni and leaving for France. Brandt writes that this act led to 'much consternation and malicious rumour' in the abandoned army.

French officers leaving Russia in a sledge in December 1812.

CHAPTER XXII

GENERAL LAVAL DIES – MOSQUITOES – WE ATTACK BERCEYTE AND PUT IT TO THE SACK – A SPANISH ATTACK – COLONEL PASCAL SAVES THE DAY – SURRENDER OF TORTOSA

In the closing days of August I was charged with the task of escorting the dying General Laval over to Suchet's headquarters at Mora. It was a difficult and dangerous journey. We would have to effect a crossing to the right bank of the Ebro at Xerta. The crossing was impossible during the day as it was in range of the Spanish posts at Tortosa, on the other bank. During the night there was at least a chance of managing to get across, as the enemy could not see properly and would, and always did, aim in the general direction of any noise.

Thus it was in these pleasant circumstances that we started out on this expedition. There were 160 men in my company, of whom some thirty were occupied in carrying the general's litter. During the night crossing we were shot at many times but fortunately without effect. After moving beyond Xerta the dangers became even greater. We were passing through a region in which the guerrillas flourished. There was in particular a series of defiles where our troops coming to camp, or vice versa, were always attacked. One of these passes, the last one before the descent to Mora, would have been wonderfully beautiful in peacetime but could not have been more disagreeable now, especially for troops, like us, who were coming from Tortosa. Imagine moving along a path on the edge of a precipice, with a massive drop beneath you and dominated on the other side by a huge mountain, the slopes of which were covered by boulders! This was the guerrilla's favourite position for an ambush.

As I knew the region quite well I took careful precautions. Before we reached the dangerous pass I sent a detachment of my best marchers out onto our flank with orders to scale the heights opposite. This they could do without attracting any attention, as the enemy would be too absorbed in watching the progress of the main body. Meanwhile another detachment, acting as vanguard, pushed on ahead and, along the difficult part of the road, were fired on by the enemy and returned their fire. However, the Spanish suddenly found themselves fired on in front and assailed in the rear by my mountaineers, who had turned their position. They thought they must have been attacked by a superior force attempting to cut their retreat and they disengaged with great haste. If we had not been able to distract them by this little ruse, the escort, moving slowly under the fire of the enemy, would surely have suffered terrible casualties in the pass. As the general himself realised, the Spanish would have hailed that as a great victory in their bulletins.

Laval only had a few days left to live and he in fact died shortly after our arrival at Mora. He was replaced by General Harispe.

We were to have countless days of horror before this interminable siege was to come to an end. After two months of unbearable heat, the weather turned dramatically in September and we were drenched by heavy downpours. For more than a week it rained *a cantaras* (in buckets), as the Spanish put it. The Huerta looked like an enormous lake and had the rain persisted we would have had to withdraw to the heights to avoid being flooded. With the floods came clouds of mosquitoes, brought in by a sea breeze on the evening of 24 September. These disgusting insects formed a thick cloud, hovering above the ground, a veritable humming and stinging fog. We burnt masses of powder to try and drive them off, though this gained us but a brief respite and the cloud reformed and descended upon us once again. Of all the plagues with which Moses smote Egypt, none were as cruel as this. History has examples of how this scourge had actually changed the course of military events, such as when mosquitoes forced Marshal Hocquincourt to abandon the six-month siege of Grenada in 1653. We, too, were about to abandon our positions to these new allies of the Spanish, when they were suddenly blown away by an abrupt shift of the wind to the north, on the evening of the 25th.

The Tortosa garrison left us pretty much in peace but new military events in Catalonia and Aragon rendered the position of the investing troops difficult and postponed any completion of the siege. On the 26th a force of all arms was directed towards Berceyte, the 'Black Town', as the French called it, on account of its population being our implacable enemies. Our division supplied four companies for this enterprise, one of which was mine. Two other companies, sent via Alcañiz, later rejoined us at Xerta.

A deathly silence reigned in the Black Town as all the inhabitants had fled. As many of our soldiers who had been taken prisoner had been sorely mistreated here, we deliberately and methodically sacked the town. We burnt down the olive groves, tore up the vines and so on.

Our approach to the town had only been resisted by mosquitoes but it was a different story on the way back. As we were in the process of passing through a deep gorge we came under attack from the very same locals as we had come to pacify. They had blocked off the exit to the defile by means of a kind of barricade and my voltigeurs were having great difficulty in demolishing this obstacle. Meanwhile the Spanish were showering the column with huge chunks of rock and boulders and were making great efforts to pick out the officers, most of whom ended up wounded, more or less severely. This inevitably put the column into disarray. Some soldiers kept order, others ran this way or that and seemed like they could not get away quick enough. The six companies formed one huge disordered mass, the enemy were firing into the crowd, the morale of the men plummeted and I am not sure how all this might have ended had not Colonel Pascal, the expedition's commander, shown exceptional energy. His horse had been killed and a bullet had pierced his arm and yet he put on a totally unconcerned appearance.

'You scoundrels of conscripts!' he shouted in a voice so resonant it could be heard above the tumult, 'you have only got your lives to lose because you've already lost your honour to these damned brigands! It'll be a good thing if you do get killed as you don't deserve to live!'

He then paused to interrogate two monks who we were taking with us as hostages and who had been busy organising the insurrection that brought us here. After this brief lull, he continued: 'Let these dogs stay here for good, but the French – follow me!'

Now, our Poles had not understood a word of this soldierly speech but it proved to have the exact same effect on them, as they understood the unequivocal gestures of the colonel, and neither did the execution of the two monks, I must add, trouble them in the least.

We redoubled our efforts and at last broke free from the trap. Towards the end of the battle Pascal, who was now the target for most of the Spanish sharpshooters, was hit by a bullet which shattered his jaw and finally put him out of action. But the soldiers he had so rudely insulted would not abandon him – so great is the prestige of courage. They carried him over six miles through the mountains supported on crossed muskets, all the while being pursued by the enemy, before being able to pause and improvise a more comfortable stretcher.

In this battle we had lost our entire baggage, along with all the booty we had taken at the Black Town, but fewer men than might be thought. Seven men had been killed in my company.

For the last two months of the siege, or blockade, of Tortosa, the Spanish garrison had been almost totally inert. We thought this might be due to the fact that large parts of the garrison had been pulled out of the town. We, on the other hand, were constantly fighting in those parts of Catalonia and

Aragon we had grown familiar with the previous winter – around Teruel and Vilel. At the end of October, General Chlopicki was sent against that indefatigable partisan Villacampa, with troops drawn off from the besieging force and including men from the 1st and 2nd Regiments of the Vistula. However, this time, to our great regret, we were not included in their number. It was during this expedition that my friend Zarski, of the 1st's grenadiers, was mortally wounded in a battle near Fuente Sande,[56] near Teruel, on 12 November, as our captain wizard had predicted. Beware of the mountains!

At last, in the first half of December, we had surmounted the majority of our difficulties and found ourselves in a position to attack Tortosa. On the night of the 15th, Chlopicki's brigade moved over the Ebro at Xerta and it seemed that we would at last play a more active part in the siege. After two weeks of digging trenches we had occupied some of the outer defences and thought that now the street fighting would begin, as it had at Saragossa, especially as some positions seemed eminently defensible. This time, however, it was all quite different.

The Spanish capitulated on 2 January, forgetting the solemn oath they had made to O'Donnell on 3 August, the day of the sortie, 'to vanquish or to die'.

---

[56] This expedition consisted of two battalions of the 121st Line, the élite companies of the 1st Regiment of the Vistula Legion, under Fondzelski, and the line companies of the 2nd Regiment of the Vistula Legion under Colonel Kousinowski. At Fuente Sande, Zarski was killed, two officers of the 1st were wounded, four officers of the 121st were killed and three wounded.

CHAPTER XXIII

Our brigade was charged with escorting the garrison of some 9,000 men
into captivity at Bayonne and we were given orders to fire on anyone seen
trying to escape. During the first part of our march, that between Tortosa
and Xerta, each morning was marked by the detonations of muskets and
confirmed that this order was being rigorously executed.

We camped in the open outside Xerta in the cold and without fires. The
prisoners suffered horribly and we were doing little better. We were under
arms twenty-four hours a day and there was no time to make soup as we
were worried that the prisoners, who outnumbered us, would all make
off. On the next day we made better arrangements to keep them under
surveillance and thereby avoid the need for drastic measures. But we could
not keep the soldiers from being unhappy with their duty and from venting
their frustrations on those they were supposed to be escorting. In the
beginning, especially, they would beat up those that tried to escape or just
hit out at someone simply because they felt like doing so, and the marks and
bruises on many of the prisoners bore testament to this.

We passed through the camp of Prince Pignatelli's Neapolitan division
and this left nothing to be desired, especially the turnout of the men: they
all looked superb. These gentlemen welcomed us in the most hospitable
manner, perhaps in too hospitable a manner. The officers plied us with
drinks and gambled with us whilst their soldiers relieved ours from guard
duty over the Spanish. It was only the next morning that we discovered
that we had all been unlucky at cards and that many of the prisoners had
escaped. Only some time later did we find out what Suchet has subsequently related, that this division had been recruited from amongst the

worst robbers and thieves.[57] This led us to believe that we may indeed have been robbed by our hosts whilst their soldiers were soliciting bribes from the Spanish and letting them escape for money.

I have forgotten to add that before we fell into this little mess we passed through, on 5 January, perhaps the most beautiful pass in the whole of Spain – that of Las Armas or Trincheras. This was named after the heraldic arms of James the Conqueror, the King of Aragon, which were carved in the rocks high above us.

We passed down the superb road Suchet had had built in order to ease the transport of military supplies and materials necessary for the siege of Tortosa, between Mequinenza and Xerta. This road, apart from its immediate purpose, was of considerable benefit to the region as a whole.

Thanks to Suchet's wise administration the whole of Aragon was beginning to get accustomed to French occupation. On the 8th we reached Caspe where I had once stayed, but in very different circumstances; everything now seemed to be flourishing. I sought out my former host and he seemed to be doing very well. He, and many other inhabitants of the region, was doing good business with the French by providing food for the army.

At Saragossa, where we arrived on the 11th, it had been impossible to erase the traces of war so quickly. Indeed, the trenches and barricades had gone and the breaches had been repaired, but in many places the ruins of houses or monasteries littered the ground, sheltering poor families in their ruins. The squares, the streets, even the famous Coso were deserted. It was the same in the once fashionable Pasco which runs from the canal to the Huerva. Most of the trees had been smashed and those that remained were riddled with shot and shell.

Saragossa still had, on the whole, the mournful look of a besieged town. Apart from a few places, as by the Church of the Pilar (always packed with the faithful coming to implore the Virgin to rid them of the French), military patrols and French sentries easily outnumbered actual inhabitants. Much work had gone into converting key buildings into defensive positions inside the town, which measure was designed to arrest the least sign of any insurrection against us. The biggest of these defences was easily the Palace of the Inquisition, the *Aljaferia*, which had been palisaded and equipped with a good stockpile of supplies so that it could hold out under siege. I visited the mournful court-room (*Audencia*) where many unfortunates had doubtless heard the judges pronounce a sentence of death. The room's

---

[57] Suchet says of Pignatelli's Neapolitans that, 'they were good-looking men, badly clothed and armed. They gave themselves over to pillage and desertion; vices only tempered by the bravery of the majority and the goodwill of their officers.' These Neapolitans were on loan to Suchet from the Army of Catalonia.

interior was well suited to its purpose, as the walls were all black with just a white border; behind the inquisitors' bench was a huge black crucifix bearing an ivory Christ and in front of it a black table with another crucifix and a skull. The cells, of which there were a few, had little of interest, but the concierge had put together a pretty little collection of instruments of torture, iron spikes and saw blades, 'to tickle the visitors' fancy' as one of my fellow officers put it.

One day I was accosted in a shop by an ancient Spaniard and a Spanish woman no less old. He greeted me by calling me *senor capitan*. It was my old acquaintance the Count of Atocha. The old man seemed rather bemused but his wife spoke and gestured enough for two. She related, with all the excitability of the Southern temperament, that many people had since accused him of treason, him – the best and least offensive (certainly not very keen on offensives) man in the world. I managed to make my escape with a few pleasant generalities. He certainly had been no traitor, but there had been nothing heroic about his conduct.

After Saragossa our next stop was Alagon, of which I had bitter memories, on 17 January. It was hardly recognisable; everything seemed quiet and affluent. The inhabitants had all long since returned and looked upon the comings and goings of the soldiers, and their money, with some pleasure.

As I had a little free time here, I went to have a look at the convent or hospital from which I had narrowly escaped death. This place still looked sad and a little dirty (not unusual in Spanish convents), revealing nothing of its sinister past; only in the cemetery did the undulations of the tombs show that the homicidal wishes of the gravediggers had, to some extent, been granted.

I grew pensive here in this town where I had experienced so much horror. As I thought of all the dangers I had survived since then, of all the close friends I had lost and of my heartbreaking experience which I hardly survived, I found my eyes filling with tears. The sun was beginning to set as I made my way through the town. Almost instinctively, I went into a church; it was deserted but for an old priest praying by the side of a coffin. The opened coffin contained the body of a young nun, perhaps the same age as Ines and wearing the robes of the Order of Mary. One last ray of light seemed to make her almost seem alive as it shone on her. Filled with emotion, I slipped out of the chapel and fell on my knees uttering the most fervent prayer I have ever prayed in my life. The priest obviously noticed, as when I saw him at the entrance to the church he waved at me in a friendly manner and blessed me. I hope God forgives him for having blessed a heretic.

Two days later I witnessed another moving scene. There were many

151

Aragonese volunteers among the troops we were escorting to France. These poor devils were shedding streams of tears as they passed over the Aragon river (a tributary of the Ebro), the boundary of their country. They stooped down to the water and seemed to be bidding farewell to the land which they believed they would never ever see again. The sad word *jamas, jamas* was repeated again and again by these despairing men. This heartfelt emotion and their poetical suffering, made for a strange contrast with the more forbidding appearance of the majority of the prisoners.

At the next halt, Tafalla, we met a Polish march battalion,[58] most of which was absorbed directly into our regiment. They were good men, well equipped and used to handling arms. They still had not had their baptism of fire but this would soon be liberally conferred on them. Incidentally, this battalion was the fifth such to come into Spain from the Duchy of Warsaw alone. From this it is quite clear how many men were being consumed by this Peninsular War.

Pamplona, which we reached on the 22nd, was lively and seemed so much cleaner than any other Spanish town of the period, which was not very difficult. But the atmosphere was quite unreal as it was populated solely by French soldiers and only in a few of the more luxurious cafés could some natives be found. The garrison was constantly on the alert and our reign over the region stretched for just a musket-shot beyond the walls.

We did not reach Saint Jean de Luz, the first halt in France, until the 28th, and that after some hard marching. The main road was swamped with other troops and we had to take the side-roads. Finally, on the 29th, we reached Bayonne, our destination. I must add, to the credit of the Polish soldiers, that feelings between the guards and the prisoners were now much improved and were almost affectionate. We officers tried to do our best to lessen the sufferings of these people and they in turn were grateful for our efforts. I saw, on more than one occasion, instances of how the good intentions of the soldiers improved the lot of the prisoners. When we halted for the night at some fortified town and guard duty fell to the lot of some other troops, the prisoners always seemed so relieved to find themselves once more under our care the next morning. They often exclaimed amongst themselves, *quel buena gente los Polacos!* Most of them seemed sad when the time came for us to separate at Bayonne. That, in truth, was the only good to have come from this convoy duty and we were very glad it had come to an end.

---

[58] A march battalion was a temporary unit used to transfer replacements from the depot to the regiments in the field.

CHAPTER XXIV

TWO DAYS' LEAVE AT BAYONNE – CURIOUS ADVENTURE IN THE
THEATRE – ESCORTING A CONVOY INTO SPAIN – BAD WEATHER AND
GOOD LUCK – CARDINAL RICHELIEU AND A VETERAN AGREE ON THE
SPANISH METHOD OF WAGING WAR

At Bayonne we were given two days' leave. We were exactly like sailors
returning to dry land after a long and drawn-out voyage. A lot happened in
those two days and I am sure most of the town's population went without
sleep the whole time we were there, but they looked upon us with a certain
indulgence, saying, 'Good God! These good men brave death every day and
suffer the most bitter hardships year on end. In a few hours they will return
to that horrible life once more, the least we can do is allow them to enjoy
themselves for a short while.'

I remember that I went to the theatre on the second evening. They were
performing some melodrama. The audience consisted largely of soldiers
and they were making a tremendous row, so very little of the play could be
heard in any case. The civilians, however, could not or dared not complain.
A Hussar officer, in one of the boxes, had got rather out of control. It must
be said that the theatre was not very well put together and there were many
gaps between the floorboards. Anyway, a lady in a box above the Hussar's
box dropped a perfume bottle containing eau de cologne and it broke, and
the contents dribbled out and between the floorboards and right onto the
head of the Hussar. He, very drunk and consequently unable to use his sense
of smell, quite mistook this liquid and jumped to the wrong conclusion
altogether. He stood up and bawled out to the Police Commissioner, 'Look
here, Sir, they are pissing on us! It is an insult to me and to the whole Army!'
The house was in uproar and the Police Commissioner and Mayor determined to have the Hussar expelled. He was now exclaiming that he
would rather be cut to pieces than leave the theatre. Finally a truce was
called and the Hussar gave his word of honour that he would not disturb
the peace as long as they did not disturb his peace. This treaty was agreed

and carried out. I mention this trivial anecdote only because it is a reflection of how indulgent, and more, they were to soldiers in France.

The evening before we were due to leave we were informed of our new destination. We were going to have to escort a large convoy of arms and money. This was not exactly to our liking, especially as we now knew from experience what this would entail. As soon as an escort reached its destination the units were broken up and assigned here and there or in guarding other convoys, and only gradually brought back together, having sustained considerable losses in the meantime.

The defensive measures for this particular convoy seemed sadly lax and did not inspire confidence. We were ready very early but did not manage to get under way until much later. We were joined, as a reinforcement, by a newly-formed unit of foot gendarmes, well equipped but with no discipline. As we left Bayonne we could see many of them were drunk and quite a few could not keep up.

We crossed into Spain in horrible conditions; there was an icy rain which kept us company as far as Tolosa and by the time we got there on 4 February we were soaked to the skin and freezing cold. Here the troops were broken up, as predicted. Parts of our brigade were sent off in different directions whilst the remainder and the gendarmes continued on as escort to the convoy. At Tolosa our arrival coincided with that of a still more badly-organised convoy coming the other way and consisting of carriages and wagons, accompanied by many *cantinières* and women. Mina, whose territory we were crossing, could have made much from such chaos. The disorder thrown up by this nocturnal meeting was beyond belief.

I had a little adventure myself that evening. I had been detached and sent towards Allegria to organise the pickets in that direction and I was sheltering from the storm and the rain in a small house by a vineyard. It was close on midnight when I was informed that some sighing and groaning had been heard. It turned out to be a young and pretty Polish woman, dragging a mule on which was slumped an old man in a bad way. She said this man was her husband and that he had been serving in a Polish regiment until recently, when he had obtained permission, on the grounds of health, to return to Warsaw. However, at Vittoria he had got worse and they had to let the convoy (the same we ran into) go on without them. He recovered a little and was so impatient to leave Spain that they determined to continue at all costs. More than once she had felt that their time had come but fate had not yet abandoned them and here they were among their countrymen. I replied that in a country such as this I could not be as hospitable as I should like. I began by making her husband a large cup of coffee which seemed to do him infinite good. He fell asleep at once and I have never seen anyone sleep as soundly. The woman seemed very wide awake and I comforted her as well as I was able. On the next day, as the husband came out of his slumbers, I could see my treatment had worked wonders. I gave the couple a hearty breakfast and gave the husband a letter of introduction he could use with one of our Legion's officers who was in charge of the convalescents in Bayonne.

I met the woman again years later in Warsaw and she told me that they had arrived at their destination without further incident.

We were attacked on the next day, close by Ormaistegui in the territory of the infamous Antonio Chapalangarra, but the attack was not pressed home. This first shock had the excellent effect of tightening discipline, of which there was great need, and putting some order into our caravan. We suffered another attack between Bergara and Mondragon, where the Spanish vainly tried to block the exit to a defile after the vanguard had gone through. We were again attacked, this time much more strongly, in the Salinas defile, which was ideally suited to such operations,[59] but the Polish voltigeurs knew the area so well that the enemy dared not really show themselves. This expedition introduced me to the plain of Vittoria, rendered famous by the battle that took place there on 21 June 1813 and which decided the fate of the Peninsula.[60] This town was the destination of the convoy and consequently our mission was over. In February 1811 Vittoria was occupied by the Young Guard under General Dorsenne.[61]

We did not expect to be sent back to Suchet's Army and our expectations were met and surpassed: we were sent back to Pamplona on 12 February. We passed through Mina's territory without being seriously molested. The situation at Pamplona was still the same. The town centre was calm and orderly but on departing the town every Frenchman left security behind and found himself plunged into complete danger. Death was hidden behind every rock and every tree trunk. On the one day of leave we had at Pamplona I visited the citadel in company with an artillery sergeant wounded at Saragossa and then decorated at Wagram. I suddenly heard shots being fired close by the ramparts.

---

[59] The Salina Pass was the scene, on 9 April 1812, of one of Mina's greatest raids. He ambushed a huge convoy, escorted by the 7th Line of the Grand Duchy of Warsaw, scattered the escort, liberated 500 prisoners and took the entire baggage train. One account states that the Poles had taken no precautions and had their muskets transported in the wagons to make marching easier.

[60] The battle of Vittoria saw Wellington defeat a concentration of French forces commanded by Joseph Napoleon.

[61] General Count Jean-Marie Dorsenne (1773–1812) commanded two divisions of Young Guard (under Roguet and Dumoustier), detachments of Sailors of the Guard and the Neufchatel Battalion (under Baste) and detachments of Guard cavalry. He also had three companies of newly-formed 'conscript artillery'.

'It's only the insurgents chasing one of our soldiers,' said the veteran. And when I expressed surprise that they could insult a strongly defended fortress in such a way the poor man declared, 'Mr Lieutenant, what goes on here breaks the hearts of the old veterans of Jena, Eylau and Wagram. Not a week passes without some outrage committed by this rabble who don't even have the courage to cross swords with us, man to man, as they did in Prussia, Austria and Poland. If our officers just hang about in this place then they will end up by coming in here to get us. It is time the Emperor came and saw for himself what was going on here. The war is conducted too half-heartedly – neither the generals nor the soldiers do their duty and that's why it is all going to the dogs. A few determined and well organised columns sent out at night and again during the day would soon put a stop to this brigandage.'

This old veteran was also of the opinion, shared by no less a person than that seventeenth-century genius, Cardinal Richelieu, that 'he who attacks the Spaniard vigorously is right and he who intends to reduce them through patience will not succeed.' The success of this theory was later clearly demonstrated by the flying columns Chlopicki used in Navarre during the siege of Tarragona.

CHAPTER XXV

OPERATIONS AGAINST MINA – IN THE MOUNTAINS OF NAVARRE – AYBAR
– LUMBIER AND THE IRATI VALLEY – A MAGISTRATE IS PUNISHED –
SANGUESSA – SADOVA – AMBUSH AT LA CARBONARA – A MUTINY

On 16 February we once more left Pamplona and headed, via Tafalla,
towards that part of the country the Spanish called Mina's Storehouse
(*almacen*).

On the 16th, after a running battle, we occupied San Martin. As we had
been shot at from several of the town's houses, the soldiers took the liberty
of putting all the houses to the sack in order to teach the inhabitants a
lesson. To be frank it was rather an extreme sort of lesson.

On the 17th my regiment took up an excellent defensive position at
Aybar on the Aragon river and we stayed there until the 27th. Detachments
were sent out daily in different directions in pursuit of guerrilla bands. I
was billeted on a retired captain of the Royal Spanish Guard and he treated
me very well. As he was still collecting his pension he was branded as being
something of an *Afrancesado*, which allegation he refuted by saying that
although he accepted money from the usurper he only accepted it in
Spanish coins!

On the 27th we headed for Lumbier to disperse guerrillas gathering in
that town and in the Irati valley. The bulk of the troops kept close to the
Aragon river, but I covered the march with my voltigeurs along the crests
of the hills. This was a difficult route but the view was tremendous. We
could see, in the west, the valleys of the Aragon and the Salazar, and to the
north that of the Irati – a torrent that fed the former two rivers after
bursting down from the mountains. The nearer we drew to Lumbier, the
more magnificent the scenery became. The great Pyrenees, with snow-
capped peaks, formed a superb background to all this.

As we arrived above Lumbier I made a final reconnaissance along the
Irati valley, going as far as the picturesque gorge, and then linked up with
the regiment at the Devil's Bridge. This was in such a beautiful location

that even the soldiers were lost in admiration. Why is it that these beautiful places are always the setting for scenes of carnage?

I hoped to have been able to see these scenes again but we were sent in quite a different direction, towards Montreal and Irozin, to keep our lines of communication with Pamplona open. This region was Mina's birthplace and always full of his people. At Irozin I was ordered to burn down his house. This would have made me a welcome visitor to his camp, had I been captured.

Before returning to Lumbier we made a dash at Izaal, a small market-town in the Salazar mountains where the guerrillas had a magazine and storehouse. We struck so quickly that the enemy had no time to evacuate and, consequently, we had to overcome some spirited resistance. At first it seemed doubtful that we would ever lay our hands on the supplies as we had searched all the houses thoroughly and found nothing. The *alcade* swore there was nothing to hide. But the major knew what he was looking for and the meek posture the *alcade* struck up did not convince him; he hit him twenty times with his cane to give him an indication of what he might expect. The Spaniard turned as pale as death but kept silent. The dose was administered again but with the same lack of success. Then, from among the bystanders, who were stood around smoking cigarettes, a man stepped forward, went up to the *alcade* and whispered some words to him. The *alcade* then turned to the major and asked, 'Will you promise to spare the life of this man if he tells you the truth?'

The major gave his word, and the *alcade* pointed out some isolated build-ings which had hitherto escaped our attentions and in which we discovered a huge quantity of ammunition.

The partisans would never have been able to make good such losses or continue the struggle so long had it not been for the assistance and help of the English.

From this lost land we were sent over to Sanguessa, where the population welcomed our soldiers with open arms whilst slipping them proclamations calling upon them to desert. These leaflets, so full of mistakes, were printed in French, German, Polish and Italian.

From Sanguessa we were sent into the region of Cinco Villas, which was more firmly under French domination and more often harassed by the guerrillas for this very reason. These five towns – Sos del Rey, Un Castillo, Sadava, Exea and Tauste – had a degree of autonomy which had been conferred upon them for their loyalty to Philip V during the War of the Spanish Succession. The 2nd Regiment of the Vistula occupied the first four of these towns and my battalion was in Sadava, a small town with a Moorish castle situated in a fertile plain.

We had only just arrived when we were sent off to surprise an enemy

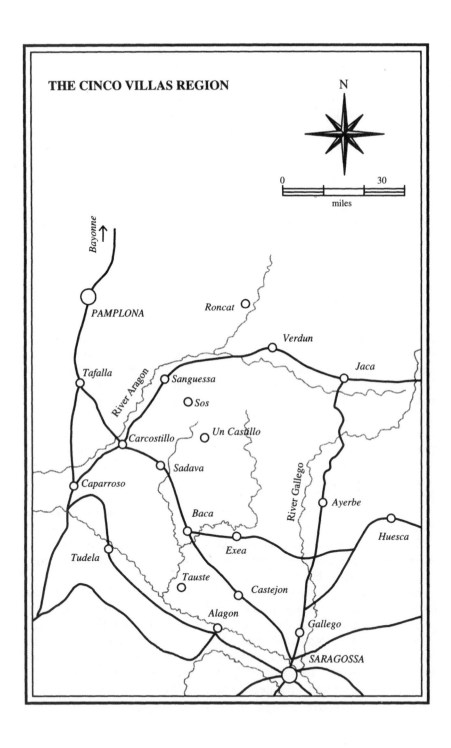

THE CINCO VILLAS REGION

N

0   30
miles

Bayonne

PAMPLONA

Roncat

Verdun

Jaca

Tafalla

River Aragon

Sanguessa

Sos

Un Castillo

Carcostillo

Sadava

Caparroso

River Gallego

Baca

Ayerbe

Exea

Huesca

Tudela

Tauste

Castejon

Alagon

Gallego

SARAGOSSA

detachment at La Carbonara, a hamlet beyond the Biel river in the mountains, and some fifteen miles away from our new base.

After marching along terrible roads for the greater part of the night we arrived at our destination without being spotted. We surrounded the town and stormed it in textbook fashion. Unfortunately most of the enemy were out on an expedition and we only took one officer and some dozen soldiers. However, we made a sizeable haul of forage and food. We took what we could and invited the inhabitants to take the rest to Exea for us whilst taking care to promise a second, less pleasant, visit should they fail to do so. At ten in the evening we were back in Sadava after having covered thirty miles in full kit, at night and across difficult terrain, in less than twenty-four hours.

We stayed in the vicinity of the town until 24 March. We usually had to seek high and low for our enemies, but they were sometimes closer than we imagined. One day some of our soldiers were using a haystack for firing practice in a field just outside the town when they were suddenly ambushed and shot up by some of the enemy who had been hiding behind the haystack.

On the 25th we were called to Exea and found that the whole regiment had been gathered in after being split up for so long. This reunion was marked by an unfortunate incident. A violent quarrel erupted between a captain and a lieutenant after a game of cards. The captain was blamed for the quarrel by the majority of officers and they formed what one of their number chose to call a confederation: meaning that the adversaries of the captain collectively declared in writing that they would not serve under him and would thus oblige him to change regiment. He protested to the colonel, declared he would have none of this and would register his complaint with the general. It was well known that Chlopicki was a strict disciplinarian and would not countenance anything that might hint of insubordination. Therefore the majority of the 'confederates' dropped out of the protest, with only a stubborn dozen persisting. I must add that I was one of their number.

This matter, for signing a declaration, illegally, in the name of the officer corps, earned us eight days' arrest. The affair ended thus but it left strong resentments, deeply buried.

As the Cinco Villas seemed at peace the 2nd Regiment of the Vistula was ordered to march for Saragossa to refit and prepare for new campaigns. The soldiers had a desperate need for cloth and shoes and they had not been paid for months. These matters, however, were not destined to be put right. No sooner had we arrived than we got an order to return to the Five Towns and the area we had just left. It transpired that Mina had reappeared and inflicted a sharp defeat on a detachment less experienced in this kind of warfare than ourselves.

As an unfortunate coincidence, our colonel was on leave and we were commanded by the major with whom I once fell out over supplies for my soldiers and who was very unpopular with the regiment as a whole. He was blamed for his style of living, for bringing his wife on campaign, for the delay in the issue of new clothing and even for the delay in pay. Quite possibly some of the Spanish propaganda was also taking effect. These circumstances, all told, had disastrous consequences on the morning of departure.

The major appeared at the head of the regiment and issued the command 'shoulder arms'. Not one company, excepting my own, obeyed. He repeated the order and was met from all parts by indignant cries and sniggering: this time it was a real mutiny. Some of the captains went among the ranks to cajole their men, but without success. Meanwhile, the major put on a brave face and carried on giving orders as though nothing had happened; 'By the right, forward march!' Despite the chaos, I had my company perform this manoeuvre and this brought us across the front of the rest of the regiment. This example of submission gave the impulse, instinctively, to the other companies to follow suit. But all was not yet over. When we drew near to the first battalion, where the sedition was the strongest, some of the soldiers rushed in front of me shouting at me to stop. I threatened to run through anyone who tried to stop me. One soldier, obviously drunk, went for me and I grazed him in the arm. This was enough to dishearten the mutineers. We continued our march and the first battalion fell in. This was just as well as an artillery battery, which had been drilling in the square, had unlimbered and had aimed their cannon at us. We left Saragossa, drums to the fore, as though nothing had happened.

We spent the night at Villanuova. On the next morning, as we were about to march off, the regiment was drawn up in a square. Rechowicz, who commanded the first battalion – where the trouble began – was given a severe rebuke and the trouble-makers were ordered to identify themselves. Some of the older NCOs and soldiers stepped forward and declared that they were all, more or less, guilty, that they were all sorry and that the most quarrelsome troops had been drunk and therefore did not know what they were doing. There was probably much truth in this as drunkenness has always played a leading role in both military and civil disorder, even in those which are ultimately assigned the triumphal label of revolution. This time, for a variety of reasons, they treated the affair with much leniency, and they were right to do so.

The commander-in-chief thought so too. In September, when we met up with him again at Saragossa, he issued a relatively benign reprimand to the troops themselves, reserving more severe language for the officers concerned and accusing them of not showing sufficient energy in attending to their duties. He concluded by adding, 'Gentlemen, only one of you performed his duty to the fullest extent and that was Lieutenant Brandt, the youngest amongst you. But since the entire regiment has always performed well before and after this unfortunate affair, I am willing to forget the incident.'

Apparently, the major was given a severe reprimand and he had been at best imprudent. From that day on this officer and his wife ceased to ride around in their gig, as they had habitually done until then.

CHAPTER XXVI

Marshal Suchet outlined in his memoirs the grave and pressing reasons
which determined his leaving Chlopicki on the right bank of the Ebro
rather than have him participate in the siege of Tarragona. He entrusted
him with the vital task of shadowing Mina and bringing him to battle
should that 'redoubtable leader attempt to link up with the Catalans or
foment revolt amongst the Aragonese and thus isolate the French army and
compromise supplies to our besieging troops'.

The commander-in-chief's confidence in Chlopicki was fully rewarded.
For almost three months the Polish general, by sheer vigilance and energy,
managed to keep in check an enemy renowned in this kind of warfare and
keep the peace in the Cinco Villas, from which our army drew most of its
supplies. Thanks to him – thanks to us – not one ration failed to reach its
destination. He was the terror of the guerrillas. A mere rumour of his
approach or the words '*El general de los Polacos*' would suffice for the
guerrillas to make for the hills. But God only knows at what cost these
results were obtained. We marched incessantly, usually twenty to thirty
miles a day along poor bridleways, climbed sheer rock faces, slid down
precipices, endured time and time again in quick succession the burning
heat of the lowlands and the icy winds of the heights, and all to get at a
slippery enemy, so that we could foil their designs, or, at best, disperse them
and force them to seek sanctuary some distance away – to which we would
pursue them and start all over again. During the course of these forays we
had some solace in the wonderful views of the Pyrenees, but had little time
to fully appreciate their charms. After all, the spectacle of these icy peaks
glistening in the sun could not improve either the roads or our dinners.

One of our toughest assignments was that of 17 March: an expedition
against Sos a Tiermas – so called from the thermal waters of the region –

where the enemy were trying to concentrate their forces.[62] We had to move upstream along the crest of the escarpment which dominates the Onzella valley. The quickest way of doing this would have been to pass through Sanguessa but as it was vital that our march remain a secret, and as Mina had spies in this town, we had to take the most deserted, difficult and convoluted road, as was usually the case. After crossing the Onzella, we scaled the heights, which were steep and covered in young oak trees. As we issued from this wooded sierra we found ourselves in terrain of a very different nature, overlooking the Aragon river. This meandering torrent swept along, sometimes stormy, sometimes calm. Before us, upstream, 1,000 yards ahead, we could see Tiermas perched there like a vulture's nest. We expected the enemy would try and hold such a strong position and how we looked forward to taking it! Compared to what we had been through, a battle, even under such difficult conditions, was so much more preferable to endless pursuit. As we made our way up the winding path that led to the village we were met by the civic authorities who, with much eloquence, tried to convince us of their innocence and poverty. They were certainly not lying about the poverty. I have never seen such a deserted or piteous region. There were some greyish stables scattered about. I went to see the famous springs in a kind of hut, where some intrepid people were attempting to bathe. Even in Spain, I have never seen anything quite so dirty!

Tired out by our exertions, we sought to buy some food and wine. The inevitable reply went: 'There is nothing here, this is a poor village, we have nothing to sell.' We were at a loss to understand how anyone could have come up with the idea of living in such a place. Most of the houses were literally clinging on the edge of a precipice and managed to give us vertigo despite having had plenty of climbing experience in this war.

We stayed for quite a long time and the inhabitants were as welcoming as when we first arrived. They also continued with their attempts to get men to desert, and not without success. We lost, in a couple of days, some forty men, as many French as Poles. This unfortunate incident led to an inquiry but only one culprit was ever found out: a tavern-keeper who sold wine to the soldiers at inflated prices and who was accused of offering them money to escape to Puente la Reyna, where, so it was said, a foreign legion in Spanish service was supposed to be organising.[63] This man swore by the *santissima madre de Dios* that he was innocent but he was condemned by

---

[62] The expedition was directed against Antonio Cruchaga, one of Mina's subordinates.
[63] Many deserters from the French armies in Spain were absorbed into Swiss regiments in Spanish service or into the one battalion of the Legion Estrangera. However, in December 1809 fifty Poles had been killed or captured fighting in the ranks of Miguel Sarasa's guerrilla band during a battle at Novales.

a court-martial and shot, despite his compatriots offering a sum of money should he be reprieved.

In this campaign we always managed to harass the enemy but never to destroy him completely. In order to do that we would have needed assistance from the other corps, something which, for one reason or another, was never granted to us. One of the best examples concerns our attack on Acaejs on 29 March, in which our entire brigade took part. Mina had massed his forces in this town some ten miles from Pamplona. Part of the Pamplona garrison was manoeuvring to his rear in order to cut off his retreat. But when the assault came the Spanish managed to escape as the Pamplona troops had failed to reach the designated position and Mina, although surprised, got off protected by his rearguard.

Chlopicki showed a remarkable aptitude for this mountainous warfare and did all that was possible in those terrible conditions and with the troops to hand. This was shown when, at the end of July, he moved out of the region and Mina immediately reappeared on the right bank of the Ebro and, despite being faced by other troops, raided as far as Saragossa.

I was in Saragossa on 2 July when I heard news of the fall of Tarragona. This news was met with much rejoicing at Saragossa, not only by the French but also by quite a few of the Spanish. They organised a series of bullfights, but these, and the bulls, were a real fiasco. I also helped organise a theatrical production in a badly lit and dirty room, Saragossa's only venue for such performances. I saw the bolero and fandango performed there in a most superb style by a dancer who had captured the hearts of the Aragonese public. She did not belong to a particular dancing troupe but was the daughter of a tailor and performed merely for the love of dancing. She was known only by the name of *Sastre* (the tailor).

The Spanish are so passionate about dance that it dominates the hearts of people of all ages and all classes. How many times have I witnessed, in the midst of that terrible war, an improvised evening dance in a humble village where the people gather round a singer sat on the steps of the fountain or by the well? No sooner does he start to sing than the people start to dance, clicking their fingers for want of castanets.

CHAPTER XXVII

SADAVA, AGAIN – THE ADVENTURES OF A JEW FROM ALSACE – BANQUET IN HONOUR OF SUCHET'S WIFE – PRECAUTIONS TAKEN FOR HER SECURITY – ANOTHER RAID IN THE CINCO VILLAS – HEADING FOR VALENCIA

During the final few weeks of our stay in the Cinco Villas, my battalion was billeted in Sadava, as was the general. He was lodged with a very patriotic marchioness who was practical enough to adapt to changing circumstances. She had first met us in February, during our first visit, and in the meantime had acted as hostess to Mina himself and he had asked her many questions about Chlopicki and about us. It was most likely that she was gathering information on us by getting to know the general well and by inviting officers to soirées from time to time. I never usually had the opportunity of going to these as I was frequently on duty at the outposts.

However, one day one of my fellow-officers came and relieved me and passed on an invitation from the general that I might come and spend the evening with him. I was intrigued, went off to put on my best uniform and made my way over to the general's quarters. I was presented to the marchioness and found that she was not very young but was still quite sprightly.

'You are the commander of the *Cazadores*?' she asked. 'I am sorry that your duties have kept you from us.'[64]

I do not remember what I said in reply but I noticed that all the women were looking at me in the most curious fashion and that not a few of them were obviously gossiping about me with my fellow officers.

As I wondered why this might be a brief musical interlude occurred. One of our lieutenants was a very talented violin player and Gulicz, my good friend the surgeon, was quite good on the flute. The general requested they play a *mazurka* which they did, and to which the other Poles danced, to the

---

[64] *Cazadores* was the Spanish term for light infantry.

great astonishment of the Spanish ladies, who had never before seen such a dance. After the *mazurka* came a waltz which caused even more surprise and perhaps not a little scandal. The Spanish were very keen to know whether the ladies and gentlemen really embraced and held each other so close during a waltz.

Meanwhile, as I noticed that most of the ladies were continuing to stare at me as though I was an exotic animal, I managed to draw one of my comrades aside and ask him to explain the meaning of all this. I learnt from him that the marchioness had asked the general whether or not it was true that there were heretics among our soldiers and officers and wanted to know if it was possible for her to meet one. It was therefore in my capacity as a Lutheran that I was invited to the party. It has to be said that a Capuchin monk somewhat tarnished my glory by saying that, in fact, I was only a schismatic...

In the Spain of that period many people believed that a Jew or heretic was some kind of devil, with horns and a tail to prove it! Many of the quite affluent classes, especially the women, were convinced this was so and it was therefore with some surprise that they noticed we were in fact just like anybody else.

A strange incident a few days later clearly demonstrated that such beliefs also held sway among the lower classes. The 14th Line, which garrisoned Tauste, had a Jew from Alsace called Salomon who provided food and wine for them, and this man was often in contact with the locals, buying victuals and supplies. Now, he paid quite well for the items he bought and so was quite popular with the people and believed he had nothing to fear from them. One day he went off with a detachment on reconnaissance and stayed on in a village against the advice of the commander but believing he would be safe. As he did not reappear, a patrol was sent out and they found him sprawled naked in the middle of the road, half dead from fear. A band of people had jumped on him as he came out of the village and pulled off his clothes and as they left they were shouting, 'He is not a Jew, he hasn't got any horns or a tail!' His little cart and his clothes were later found intact and proves that these people had not wanted to rob him.

The commander-in-chief, who became a marshal after the fall of Tarragona, had almost absolute power in the provinces we occupied and was determined to bring his wife into Spain to be with him. We were not notified of this until almost the last moment. One day the voltigeurs of the 2nd Regiment of the Vistula were ordered to carry out a thorough reconnaissance towards Ayerbe on the right bank of the Gallego. We were at a loss to understand why it was we were being sent into a region so completely outside our normal sphere of operations. The heat was unbearable and the roads were as bad as any in the peninsula. In addition a fog hung close about, one of those fogs the Spanish christened a *calina*. This gracious name disguises something quite horrible, a mist of vapour which literally takes your breath away. We were in an endless *calina* all the way to the region between the Gallego and the Isuela. As per our instructions we passed through Ayerbe, Bolea and Huesca and then returned to Ayerbe to make our report to the commander of the place. The report was quite brief: we had seen nothing nor heard anything of the enemy. On 10 August, after a long and tiring march, we got back to Exea in the Cinco Villas, where headquarters had been transferred on 30 July.

On the next day the marshal suddenly appeared among us and only then were we informed of the purpose of our mission. The marshal's wife was expected at any moment. It would have been impossible to have taken too many precautions in such a situation and so we set off once more and our flying column scoured the area around Ayerbe just before her expected arrival; in fact she arrived there on the 19th.

She was met with the kind of honours usually reserved for monarchs. Beneath her eyes thousands of young men, armed to the teeth, danced some kind of war dance, *bailadoras* performed endless boleros and fandangos and a guitarist played *jotas* before the marshal. This nocturnal scene, lit by burning torches, had a kind of picturesque beauty. The marshal and his wife circulated amongst us, she seemed cheerful and full of confidence. But it seems that this confidence was not infallible as no officers were invited to supper and we were all despatched to the pickets with the recommendation that we be especially wary. These precautions were necessary as there were a few guerrilla leaders who would have liked to interrupt the celebrations.

My company formed part of an élite battalion which was to accompany the marshal's wife from Ayerbe to Sanguessa. During this five-day journey we came across a few enemy scouts, who stayed well clear of us. We arrived at Sanguessa, without incident, on the 24th. Before leaving the region entirely we took part in one more punitive raid, which yielded considerable success.

When we reached Un Castillo on the 30th, we were informed that Pesaduro,[65] one of Mina's best lieutenants, was at Pentano, only some twelve miles from where we were, and accompanied by just a small escort. We made dispositions which indicated we were preparing to return to Exea, in the opposite direction. But when night fell we made a dash to the north, towards Lobera. After a six-hour forced march through the mountains, we reached Pentano just before dawn, the best time to surprise anyone.

Unfortunately a man in Lobera, who had once been accused of collabor-

---

[65] Mariano Larrode (the Pesaduro) was active in the Cinco Villas region but was captured by French troops in 1811 and hanged on 21 September.

ation and was burning to be rehabilitated, had run to warn Pesaduro, who quickly made his getaway with most of his men. But he lost his food, his baggage and his rearguard. I was charged to conduct the prisoners to Exea. As Pesaduro's brother was one of their number, I was sure I would be attacked at some point of the journey. I therefore placed the man on a mule, roped the rest together in threes and made it quite clear that I would be treating them all as soldiers – that is, if anyone tried to escape I would shoot the lot of them. My little speech had its required effect. We were shot at many times on the way to Exea, but I delivered all my prisoners.

We were finally relieved in September by new troops moving in from Navarre; good men, well supplied but more used to sleeping in barracks than in the open. We went to Saragossa with Suchet as he wanted us to form part of his difficult but glorious expedition to Valencia. We returned to the excellent region around Morella and San Mateo with which we became familiar at the time of the siege of Tortosa. The nights were now superb and it was even possible to see the famous comet which was considered – after the event – to augur the fall of Napoleon.

CHAPTER XXVIII

~

A FINAL INTERVIEW WITH SUCHET – I ESCORT GENERAL BLAKE INTO
CAPTIVITY IN FRANCE – INCIDENTS ALONG THE WAY – COLONEL PÉPÉ'S
INTERFERENCE WITH MY MISSION – I FALL ILL

The day after the surrender of Valencia (10 January 1812) I was ordered
with my company to Murviedro, where Suchet was based, as the marshal
wished to speak with me.

'I have selected you to command the escort of General Blake. You will
see that all honours due to an officer of rank are accorded to him but you
should watch him like a hawk. You will get a list of people who will be
accompanying Blake to France from my adjutant. Be ready to leave the next
morning. I have always had good reason to trust you and I have no doubt
we will be satisfied with your conduct and the way you carry out this *rather
delicate* mission. Farewell, and I shall see you again upon your return to
Valencia.' This is literally what he told me. But it so happened that I would
never see Suchet or Valencia again.

In this final interview he did not seem at all well and in fact not long afterwards he fell seriously ill. I will always remember him with great warmth.
Even though I am not personally named in his memoirs, I cannot forget that
he always spoke of me as being one of the most reliable young officers,
that he cited my name in orders of the day, and that he came to personally
decorate me with the Legion of Honour as I lay wounded in Teruel.

The list of those who I would be escorting to France consisted of eleven
people, namely: Generals Blake, Zogas,[66] Carlos O'Donnell and their aides-
de-camp as well as some officers from foreign regiments, most notably two
future Prussian generals, Major Grolmann and Lieutenant Lützow.[67]

---

[66] Although Brandt says Zogas, he must have meant Zayas, Blake's chief of staff.
[67] Grolmann and Lützow were Prussian volunteers in Spanish service. They
surrendered with their unit, the Legion Estrangera. It is interesting to note that Brandt
says these two officers were exchanged, whereas most Prussian histories have it that
they escaped.

Lützow was to play a leading role in the events of 1813. However, these two officers were struck from the list as they would be remaining in Spain to be exchanged. This was fortunate indeed for them, especially for Lützow as he would thus be allowed to return to Prussia, where he would ultimately raise his legendary *Freikorps*.[68]

Our convoy consisted of the captain-general's carriage, which was quite old-fashioned, a coach which contained some personal items and a few other covered wagons in which the other officers, aides and servants sat side by side as people do today in an omnibus. At the first halt, I had an excellent opportunity to study my principal prisoner at close quarters, as he invited me to dinner. He was aged about sixty, resembled Frederick the Great (in appearance) and was of a sad and introverted disposition.

At Castellonde de la Plana, where we arrived on the 12th in the evening, Blake wanted two whole days to be set aside for mass. I did not oppose this but made sure the doors of the church were well guarded. He came out of the church looking sad: for the whole of the ceremony he had heard people whispering the words 'coward' and 'traitor' at him. At the next stop, Oropesa, the captain-general was given another form of entertainment. As he arrived, the commandant of the town, a former captain from my regiment, wanted to give the regulation number of shots prescribed as a gun salute for a general, despite Blake himself, naturally for one in his position, not really wanting to announce his arrival. 'Your captain likes his artillery,' was all he would say.

On the next day, as we followed the coast, time and time again we came across troops taking part in the siege of Peñiscola. This fort, perched like an eagle's nest some 2,500 yards up, was deemed impregnable.[69] The garrison, however, surrendered some three weeks later. At the next halt, Benicarlo, the conversation around the dinner table turned to the Duke of Vendôme, the victor of Villa-Viciosa, who died of indigestion at Vinaroz, not far from Benicarlo, on 11 June 1712. 'It was good that he did,' said Blake mournfully, 'for it is a good thing to die at the peak of a military career in a full blaze of glory.'

On the 17th we crossed the Cenia, which marked the end of Valencian territory. I said my farewells to this land, farewells I never would have guessed as being final. The Spanish proverb is most apt: 'Valencia is a paradise but its people are devils.' All I can add is that they have more Moorish blood in their veins than do the people of Aragon and Castile.

---

[68] Lützow's *Freikorps* made a number of highly successful raids behind French lines in the 1813 campaign in Germany.

[69] Peñiscola was known as 'Little Gibraltar' on account of its resemblance to that formidable defensive position.

Uldecona, where we were to spend the night, was infamous for ambushes and it certainly looked as though it justified its reputation. It is a small town in a woody region and is located at the exact point that the borders of Aragon, Valencia and Catalonia meet. To our great surprise the town was not provided with a garrison. I therefore camped in military style and set constant patrols around the house *my* general was quartered in. Such measures were necessary as there was a garden full of enormous trees which touched the surrounding woods of the sierra. The general's room also had a door which opened onto the balcony. It is hard to imagine a place more fit for an escape attempt.

The specific measures I took included pickets at designated posts around the house and on a neighbouring piece of high ground. After dinner, which dragged on quite late, I took my leave of the general and instead of going to bed, set out to ensure all the orders I had given had been carried out as intended. This took me until the middle of the night. At one in the morning, as I was in the garden, I had the idea of getting onto the balcony.

I had been on the balcony for a short time when I heard the general's door open. It was the general and he was still dressed even at this late hour! He caught sight of me and asked who was there. I replied, with as much respect as I could muster that I was *El commandante de la gardia*. By way of reply he muttered *entendo, entendo*, and went back into his room. On the next day, as I went to pay my respects and to inform him as to the time we should depart, I was not well received and he sent his reply by way of an aide.

After a few hours' march we found ourselves in the pleasant and fertile area around Tortosa which was more than familiar to us. From time to time we would come across detachments from the French garrison out on patrol; we always had to be on our guard against guerrillas even after great victories. My voltigeurs had served as scouts and lookouts at the time of the siege and recognised each clump of trees, each house and even those places where they had buried their comrades. As for myself, I was acutely aware and heart-broken by the fact that in less than a year at least half of my company had perished in Navarre, Aragon or before Sagunto and Valencia.

As we drew closer to Tortosa I caught sight of a Neapolitan colonel who I had seen but a few days earlier at Castellonde, where he had had a long conversation with Blake at his carriage door. He stopped me and reproached me for having insulted a gentleman in unfortunate circumstances by keeping him under a repugnant surveillance.

'Sir, I am only carrying out orders given to me personally by the marshal'.

'Be quiet!' he shouted in a fit of passion, 'you obviously haven't understood your orders. I will report at once to the marshal!'[70]

After that strange outburst he mounted, thrashed his horse and disappeared.

His behaviour was so odd and yet I might justly be accused of being overcautious. However, I had, with my own eyes, seen four Spanish generals (O'Donoja, Renovales, Villacampa and Campo Verde) escape in similar circumstances, despite the first two having given their word of honour not to try to get away.

I was as yet ignorant of the officer's name and never discovered what right he had to address me thus. But, as I mentioned before, the Neapolitans were hardly saints and my first thought was that he was in league with Blake and would try to rescue him.

A few hours later the governor of Tortosa told me that his name was Pépé and that he was somehow supposed to oversee Blake's escort and exercise a kind of control over the details of the mission. Possibly the marshal had ordered him to do this, but he had told me nothing about it at our interview on the eve of departure.

This information put me in a tricky situation with the colonel. I went to look for him in order to explain myself, but he told me he had no time to see me. In addition, I was not invited to the general's table as I had been until then. But then something happened and I wrote to Colonel Pépé and informed him that due to a violent bout of fever I was forced to relinquish my command of the escort to a second lieutenant. I added that I had taken to my bed and that for the last few months my voltigeurs and myself had been employed without relief in the trenches of siege-works and in hunting guerrillas. I was therefore at the end of my strength and my tether.

Ten years later this man, made a general, played such a devious role in the Neapolitan revolution that my old suspicions seemed confirmed.[71] Even so, had he managed to free Blake and had the Junta in Cadiz promoted him to general and rewarded him with his own army, Pépé would in all likelihood have rendered a tremendous service to France.

---

[70] Suchet, in his memoirs, states that, 'Florestan Pépé was charged by the Marshal to accompany General Blake to the frontier'.

[71] Brandt here confuses Florestan Pépé with another officer in Neapolitan service, General Guglielmo Pépé. It was this latter officer who raised the standard of revolt against Bourbon rule in Sicily in 1821, only to come to terms with the Bourbons when they appeased him by offering him command of their armies.

CHAPTER XXIX

I managed to obtain permission from the governor, a major of the 44th Line called Miller who I was acquainted with and who took my side in the dispute with the Neapolitan, to remain a while in Tortosa. I was bedridden for the whole time Blake was in Tortosa but I managed to make a full recovery before he ever tried coming to ask how I was. I profited from this almost miraculous recovery by going out and examining the positions we held during the siege. Almost everything had changed beyond recognition. In addition, the plough had long since passed over the graves of my poor friends Boll and Solnicki and I found it impossible to discover their exact location.

I spent about three weeks at Tortosa, in which time I saw convoys of Valencian prisoners arrive day after day, escorted to France in the wake of their unhappy general. These men were short and stocky and dark and seemed quite lively. I much wanted to talk to them but I was at a loss to understand their dialect. They were well treated and seemed to be getting on well with their escort and seemed resigned to their fate. At the various halts they broke up into groups. Some played cards, others listened to a guitar or to a kind of flute which resembled that used by Caucasian tribes. They all ended up jumping and dancing as though they were still in their native villages. For a Spaniard, dance is as vital as food. The most cheerful men were the 300 or 400 who had served in the artillery, who could be recognised by their huge red cockades. From their ranks came the best guitar players and the most amazing dancers. One day I got sight of another convoy but this time of some 400 or 500 surly-looking men; these had taken part in the defence of Valencia and had attempted to instigate a revolt after the surrender. A few of the mutineers had been shot and the rest were now being sent on to France. The escort of this shackled group was composed

174

of some companies of the 2nd and 3rd of the Vistula, commanded by a staff officer. The convoy included various monks from different orders and therefore in variously-coloured garments – brown, black, grey, etc. The commanding officer had mixed all the orders together and so the column resembled a huge moving mosaic. As long as they were in Valencia they were treated as martyrs and were well looked after with all the best portions going to them. Mothers even held out their babies to be blessed by them as they passed. It would be altogether different in Aragon and still more different in France.

Some sixteen battalions from Suchet's army were assigned to the escort of these prisoners to France and mine was among their number. The convoys lasted at least two weeks when our lines of communication were unmolested, and that was not always the case. To maintain and safeguard communications meant detaching large numbers of troops and being constantly on our guard.

On 21 January, three companies of my regiment passed through Tortosa. I went to meet Major Beyer, who was in charge of these companies, and explained what had happened between Colonel Pépé and myself. He advised me to wait for the battalion to come back through Tortosa as it was impossible to guess what the Colonel had reported to the Marshal and how he might react.

Two weeks later my battalion had still not come back. I set off for Saragossa, hoping I might encounter it on the way there. By chance, I ran into one of Chlopicki's aides. He informed me that the order was out for all the Vistula Regiments to return to France at once as it seemed likely they would take part in the coming war with Russia. This order was carried out with amazing speed.

I set out from Tortosa on 10 February with the last of the 2nd's battalions, which had been involved in the siege of Peñiscola, and a part of the 1st Regiment which had been escorting prisoners. Some of the prisoners were chained together. These were men from Valencia who had allegedly taken part in the massacre of the French in the uprising of 1808.[72]

This time we were leaving Spain for good. Yet news of the new war was not terribly well received by our brave and patient soldiers. Those that hailed from the area around Pultusk and Ostrolenka spread word of how they had seen the abandoned wounded dying in the mud in the terrible winter campaign of 1807. Chlopicki, who had once served under Suvorov

---

[72] Interestingly, if this was the case, then this act was in breach of the surrender agreement, Article II of which stated that 'there would be no investigation into the former activities of citizens of Valencia or into the pasts of those who have taken part in the war or the revolution.'

against the Turks and had fought the Russians in the 1794 insurrection and again in Italy, considered this new twist in events most serious.[73] He remarked, 'Napoleon has now grasped the candle with both hands and will probably get his fingers burnt!'

As we moved from Saragossa to Jaca (18–29 February) our soldiers showed themselves to be thoroughly sick of acting as mobile prison wardens and let a large number of prisoners escape. Jaca, the principal town of upper Aragon and militarily significant, was occupied by a strong French garrison. I really wanted to be able to go and see one of the main Spanish pilgrim sights, the monastery of San Juan de la Pena, where the tombs of the kings of Aragon could be found, but I would have needed an entire battalion to serve as my escort for this pretty little excursion.

Crossing the Pyrenees in the middle of winter was as difficult as could be expected especially as we were taking a short cut along a track that was impossible for vehicles. Our wagons had to make a wide detour via Tudela and Pamplona and only linked up with us again at Bayonne.

Our suffering was especially pronounced between Jaca and Lanfranc and particularly by the miserable little village of Castello, where the steep climbing begins. The cavalry had to dismount and we all had to scramble up a steep road on which tree trunks, cut down and laid on the ground, formed a kind of staircase. The way was as picturesque as it was exhausting. We were surrounded by verdant valleys in which streams ran their torrential course and drowned the sound of our marching with their noise. Above us were the snowy peaks, steadily drawing closer and closer. When we passed the village of Villa Nueva, we found that the path became even more tortuous and dangerous. In one particular place there was a ledge, high above a precipice, along which the horses and mules could pass only one at a time. As luck would have it we were hit by a little avalanche just as we were attempting to cross over the narrow ledge. Quite a few horses and mules were swept into the abyss and a Spanish officer who had been holding onto his horse's bridle for support could not get free before he too was swept away.

---

[73] Field Marshal Alexander Vasilevitch Suvorov (1729–1800) was the most famous Russian commander of the Revolutionary Wars. Many Polish officers had served under him in the wars against the Turks and at such battles as Rymnyk and Focsany and the sieges of Jassy and Ismail.

CHAPTER XXX

At the French Frontier – One Last Look at Spain – The Wizard – Bizarre Incident – Napoleon and Captain Smitt – Our *Cantinière* – Bernadotte's House

After a two-day march in such conditions, we passed through Candols, the last Spanish village, and finally crossed the French frontier. Here there was an amazingly emotional scene. Instinctively, we all turned to look at Spain. We bade it farewell as you would to an old friend who you knew you would never be seeing again, and remembered all the many friends who would be staying there forever.

Suddenly I heard my name called out by a voice, the sound of which froze my blood. It was Rakowski. It was the first time he had spoken to me since the words we exchanged in the trenches surrounding Tortosa after I heard of Zarski's death.

'Well', he said, 'are you thinking of your friend, Lieutenant Brandt? I sometimes think about him. Yesterday it was his turn. Tomorrow will be ours. I know the Russians. They are tough opponents!'

And, without waiting for my answer he stalked over to a little knoll and stood there looking at Spain for some time.

'What did the old wizard say to you?' asked a lieutenant from his company. 'He is a real bird of ill omen. This morning he was drivelling on about Suvorov, Trebbia and Novi.[74] He reckons that up to now we haven't really known what war is, we young ones, but that we will soon find out.'

This one would indeed find out and would not survive the experience.

There was a bizarre incident a little later which served as a useful

---

[74] The battle of Trebbia, 17–19 June 1799, was a Russian and Austrian victory over General MacDonald's French. General Dombrowski's Polish Legion fought on the French side and suffered heavy casualties. The battle of Novi took place on 15 August 1799 and witnessed another defeat of the French, under Joubert, at the hands of the Russians and Austrians. Again, the Polish Legion was present and suffered heavily.

distraction from our melancholy thoughts. Not a few of the soldiers were amusing themselves by climbing up some of the rocks to get a better view of the surroundings. One of them, perched high on a rock above which served as a kind of pedestal, suddenly pulled down his trousers, stuck his posterior towards Spain and shouted out, 'There you are, cursed country which has devoured so many of my comrades!'

This unique farewell was appreciated by many, but a captain called Smitt, no friend of Napoleon's, observed that 'the soldier was mistaken. The country was not cursed, as it was the man she had to defend herself against who was the real guilty party.'

This grudge against Napoleon dated back to something that happened in Bayonne in 1808 as the Emperor reviewed our regiment, then passing through on its way into Spain. On that particular day Napoleon had just finished an interview with the Bourbons. Unusually, he was in a carriage and in court dress – good shoes, silk stockings. He was also in a foul temper. Some badly executed drill caused him to burst out and shout, 'The Prefect of Cassel is quite right when he writes that the officers of these regiments do nothing but gamble and the soldiers do nothing but guzzle food, but I will set you straight'. When he spotted a major perched, it must be said, rather badly on his horse he screamed: 'You ride like Frederick the Great.'

However, he reserved his full wrath for Smitt's company. I must mention that, by some unfortunate fluke, the three senior officers of this company verged almost upon the grotesque in appearance. The captain was short and thin; the first lieutenant was still thinner; and the second lieutenant was as short as the captain but as round as a ball. The Emperor, after contemplating this trio for a moment, then whispered something to the colonel in so quiet a voice that no one heard what was in fact said. But some of the young officers who did not like Smitt pretended that they had heard Napoleon order that the lieutenants and, upon reflection, the captain too be sent to the depot. Whether this story is true or not, it took hold in the regiment and that is how Napoleon had the misfortune of getting on the wrong side of Captain Smitt.

When we reached Urdos, the first French town, I was surprised to notice the little wagon of Mrs Lewczakowa, our *cantinière*, come bouncing down the now well-surfaced road. She was a brave woman who I had seen, on more than one occasion, in the midst of battle tending and assisting the wounded. Despite orders to the contrary, she had not left the column but had reached an agreement with some Spanish prisoners who had taken the wagon apart and carried the various pieces, along with her stores and provisions, through the mountains with us. This had cost her just a few cups of hot chocolate and some glasses of schnapps.

All the *cantinières*, Polish as well as French, were noted for their courage.

On the other hand their merry and handsome husbands were usually the worst soldiers and would find a thousand excuses not to be counted in the ranks during a battle.

Our passage through France as far as Paris was without incident and made in the best possible conditions. At Pau my company and I were lodged in a posting house where Bernadotte had been brought up and had spent his early years. A woman there remembered having frequently seen him in his youth and how, on occasion, he had been pressed into service as a courier. It seems, too, that the future king of Sweden did not scorn the offer of tips! All this brought to mind thoughts on one of the most astonishing cases of good fortune our century had produced, and all from this little two-storey house with its three windows and its green shutters, all of which seemed so modest.[75]

As we passed through the Bordeaux region, our soldiers were enchanted by the warm welcome they were accorded by the inhabitants and by the good wines. Many talked about coming to retire in this lovely region one day. Alas! Of those that dreamt thus in March 1812, not one would realise their wish. Less than one year later, most were dead!

---

[75] Jean-Baptiste Jules Bernadotte joined the army in 1780 and was a general by 1794. He became a marshal and, in 1810, was elected Crown Prince of Sweden by Swedish notables grateful for his treatment of Swedish prisoners in 1806. He was adopted by the king of Sweden, changed his name to Charles-Jean and was crowned king himself in 1818.

Part II
IN RUSSIA

CHAPTER XXXI

~

REVIEW OF 22 MARCH – THOSE ABOUT TO DIE SALUTE YOU – TRIP TO
VINCENNES – SEDAN – METZ – SIGNS OF DISCONTENT – BRILLIANT
ORGANISATION ALONG THE ROUTE

On 22 March 1812 those Polish regiments withdrawn from Spain formed
up in the Place du Carousel for the Emperor to pass them in review.[76] To
really understand how momentous an occasion like this was in those days,
and how the emotions would grip the heart of the bravest at the sight of that
extraordinary man, you have to have experienced such an event.

Those officers of the Vistula Legion who had been present at the
Bayonne review of 1808 did little to boost our confidence.

To our left was placed a regiment of the Old Guard, the officers of which
were our hosts, whilst on the balcony stood the Empress and many of the
ladies of the court, famed for their beauty.

After waiting for an hour the word 'Attention!' rang out and echoed
through the ranks and we caught sight of Napoleon arriving just to the right
of the division, accompanied by Berthier and numerous other generals.
As he was passing our battalion, he stopped right in front of me and
demanded, 'How many wounded men in your company?'

'Twelve, Sire, and a few bruised.'

'Good. You are still young but you will make captain.'

One soldier in the second rank, quite portly for a voltigeur, caught the
Emperor's attention and, gesturing at the man, he turned and requested
General Krasinski[77] to ask the voltigeur where he got so fat. The soldier

---

[76] These regiments were the 1st, 2nd and 3rd Regiments of the Vistula Legion, the 8th
Chevaux-légers Lanciers and the 4th, 7th and 9th Line Regiments of the Grand Duchy
of Warsaw.

[77] Krasinski, General Vincent Corvin (1782–1856). He served under Dombrowski in
Italy and in 1807 was given the task of organising the Polish lancers attached to the
Imperial Guard. This regiment later became the Polish Light Horse Lancers of the
Imperial Guard and Krasinski acted as its colonel. In 1814 he took command of all
Polish troops in French service. He later served the Russians as viceroy to the Congress
kingdom of Poland, the Russian equivalent of Napoleon's Grand Duchy of Warsaw.

replied, 'in France.' Napoleon, laughing, went on, 'Tell him to put himself on a diet, for soon we'll all be fasting.'

The Emperor did not realise how true he spoke.

He tasted the bread ration – this was a habit of his – and had one of the soldiers step forward from the ranks in order to examine the soldier's turn-out in detail. Then he turned to the colonel and said, 'One would never have guessed this regiment had just come from such a tough campaign. I am satisfied with its dress, equipment and turnout. You may tell that to the regiment.'

As we filed passed, the Poles, who thought that this new war heralded a total restoration of their country, cried '*Vive l'Empereur!*' with tremendous enthusiasm. It was indeed, for most of us, the final salute of the Roman gladiators: 'Those about to die salute you!'[78]

Our departure was fixed for the 26th and so there were only three days for the Polish officers, lodged at Vaugirard, to see Paris.

As you can imagine we did not spend much time in our quarters, only being there for as long as it took to get ourselves ready in the mornings. Our hostess, a young and intelligent woman, once asked us why it was that we were less clever than the French, who never frittered away their money and risked their health as we were doing.

'It should be no surprise, Madame,' one of us replied, 'as the French can come to Paris any time they choose whereas we can't and must make the most of the occasion.'

As part of our itinerary we did not forget the château de Vincennes. But as soon as one of us mentioned the Duc d'Enghien[79] the porter, a former non-commissioned officer in the artillery, exclaimed, 'normally people come here to see the military buildings and I am ready to give you a tour of them.' Only when he had taken leave of the other visitors at the drawbridge did his wife approach us and discreetly offer to let us have a look at 'the not so strictly military sights'. After having showed us the cells where various famous people had been held she whispered, 'I know how things are; if you would like to see the place where the fate of that young man was sealed, I can take you there.'

Inevitably, this extra bonus came at a price. I should think that this secretive little performance not only allowed them to break the rules but also make a profit from doing so.

---

[78] In a conversation in February 1812, Napoleon had declared to Caulaincourt: 'I am not thinking of the restoration of Poland; and although it would be politic and in the interests of civilisation, I am not planning it. That would be too great an undertaking, on account of Austria.'

[79] The Duc d'Enghien (1772–1804), a high-ranking Royalist émigré, was kidnapped from Ettenheim in Baden in March 1804, on Napoleon's orders, implicated in a Royalist assassination attempt on Napoleon, and shot at Vincennes.

I also remember how one of my fellow-officers felt rather let down by Paris. He noticed an area of the city marked Little Poland on a map and set out with high hopes; he returned furious, demanding how it was they could give such a name to so vile a series of alleys and most loathsome parts of Paris.

The impressions Paris made on our soldiers varied. Many took the statue of Napoleon dressed in imperial robes on the Vendôme Column to be the statue of some saint. When they were told it was Napoleon, who they had seen at the review dressed in his grey coat and legendary hat, they refused to believe it.

The Invalides seemed to impress them most and here they were able to meet up with some of their comrades wounded at Saragossa and who sang the praises of the hospital.

The consequences of the review were not as we might have wished. Many had hoped for promotion, decorations or rewards. In all there were just thirty for the 2nd Regiment of the Vistula Legion which, for nigh on four years had lived, or rather died, in an atmosphere thick with shot and shell. In my company there was not one man who had not been wounded since 1809 and we were accorded but two decorations.

Soon another source for potential dissatisfaction appeared. When we arrived at Sedan, which had always been the Legion's depot, on 4 April, we learnt that the 2nd Regiment was to form part of Claparède's division and that that general would now review us. If Poland was to be resurrected this breaking up of the Polish regiments throughout the army did not augur well. Neither did the rude manners of the French general allay our fears.

Rechowicz, our Adjutant, said that 'he does not seem a very good fellow and looks like he might like finding fault.'

In truth, Claparède was never happier than when he was criticising his subordinates. Indeed, on the occasion of our first meeting I had just such an experience. As I was the only officer of my rank to have received two decorations, the general growled out 'so this young man is so very brave that...'

'This young man, general, has had the good fortune to have carried out his duties to the full under the eyes of Marshal Suchet and General Chlopicki who nominated him for the decorations he is wearing.'

'Don't get so excited about it,' snapped Claparède, ignoring me and carrying on with his inspection.

In order to understand why I was so sensitive, it must be remembered that in those days the words 'young man' were synonymous with greenhorn and were deemed very insulting. Between officers of the same rank they were often cause for a duel.

At Sedan we busied ourselves with the administrative work surrounding the formation of a third battalion – which was to come into being when we got to Poland proper.[80] I was appointed, as a first lieutenant, commander of one of the new voltigeur companies. In a wise move Napoleon ordered that those officers charged with these duties be sent on ahead. We left the next day whilst the rest of the regiment waited in Sedan.

At Metz, where we arrived on 11 April, I was very well looked after by the good-natured artillery officer Robert, who took me to see the citadel. A few months later, I saw him among the dead in the Grand Redoubt at Borodino.

As we passed through Alsace and Lorraine I was able to notice, for the first time, some unequivocal signs of discontent. People were growing tired of the continual passage of troops, despite the money that was thus being spread along the way. On our part we could only admire the way in which the various stages of the march were organised. Everywhere one could see, in the smallest of details, the aura of a master perfectly obeyed. As all orders concerning troops on the march emanated from the Ministry, all the quartermasters and commissaries knew where to meet us at the various stops and the Ministry knew exactly which troops would be where and when. When we reached a halt, the quartermasters would first obtain a permit from the commander of the place or from the commissioner and then a list of billets from the town hall and receipts for food, supplies and wagons which they would hand over to the suppliers. Collection of the meat ration could either be individual or as a whole, but bread was always as a whole. Companies to be billeted in villages alongside the main road picked up their rations as they were passing through or were obliged to come in and get them.

This organisation, imitated by each of the great powers since, worked with a precision and ease unimaginable. It was rare indeed that any complaints were forthcoming. As far as the Poles were concerned they even knew that we *Frenchmen of the North* preferred quantity over quality and distributed rations in accordance.

---

[80] The third battalions were decreed to be formed on 3 March 1812.

CHAPTER XXXII

∾

We reached Mayence on 22 April and it presented the appearance of a huge warehouse. Infantry, cavalry and artillery trains filed over the Cassel bridge in a never-ending column. Frankfurt seemed very much a French town and it seemed that German was only spoken in the country and by the Foot Guards of the Grand Duke.[81]

Things seemed to be becoming more and more urgent and we were transported in wagons as far as Hanau. This part of the journey, however, was very tiring as the transport consisted of the most basic kind of wagons and the roads were, at that time, only paved in the towns and in those places which would have been impassable had something not been done. The jolting of the wagons was frequently so rough that it was often preferable for us to walk. We were blinded by billowing clouds of dust, jolted to pieces by large rocks, and brought to a halt by muddy ruts. Such a journey does not encourage admiration for the scenery, and the Elbe, the Spree and the Oder all seemed insignificant next to the French rivers we had seen. The sky, full of clouds, was a poor contrast to the blue horizons of Spain, as was the sombre green of the pines to the lush palms of Valencia. And we were still only in Germany!

On 5 May we reached Posen. After four years away I found my country to be in a poor state of health. The Continental System[82] had brought the price of cereals so low as to scarcely cover the cost of growing it. Nevertheless, the hope that Poland might be entirely restored kept alive the hopes of the people. Nobody wanted a return to Prussian domination, despite believing they had been happier in the good old days.

---

[81] Frankfurt was a grand duchy in 1812. Its grand duke was the Prince Primate von Dalberg.

[82] The Continental System was Napoleon's economic blockade of Britain.

The cadres of the new battalions were lodged around Posen. We were sent to Szrem, which was a small town on the Warta about fifteen miles away. The quarters were not memorable for their cleanliness and we veterans thought them dirtier than Spanish stables.

We spent our time arming, equipping and training the new recruits. This task was so rigorously carried out that after about a week these young troops, shorn of their long hair, could drill and manoeuvre passably. I have since frequently been involved in training new troops but I have never obtained such good results in such a short space of time. Everyone, from all levels of the population, seemed so enthusiastic. In addition, as the tailors of Posen could not deal with the vast quantity required, production of the new uniforms was farmed out in the surrounding areas and cloth and instructions were sent to even the humblest of villages. Everyone who could use a needle was put to work and the uniforms for our third battalion were completed much more quickly and to a better standard than we had dared hope.

Naturally there were some ominous clouds gathering on the horizon. As soon as our men were clothed, many began to desert. Had we strictly enforced military law, our battalion would have lost a good part of its effectives before the campaign had even opened. So we used methods more appropriate to the situation. Each deserter we caught (and we caught most of them) was taken before the assembled battalion and given fifty or sixty blows to his posterior with a cane, after which he was returned to his company. This treatment produced the desired effect and the desertions stopped as if by magic. The rations that were given out also had something to do with this abrupt change. The new recruits found that they were fed and housed much better than they had ever been in their lives. Most had never slept in a bed and knew of white bread and coffee only by repute.

We officers, however, were much worse off than we had been in France and everything was more expensive. Neither was there, in the whole town, a room that was big enough or adequately furnished to allow us to all sit round a table together. We were as though stranded on a desert island and only caught snatches of news about the rest of humanity by means of the twice-weekly *Posen Gazette*.

Walking with some of the district's farmers was our only real source of entertainment. These good people welcomed us with a sincere warmth and let us partake of their best food and drink. Their houses were furnished with an ancient simplicity and it often happened that although there was only one glass in an entire household it would be passed round again and again.

On 29 May all the troops were hastily called in and concentrated at Posen, as the Emperor was expected there. However, he only arrived at nine in the evening, escorted by a detachment of French and Polish Guards. He was met by a welcome as enthusiastic as the one in 1806. There were triumphal arches, illuminations and fireworks everywhere, marking the hopes of a people confident in the future. At the entrance to the suburbs a triumphal arch bearing the inscription *Heroi invincibili* had been erected. The hero, invincible till then, was graciously received and complimented by President Rose, the mayor, a serious kind of man who has since gone on to compliment many others. I saw him once again in 1831, giving an eloquent speech in honour of the Prussian marshal Gneisenau.

At the end of the street which goes up to the Jesuits' College and which the Emperor would be passing down, you could see a second triumphal arch with the motto *Restauratori patriae* and on the doors of the College itself the words *Grati Poloni Imperatori magno*.

On the five great windows of the town hall transparencies of the town's coat of arms, the initials of Napoleon and Marie Louise, and the eagle of France and the coat of arms of the Grand Duchy of Warsaw were placed. On the clock-tower of the Bernadin church, which the Emperor could see from his window, a gigantic illumination shone forth a crown of laurels bearing the inscription *Napoleoni Magno Caesari et Victori!* A sky of southern serenity lent a beautiful aura to this solemnity and a huge crowd choked the streets, which were as light as in any daylight. The population of the surrounding countryside had gathered to take part in the celebrations and were camping in all of the town's squares, especially in the Place Napoléon which, before the year was out, would be renamed after Frederick William.[83] The veterans, and we Poles had quite a few, were rather sullen amidst the festivities. They believed that the enthusiasm was, at least in part, affected and encouraged by the authorities who wanted to selectively blind the Emperor.

---

[83] Frederick William III, king of Prussia (1770–1840). Posen was returned to Prussia by the Congress of Vienna.

CHAPTER XXXIII

On the next day we were reviewed not by the Emperor, but by Marshal
Mortier. Despite only a third of our new recruits being uniformed as they
should, he seemed satisfied with our turnout and was pleasantly surprised
that we had done so much in such a short space of time. Napoleon suddenly
arrived as we were filing past but he seemed worried and preoccupied.

'Where is the Prefect (Count Poninski)?' he demanded impatiently and
in a loud voice. 'These troops are too young. I must have men who can stand
fatigue. Young troops are fit only to fill hospitals,' he added. As he turned
aside, still talking, I was unable to hear more.

One of my old friends from university told me some details about a
reception that had taken place in its refectory. The region's nobility had
gathered attired in court dress. The Emperor had complimented them and
told them, 'Gentlemen, I would have preferred to have seen you in armour,
with swords at your sides, as your ancestors were at the approach of the
Tartars and Cossacks. We live in times when we must be armed to the teeth
and have our hands constantly on the hilts of our swords.'

A few comic incidents marred the seriousness of the evening. Among the
nobles who had come to greet the Emperor was Count Szoldrcki, a justice
of the peace and key landowner in the region. He was carrying an enamel
plaque, as big as a plate, as a mark of his rank. The Emperor either mistook
the meaning of the plaque or pretended to, and asked him, to break the ice,
how many workers he had at his porcelain factory. The count was struck
dumb and the prefect hastily interjected that this gentleman was Count
Szoldrcki, the richest landowner in the region. 'Very good,' said the
Emperor and passed on by.

A few moments later, when it was the ladies' turn to be presented, the

Countess Mycielcka, a pretty young woman aged eighteen but who seemed much older on account of her being rather fat, stepped forward. The Emperor took her to be already married and, as was his wont, asked her, 'How many children do you have?'

'But Sire, I do not have any.'

'So you are divorced?'

'No, Sire, I am still not married.'

'Well you mustn't be too picky as you've not got much time to lose!'

This exchange made everyone laugh, except, of course, the poor lady. But she must have taken the advice to heart as she did get married shortly after.

For the Polish nobility, and especially the women, this audience created a poor impression of Napoleon. One of the ladies, a high-ranking and outspoken woman, said that the event had shown that 'he (Napoleon) has not improved much since 26 November 1806' (the date of his first visit to Posen). She believed that his abrupt manners and his imperious and condescending tone contrasted painfully to the gracious charm and generosity of Prince Joséph Poniatowski. When somebody objected that charm did not make states, she replied, with an element of truth, that often more conquests were made with the heart than with the head.

When asked for his opinion of Napoleon an old chamberlain of King Stanislas,[84] the former king of Poland, replied with the Latin phrase: *Nec affabilis, nec amibilis, nec adibilis* (neither affable nor friendly nor worthy of hate).

A few days after these festivities, I received the order to rejoin my regiment, then marching to Gumbinnen. This allowed me to spend two days with my parents, who still lived at Strzelnow, on the road between Posen and Thorn. The joy of our reunion, after an absence of four years, was marred by the sight of the straits they had been reduced to. This was the part of old Poland that had suffered most. The war of 1807 and all its attendant evils had been relentlessly succeeded by the miseries of the Continental System, the diseases ravaging both men and livestock and by the new and continual passage of troops. My parents, who were once quite affluent landowners, had had the expensive privilege of hosting both Marshal Ney and the Prince of Württemberg.[85] All their forage had been spirited away by the artillery trains and the draught horses were constantly

---

[84] King Stanislas Augustus Poniatowski (1732–98), the last king of Poland, gave up his crown in 1795 and died in exile in St Petersburg.

[85] Crown Prince William of Württemberg commanded a division in III Corps until, disenchanted with the campaign, he returned to Germany and was replaced by Marchand. He became king of Württemberg in 1816 and ruled until 1864.

being requisitioned. In fact everything was being done as it would have been done in enemy territory with the exception of the issue of government vouchers, which could be cashed in after considerable delay. For me the forty-eight hours I spent in my parental home were as many hours of torture.

I found a detachment of the 2nd Regiment of the Vistula, left behind to guard the baggage, at Thorn.[86] The officer in charge recounted unpleasant details of atrocities being committed along the line of march and of the confusion and lack of discipline which reigned in certain parts of this immense army. He told me that 'everyone does what he wants and takes what he can. Frenchmen, Italians, Württemburgers, Badeners, Bavarians, even Poles, are plundering the country as they see fit. If it carries on like this we'll all end up eating each other, like starving rats. The Emperor must be blind to put up with such excess.'

Napoleon passed through Thorn on the night of 3 June. At about one in the morning, the duty officers were not a little surprised to hear the Emperor pacing his room and singing aloud Mehul's[87] song *La Chant du Départ*:

> *From North to South the trumpet sounds,*
> *And marks the course of war.*
> *Tremble, you enemies of France!*

This unaccustomed revocation of Revolutionary sentiments was inspired by the problems and perils of the coming war and made a lasting impression on those officers who chanced to overhear it. I learnt of it from the mouth of one of them, Colonel Malzewski, attached to the staff, who would take command of our regiment after the occupation of Smolensk.

On 11 June I went over to Strassberg with a forester who was close to my family. In the midst of these terrible events I had the extreme joy of reading, for the first time, Goethe's *Faust*. On the 14th I rejoined the regiment at Liebstadt. From there, as far as the Niemen, we would find the roads crowded with stragglers from the vanguard. From them the officers and soldiers heard a sorry report of the situation further ahead: the roads were appalling, the heat was unbearable and rations left much to be desired. All this had a depressing effect on the morale of the soldiers and we had desertions, something we had not experienced for some time. On the other hand a minor but positive incident was sufficient to revive our spirits

---

[86] Thorn, or Torun, was a major fortress on the Vistula and scene of a siege in 1813.

[87] Etienne Mehul (1763–1817) was a very popular composer during the French revolution. His *Chant du Départ* was at least as popular as the *Marseillaise*.

completely. So it was at Interburg, where, on the 19th, a well supplied halt once more restored our flagging spirits and our hope for new flashes of genius...

On 21 June, around Gumbinnen, we camped in the open for the first time. That particular night the weather was superb and the soldiers could stretch out at last after being squeezed like sardines into tiny rooms for so long. The weather was not to be the same at our subsequent halts, most especially at Wirballen, where we stayed for two days and two nights, as it became distinctly colder and the soldiers, camped in marshy fields, came down with fevers and ague.

On the 24th we reached Wilkowiski where, but two days before, the Emperor had issued his famous bulletin which opened with the celebrated, 'The Second Polish War has begun...'

I was a principal actor in a strange little scene which was remarkable for being one of the last occasions in which something amusing happened.

One afternoon I received the order to proceed, along with fifty voltigeurs, into the forests around Wilkowiski and Mariampol where the inhabitants grazed their livestock. We were to trap and bring back this livestock, which was to serve as food on the hoof for our division. This was not really a mission I looked forward to, but I had to obey.

So off I set with my men. We spent the night in the forest without lighting fires, so as not to alert those guarding the herds. At the crack of dawn we began our hunt and after about an hour we came across a herd of some fifty cows, guarded by a pretty girl. Upon seeing us about to make off with her herd this Amaryllis[88] began to sob and wring her hands. Finally she threw herself at my feet and begged to be left at least two cows for her parents. She seemed prepared to make great *sacrifices* to win me over but I was as generous and as careful as Scipio in Spain and I granted her request without exacting any kind of ransom. At around ten in the morning men and beasts reached Wilkowiski, only to find that the regiment had already left. I was about to follow them when I was accosted by two people, one of whom was the local priest. He suggested I visit his presbytery – which was a handsome house in which the Emperor had slept some two nights pre- viously – and partake of a light meal. I accepted the invitation but refused the meal. He showed me the bed in which Napoleon had slept, the table upon which he had signed his declaration of war and the places where he had washed and so on. As the visit was drawing to a close, the priest's com- panion spoke up. He was the owner of most of the cows I had requisitioned and asked me to return them, then changed his mind and asked that I at least leave the bulls. I had eaten plenty of bull's meat in Spain and the meat

---

[88] Amaryllis was the name given to a shepherdess in Virgil's *Eclogues*.

was tough and unpleasant. So I was generous yet again, asking nothing but a little glass of schnapps for each of my men. The bargain was sealed to the satisfaction of each of the respective parties and the priest asked that I might accept, as token of his appreciation, two bottles of liquor which had been hidden away and had, so he told me, come from the imperial cellars.

We turned up quite late with our convoy at the divisional camp, which was in the midst of a forest. I was very pleased with my little piece of good fortune and after dinner I invited my friends and the adjutant to come and hear an important announcement. There was considerable enthusiasm when I revealed that they would be able to taste a fine sample from the imperial cellars. My triumph was not set to last. The two bottles, opened with great care, contained nothing but water. Had the priest been tricked as I had been, or was he tricking me? This latter explanation seemed the most probable and many made merry at my expense. However, events soon followed which took away any cause for laughter.

CHAPTER XXXIV

CROSSING THE NIEMEN – THE CHÂTEAU AT ZAKROD – A RUSSIAN CAMP – VILNA – DIFFICULT MARCH TO MINSK – I LEAVE MY VOLTIGEUR COMPANY – LIEUTENANT ZORAWSKI'S ODYSSEY

Claparède's division crossed the Niemen at three o'clock on the afternoon of 26 June. It then went into camp in a small wood on the far side of Kovno and on the next day close to a village which was already laid waste. During the night the rain, which would not leave us until we reached Vilna, began to fall. At Szernicki, the next halt, all of the nearly ripe corn had been cut down to provide shelters with roofs and fodder for the horses. The Young Guard was marching in front of us and trailing stragglers, who could be seen stretched out along the sides of the road, mixed up with the dead horses. The population had all fled to the woods, apart from a few of the poorest people, who would come to our camp fires begging for bread.

On the 30th we camped in still more terrible weather in what had once been the gardens of the Zakrod Château. This had originally belonged to the Jesuits but was now owned by General Bennigsen,[89] and it was there that, four days before, Czar Alexander[90] had heard the first report of the crossing of the Niemen whilst attending a party.

Those troops that had arrived before us had put the whole place to the sack and the front of the house no longer had doors or windows. I managed to make a kind of glass tent out of the remains of the greenhouse and in which I hoped to be able to sleep under cover for the first time since entering Russia. But the rain even managed to seep into this shelter and I woke

---

[89] General Levin Bennigsen (1745–1826) was a senior Russian officer of Hanoverian extraction who served as the Russian chief of staff at Borodino.

[90] Alexander I (1777–1825), son of Paul I, became czar in 1801. A one-time admirer of Napoleon, he maintained an uncomfortable alliance with the French emperor between 1807 and 1812. His reign witnessed a considerable expansion of Russian territory at the expense of Sweden, the Ottoman Empire and Poland.

up in the middle of a puddle. The rain was falling so heavily that all the camp fires were extinguished.

On the following morning, as the troops were gathering to be reviewed by the colonels of the various regiments, the shout 'to arms!' rang out. Pajol's[91] and Bourdesoulle's[92] scouts had caught sight of substantial forces drawn up on the other side of Oszimana and everyone hoped there would be a battle. Claparède's division skirted around Vilna and made a forced march for a height to the east of the Jedlina road and took up position there. Just then the sky, which had cleared somewhat in the morning, clouded over again, the rain began to fall with extreme force and a thick fog enshrouded us so that we could scarcely see a few paces in front.

From out of this mist came Napoleon, mounted on a white horse. The brim of his famous hat, sagging in the rain, funnelled water onto his grey riding coat. He stared uselessly at the horizon through a telescope, turned to Berthier, who was riding behind him in a thoroughly bad mood, and said, 'This rain is terrible!' He then rode off after exchanging a few words with Claparède.

We shortly learned that the troops the cavalry had seen this morning were part of Dochtorov's[93] corps and that they were endeavouring to steal away and join up with Barclay.[94] We had only just missed trapping these troops but followed close on their heels along the Oszimana road and camped that evening in a position the Russians had occupied a short while before, probably with the intention of spending the night there themselves. Their shelters were still standing and the ground was littered with the soldiers' little note-books and other military objects thrown aside in the haste to get away, as well as piles of human excrement which served as a pungent welcome to our new quarters.

There has been much conjecture as to what would have had happened had the Russians not given up Vilna without a fight. I think we would have had an indecisive battle much like that of Pultusk[95] because it was next to impossible for the artillery, the cavalry and even the infantry to manoeuvre in this quagmire.

We stayed in the Russian camp until 3 July. The weather steadily began

---

[91] General Claude Pierre Pajol (1772–1844) commanded I Corp's cavalry.
[92] General Bourdesoulle commanded the 1st and 3rd Chasseurs in Pajol's division.
[93] General Dmitri Sergiev Dochtorov (1756–1816) commanded the Russian 6 Corps.
[94] Field Marshal Mikhail Barclay de Tolly (1761–1818) had risen from being a cadet-private in 1776 to commander of the First Army of the West and Minister of War in 1812.
[95] The battle of Pultusk on 26 December 1806 was a bloody but indecisive engagement between Lannes' French and Bennigsen's Russians in the cold and mud of a Polish winter.

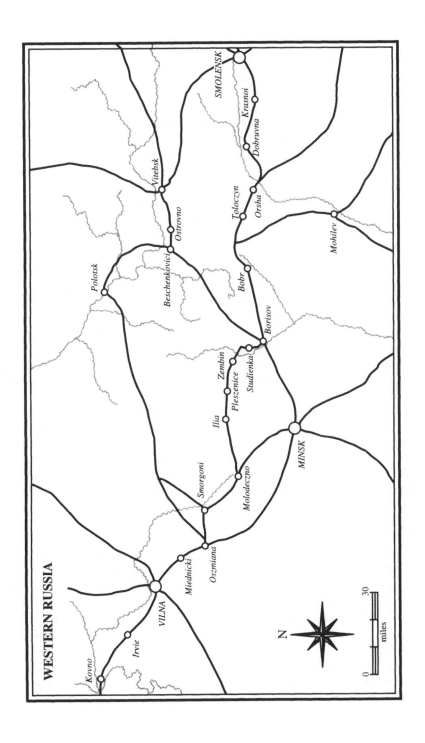

WESTERN RUSSIA

SMOLENSK
Krasnoi
Dobravna
Toloczyn
Orsha
Mohilev
Vitebsk
Ostrovno
Beschenkovici
Polotsk
Bobr
Borisov
Zembin
Studienka
Pleszenice
Ilia
Smorgoni
Molodeczno
MINSK
Miednicki
Oszmiana
VILNA
Irvie
Kovno

N

0   30
miles

to improve and the sun finally reappeared, and was welcomed by loud cheers. On the 3rd the division was ordered to Vilna and spent the night in the suburbs. Vilna, then a historic town with some 30,000 inhabitants, had dark and twisting streets and was noted for its churches, of which there were thirty Catholic and sixteen Orthodox in addition to two Protestant chapels and a mosque. The suburbs resembled little villages and consisted of huts and a few wine shops.

Despite the fact that we were Polish, the inhabitants gave us a rather frosty reception. The troops that had got here first had taken the best of both the welcome and the food. The town was already suffering severely from the ransacking that had gone on and went on throughout this campaign. I talked to one Lithuanian, a former soldier who had come to offer his services to the French Army but who found that he had to rush off in order to defend his property from being plundered. Despite all this, the demands made by the Imperial Commissary under Bignon, whose sympathy for the Polish cause was well known, were always met.

A general review by the Emperor was ordered for 4 July and we were just making our preparations when we received the order to move on Minsk with all haste. We were to be attached to the Prince of Eckmühl's corps and would in fact stay under his command until we reached Smolensk. We got to Minsk after a forced march which lasted for six hours.

Some of the events that took place over the following days were recorded in my journal as follows:

4 July: An exhausting march of thirteen miles over terrain that was alternately marshy and sandy. We camped in woods and on soaking ground, close to Miednicki, the ancient capital of Samogitie but now insignificant.

5th: We marched for Oszimana. The heat was tropical and water scarce. We camped close to the town, which had already been looted by marauders. We came across them, loaded with their loot or with wagons drawn by the small local horses, every step of the way.

6th: The bad state of the roads continues. We camped in a wood not far from a plundered village.

7th: A sharp drop in temperature with continual freezing rain. We stopped at Wismievo, a market town where not one of the population had remained. Our camp was very marshy and the wood was so damp that it was impossible to light fires.

8th: The troops, starving and drenched to the skin, arrived at the miserable little village of Rokow on the Kolenka. No rations were issued and we hunted down the marauders in order to take what they had stolen, but not so we could return it to its rightful owners. Detachments scoured the woods and brought in some livestock which the inhabitants had hidden there. All this took place not in Russia but in Samogitie, once a part of Poland.

9th: Rain. We camped in the middle of the woods. The soldiers had meat but no edible bread.

It was at about this time that I received the order to leave my voltigeur company, which I had commanded since 1809, and take on the duties of adjutant-major. These duties were sure to be a trial and fraught with difficulties in a campaign such as this. The parting almost broke my heart as the relationship between me and my men was one built on sincere affection due to us all having shared the same suffering and dangers. They were all of roughly the same age as myself and I had got to know them very well: I would read any letters they might receive from home and would write their replies for them. When I bade farewell to them they all cried as they shook me by the hand. Of those who survived this deadly campaign, and the no less murderous one which followed it, I only ever met one again. It was in 1848, at the time of the uprising in Posen. I had taken up a position with a few companies on the bridge over the Wartha. An old peasant came over towards me and grabbed my leg (I was sitting on a horse) crying, 'Sir! Thank God that I've seen you one more time!'

'Who are you?' I replied, 'What is your name?'

'Don't you recognise me? It is Wessilowski.'

'Oh yes! Now I recognise you. Your name is Cassimir. You were always out on the left flank when we marched in sections. What are you doing now?'

He was doing quite well, was married and was a father of two strong lads. Seeing this man brought back a whole flood of memories. I asked him to come and see me in Posen, where I was garrisoned, but he never did come. I think he must have died in the cholera epidemic which was sweeping the region at the time.

At the last halt before Minsk we were rejoined by a good friend of mine, a grenadier lieutenant called Zorawski, who had been granted eight days' leave whilst we were still in Poland so he could go and see his parents. Finding his way back to us had proved to be a real odyssey and his trials painted a true picture of the state of affairs to our rear. His father, a rich landowner, had made him a present of two good horses, one for him and one for his servant. Fifteen miles from home, as he paid a social call on someone, one of the horses was stolen; the other, for which no forage or oats could be had, fell dead before they had even reached the Niemen. From there on it was chaos! Forced to walk in torrential rain, my friend had the good fortune to run into a courier who, in return for a little money, agreed to carry him as far as Vilna. More than once on this leg of the journey they had to threaten to shoot marauders who attempted to seize hold of the bridle. At Vilna things were still worse. It was impossible to obtain transport of any kind, either for love or money, and our friend was forced to continue alone and on foot, following in our wake through the villainous and dangerous bands of marauders.

Since the campaign began, the soldiers of Claparède's division had not laid eyes on a single enemy apart from a few fleeting bands of cossacks on the horizon. But the ceaseless marching, the bad weather, the lack of food and the ill effects of seeing all the pillaging, had already had disastrous consequences. By Minsk each company had been reduced by at least twenty-five men. Normally it would have taken two battles to have reduced our strength so. These returns made Claparède furious but he had contributed to them by his lack of concern over the well-being of his troops and by his poor choice of places to camp. This is what Chlopicki told him in one of their heated debates on the subject.

CHAPTER XXXV

TERRIBLE EVENTS IN MINSK – DAVOUT'S ANGER – CHLUSEWICZ'S
FOREBODINGS – CHARLES XII AND NAPOLEON – THE BERESINA – THE
BEARS OF NIEMONICA

Despite being absorbed by the Russians, the people of Minsk were Polish
in their hearts. They had managed to prevent the Russians from burning
the huge stores of food as they fell back in retreat and this was the best
possible service they could have rendered the French Army.

An incident, which I witnessed as we arrived at Minsk, saw Davout
finally lose his temper over the breakdown in military discipline.

A *Te Deum* was sung in the cathedral in gratitude for the liberation of
Lithuania and the military and civic dignitaries were present, as were
representatives of various regiments. General Grouchy,[96] in full uniform,
officiated. In the middle of the ceremony it was announced that some
cuirassiers had broken into the shops and were pillaging the place just as
they would a town taken by storm. Marshal Davout sent one of his aides,
and those responsible were arrested, taken before a court-martial and shot
the next day. But this regrettable incident was the final straw for Davout,
who had already been rankled by various other such incidents. In a general
review, held on 12 July, he lost his temper and vented his spleen on a
German regiment in Compans' division which had been reduced from
a strength of four battalions to just a few hundred men despite not having
fired a shot.[97] The marshal bawled at the officers and had the regiment
march past the rest of the troops with its musket butts in the air. This was
a harsh chastisement and unfair, as those who had resisted temptation had
been punished rather than those who were in fact guilty.

I discussed this affair and its probable implications with Chlusewicz, our

---

[96] General Emmanuel Grouchy (1766–1847) commanded the III Reserve Cavalry
Corps.
[97] This was in fact a Dutch regiment – the 33rd Light.

colonel, an intelligent man full of common sense. He said, 'The Emperor will be unable to avoid Charles XII's[98] fate and will make the same mistakes. As he is drawn into the heart of Russia he leaves behind him a badly-organised Poland and a devastated Lithuania. In such a situation, the smallest setback will have terrible consequences. The whole of Germany will rise up and things will be as they were in Spain only on a much different scale. The kings are yoked to Napoleon's chariot now but they will hastily break their harnesses. Napoleon is losing much because of his neglect to do what he should.'

It was only natural that Charles XII sprang to mind as reminders of him were littered throughout this land. It was at Radoskowicz, near Minsk, that he changed his plan of campaign and began the brilliant and adventurous march to Poltava. In addition, we had in our ranks descendants of the Lithuanians who, 100 years before, had fought under the flag of Charles XII: the Radzivills, the Sapiehas, the Tysenhaus, the Chodzkos and so on.

On the 14th, after spending a few days of much-needed rest at Minsk, Claparède's division was once again set in motion – this time towards Borisov. Fine weather and abundance had once more restored a measure of good cheer. We camped in the midst of a forest which was farmed for timber and consequently there were large piles of logs around from which we borrowed without scruple. We'd not had such terrific camp fires since the opening of the campaign.

The Russians had considered contesting the crossing of the Beresina at Borisov. They had begun work on a bridgehead, which they hastily evacuated as we approached and pulled back to Mohilev. It was here that their ancestors had inflicted a momentary check on Charles XII,[99] who then put in a feint attack and crossed the river further upstream at that same ford of Studienka where Napoleon tricked Tchichagov in a similar manoeuvre as he passed back over the Beresina on 26 November 1812.[100]

On 15 July an amusing incident enlivened our crossing of the river whose name, even today, awakens melancholic but glorious memories in the hearts of the French people. The Beresina had flooded the surrounding fields after having been swollen by the recent storms and had created huge lakes of

---

[98] Charles XII, king of Sweden, invaded Russia in 1707 during the Great Northern War but was heavily defeated at Poltava and only escaped to the Ottoman Empire with a handful of followers. Napoleon carried Alderbeth's history of this campaign with him into Russia.

[99] Charles halted at Mohilev in July 1708 and awaited developments. This delay gave the Russians time to recover and marked the turning point of Charles' invasion.

[100] Admiral Pavel Tchichagov (1767–1849) commanded the Russian Army of Moldavia and almost succeeded in cutting Napoleon's retreat at the Beresina as the French retreated from Moscow.

water in which there were vast numbers of wild geese. Grouchy's cavalry, which formed the vanguard, made a devastating attack on these flocks and were vigorously supported by the Polish regiments. Less than two hours later, each soldier had one or two of these birds dangling from his knapsack.

Upon leaving the land of the goose we entered that of the bear. There were many of these creatures in the huge forests which stretched from Vilna to the Dnieper and they were especially common around Niemonica, where we made camp on the evening of the 17th. Training and exhibiting bears was as popular in this part of the world as breeding marmots is in Savoy. Voltaire said irreverently that there were two universities in Poland: one in Crakow for the clergy and one in Smorgoni for the bears. So, in many houses, there were special areas put aside for the training of cubs which had been captured during the hunt. Our soldiers took many of these along with them. Not long after, as I was coming back from headquarters one night, I tripped over one of these animals; it lost its temper and the situation could have turned out nastily as it was already quite strong. As a result of many similar such occurrences the bears were banned, to the great regret of those soldiers who had already started taming them.

CHAPTER XXXVI

BATTLE AT MOHILEV – IN PURSUIT OF THE RUSSIANS – CROSSING THE
DNIEPER – STAY AT DOBRUVNA – DEATH OF SERGEANT DACHOWICZ

My regiment was sent to Orsha to guard Davout's communications with the
Grande Armée. On 19 July we arrived in Toloczyn at around seven in the
evening. This little town was sited on the ancient frontier between Russia
and Poland determined at the time of the second partition in 1772. It was
still possible to see the huge customs buildings constructed at that time and
since rendered useless by subsequent Russian expansion. But the people of
Toloczyn had not abandoned their old habits, remembered their origins and
gave us a very warm welcome.

It was here that the main road to Smolensk began. This was wide, well-
surfaced and with a row of enormous birch trees planted on either side and
mile posts which bore the distance to Smolensk and Moscow and so on.

On the 20th we camped along the Orsha road by a puny little village
called Kochanovo. We spent two days here and were closely watched by
cossacks. We were there in order to support Colbert's[101] cavalry which was
endeavouring to seize the crossing over the Dneiper at Orsha, a position of
considerable military importance which had always played a crucial role in
all previous Russo-Polish wars. As this mission was successfully completed
we were hastily summoned, on the 22nd, to Mohilev, where a battle was
taking place.

We arrived the day after the fight in which Davout's corps had
victoriously defended itself against the numerically superior forces of
Bagration.[102] We found the battlefield still littered with the French and

---

[101] General Chabanais-Pierre David (known as Edouard) Colbert (1774–1853) commanded the 2nd (Dutch) Lancers of the Guard cavalry. His troops had been attached
to Davout's corps and were acting in support of Grouchy. Grouchy carried out the
crossing of the Dnieper and the seizure of Orsha and its rich supply depots.
[102] General Peter Bagration (1765–1812) commanded the Second Army of the West.

Russian dead. I was shown a house in which Davout himself had almost been killed. He was at the attic window observing the enemy's movements, when a cannon-ball smashed into the room and hit a beam, showering the marshal with splinters. Thirty years later I had the opportunity of discussing these events with General Achard, who had distinguished himself here as the colonel of the 108th Line. He was very enthusiastic about Davout's judicious dispositions and the bravery shown by the soldiers in this unequal struggle.

After the battle, Davout displayed considerable energy in pursuit of the enemy, despite what several badly-informed writers have said to the contrary. Despite not being supported by the king of Westphalia,[103] he still hoped to catch Bagration, make him pay dearly and prevent him from linking up with the main Russian army. For the six days that this pursuit along the right bank of the Dnieper lasted, as soon as we came to some favourable terrain or came across a building which could provide a good view, you were sure to see the marshal ride up and study the horizon through his telescope. I once saw him sitting astride the roof of a house and doing just that.

Usually we saw a few cossack detachments but nothing else. On 2 August, as we retraced our steps after a long and difficult phase of advance, we found that the troops on our flanks were being driven in by the enemy. We were too far away to hear the firing but from some raised ground we could distinguish the smoke and some sizeable columns on the march. Towards noon we crossed the Dnieper, which at that time of year was neither deep nor wide, on pontoons. Our soldiers would not believe that this was the famous Borysthene,[104] as it seemed so slight when compared to the Tagus or the Danube. 'Russia is like that. Things which seem big from far away are small close up,' said the soldiers. Their morale had improved tremendously, not just because of Davout's success but because of those achieved by the rest of the *Grande Armée* (Vitebsk,[105] Ostrovno[106] etc). They were therefore in high spirits when they crossed this river which they would be recrossing all too soon.

We camped on the left bank around the little wooden town of Dobruvna, which was situated at the confluence of the Dnieper and the Krupivna. It

[103] Jerome Bonaparte (1784–1860), king of Westphalia, commanded the right wing of the French army until 16 July, when he returned to Westphalia in protest at having to serve under Davout. Interestingly, according to Caulaincourt, had Napoleon restored Poland it is likely Jerome would have been promoted to king of that country.
[104] According to the Greeks the Borysthene was the limit of the known world.
[105] The battle of Vitebsk on 28 July 1812 saw the defeat of the Russian rearguard but the escape of the Russian main body.
[106] The clashes at Ostrovno on 25–26 July 1812 were a series of short and bloody actions which, yet again, saw the Russians pull off in an orderly retreat.

was here that Davout had to face the unhappy realisation that his adversary had given him the slip.

Whilst waiting for all of our forces to concentrate before the general assault on Smolensk was launched, the Prince of Eckmühl massed his troops in and around Dobruvna and rested them for six days. He was lodged close by the château of Prince Lubomirski, whose sons were serving in the Russian army. It was here that Davout took excellent steps towards restoring an element of discipline in the troops and furnishing them with adequate supplies.

Whilst we were here we were reinforced by several march battalions, the officers of which painted a sorry picture of the disorder existing in the wake of the army. One of them, who had served under Kosciuszko,[107] was seriously worried about how all of this would turn out and mused, 'It is all going well at the moment, while the good weather lasts, but you should not campaign in Russia when the rivers begin to freeze.'

Even so, the younger officers had regained a measure of confidence in the genius of Napoleon. He could have ordered us to conquer the moon and we would have obeyed! The older officers sneered at our enthusiasm and called us mad or possessed. We dreamt of battles and victories and we only feared one thing: that the Russians would sue for peace *too quickly*.

Whilst at Dobruvna a brave sergeant from my old voltigeur company called Dachowicz, who had been sent on reconnaissance with seventeen men, fell into a cossack ambush. He had not panicked and had managed to keep up a steady fire until he was quite close to our outposts. At the sound of the firing a detachment was sent out to help him but it either arrived too late or moved too slowly and only found corpses. I could not restrain my tears when I heard the news, as Dachowicz had been with me throughout our Spanish campaigns. He had received eleven wounds. He was one of the best and most intelligent men in the regiment and would have long since been an officer had he known how to write.

---

[107] Tadeusz Kosciuszko (1746–1817) was born in Lithuania and was the hero of Polish attempts to resist the partition of Poland, leading the revolt of 1794. After his defeat, he lead a life of exile in Paris and then Switzerland.

CHAPTER XXXVII

March on Smolensk – Assault on the City – The City is Stormed
– The Fires – A Polish Hospital Burns Down – The Wounded
Perish – Last Words of a Dying Russian – Napoleon at Valutina

Claparède's division left Dobruvna on 13 August and formed part of the
general advance on Smolensk. From that day on we were no longer under
Davout's command but were attached to the Imperial Guard. We passed
through Krasnoi on the 15th. This had been the scene of the bloody battle
between Murat's cavalry and a Russian division. The king of Naples had
taken a few cannon and some prisoners, but he himself had lost heavily,
galloping about in ground that was unsuitable for cavalry. Napoleon is
supposed to have commented that 'Murat has acted like a cadet from Saint
Cyr'.[108]

We climbed the heights before Krasnoi and from a superb vantage point
were privileged to witness a sight that is rare indeed: 200,000 men of all
arms manoeuvring over a vast landscape.

Claparède's division formed part of the reserve positioned on the heights
overlooking Smolensk, and we watched the mixed fortunes of the mass
assault on the 17th. At about four in the afternoon, at which time the
Russians were still putting up a stubborn defence, I heard our colonel say,
'You'll soon see they can't hold out much longer.' He was right and as night
fell their withdrawal began.

The next day one of Poniatowski's staff officers informed me that Count
Skorzewski had carried news of this retreat to Davout at about ten in the
evening. Skorzewski had been sent off to find out what had happened to two
battalions that had pushed too far forward and out of touch with the rest
of their division. He was chased by some Russian cavalry and actually
crossed the Dnieper in order to escape them. As luck would have it, he ran
into one of the battalions he had been sent out to find and its commander,

---

[108] Saint Cyr was the French military academy.

Rozycki,[109] told him that he had distinctly heard the sound of wagons on the move which could only have meant one thing: retreat. Skorzewski, now far from his own headquarters but close to that of the Prince of Eckmühl, felt duty bound to inform Davout of these important developments. But he was given a frosty reception by the French general, who he found in a church and who deemed his news *silly*. He went straight to Poniatowski, who limited his own comments to, 'If those gentlemen do not wish to believe it, that is not our fault.'

From the heights we could clearly see the three great infernos which dominated the end of the day. The first of these fires was among the stores and the warehouses and Napoleon aptly compared it to a volcanic eruption – it even ended with a shower of ashes. To the left of this could be seen another fire which burnt less brightly but for just as long. This was the wooden buildings in the citadel going up. Finally, a little later, we caught sight of a third fire which suddenly broke out in a suburb captured by Poniatowski's troops. A huge storehouse, being used as a temporary hospital, was hit and set on fire by Russian shells. This fire took such a hold and made such progress that it was only possible to rescue a few of the wounded; the rest perished. This cruel incident passed almost unnoticed amidst the terrible and horrible events of this campaign.

The city seemed deserted on the next day. All the inhabitants were still in the churches or the cellars. Some of the victors had gone off towards the Dnieper, others were occupied in battling against fires which were still raging in most areas. I crossed over that part of the city which, the night before, had been the scene of the fiercest fighting. Most of the casualties had been from Ney's and Poniatowski's corps. The latter had lost some sixty officers and at least 2,000 men dead and wounded. The storehouse I mentioned presented a truly horrible sight.

On the other side of the river, the Russian army made its escape along the road to Moscow, but we could easily see that their main body was protected by a strong rearguard which was still firing on us and still raining shells down on the city – particularly on that part occupied by Ney's troops.

As we were busy trying to sort out the dead from the wounded, I noticed a young Russian who had been plundered and left for dead. He had been shot and the bullet had passed through his chest and he showed no sign of life. But I saw him suddenly raise himself up only to collapse once again, uttering some unintelligible words. They tried to help this unfortunate who struggled between life and death for a few more hours. A short while before

---

[109] This was Major Samuel Rozycki of the 3rd Infantry Regiment of the Grand Duchy of Warsaw, part of the 16th Division, V Corps.

he finally passed away, he came back to full consciousness and seemed aware of what we were doing for him and in a White Russian[110] accent told the Polish surgeons, 'You are brave, but your Czar must be a wicked man. What have we ever done to him? What does he want from our country? Rise up, Holy Russia and defend yourself, your religion and your Czar!' These were his last words! 'That's how these Russians are,' said one of my comrades who had been witness to the whole scene, 'the Emperor really is taking chances!'

On the morning of the 19th Claparède's division marched through the city, parts of which were still ablaze, and established itself on the far side of the Dnieper, the bridges having been repaired, at the point where the roads to Petersburg and Moscow bisect. At about eight o'clock the noise of a cannonade started to come through to us from our right. The struggle lasted the whole of the day but was particularly fierce in the afternoon. It was the famous battle of Valutina.[111]

At around five in the evening we caught sight of the Emperor riding along the Moscow road. He seemed much displeased and galloped past the soldiers without seeming to notice their acclamations. This naturally gave rise to quite a few comments. Some assumed that the vanguard had suffered a reverse but as the Emperor did not come riding back and the noise of the firing seemed to be getting further and further away, there was sufficient proof to suggest that it was the enemy who were in fact in retreat.

What had put Napoleon in a bad mood was news of Junot's negligence, which had allowed another chance for decisive victory to slip away.[112]

---

[110] White Russia, Bielorussia, is now the Republic of Belarus.

[111] Valutina, on 19 August, was almost the battle the French had been waiting for. However, through a combination of ill-luck and bad judgement, the Russians escaped without serious loss.

[112] Junot had taken over command of the Westphalian VIII Corps after Jerome had returned to Cassel.

CHAPTER XXXVIII

~

THE BATTLEFIELD OF VALUTINA – ON THE EMPEROR'S STAFF –
THE EAGLE OF THE 127TH LINE – NAPOLEON AND PONIATOWSKI –
I AM PROMOTED – SACK OF SMOLENSK – HISTORY OF A COLONEL,
A GRENADIER OF THE OLD GUARD AND A POODLE

The following morning (20 August) the Emperor again rode by us and
along the Moscow road. My colonel was very keen to find out about what
was going on and asked me if I would join the imperial staff in order to
discover the latest developments. Consequently I soon found myself on
horseback.

We were galloping along but soon had to slow down when we began to
come across more and more wounded. Some of them cried out 'Long live
the Emperor', but others kept silent. Napoleon occasionally stopped to talk
to the wounded, of whom there were many, too many. Before long we
started to come across both French and Russian dead. The road followed a
small watercourse that had steep sides and fed irrigation channels and these
made the terrain very boggy and difficult.

We finally reached a height from which the entire battlefield could be
surveyed. The battle had taken place on a marshy plain ringed by hills and
criss-crossed by the Stragonbach, along the banks of which there had been
heavy fighting. Ney's corps was now camped by this river, surrounded by
corpses.

Napoleon's arrival produced the usual loud acclamations and some of
the most seriously wounded men were making an effort to salute him,
perhaps for one last time. He passed close to a grenadier who had been
wounded in the foot, and this brave man called out, 'Oh, Sire! Why were
you not at our head yesterday? We would have crushed the Russians!'

The battlefield presented a horrible scene, illuminated by a radiant sun.
We had to keep turning our horses to avoid them trampling on the piles of
corpses. And for all this slaughter we took not one cannon or ammunition
wagon. The only gain we made was the actual ground we stood on.

The Emperor reviewed Ney's troops and presented an Eagle to the 127th Line – a regiment which had just received its baptism of fire. This ceremony, which in itself is imposing, took on a whole new aspect in such a setting. The regiment formed a square. Many of the faces in the ranks were still stained black with powder and uniforms and equipment were bloodstained. The colonel and the officers were gathered in a semi-circle around the Emperor. 'Soldiers!' he began, 'here is your Eagle! It will serve as your rallying point in moments of danger. Swear to me that you will never forsake it, that you will always be true to the path of honour, that you will defend the fatherland and keep France, our France,[113] free from insult!' All replied as one man: 'We swear it!' The Emperor took the Eagle from Berthier's[114] hands and passed it to the colonel, who handed it on to the standard-bearer. Then the square opened up and formed line and the standard-bearer, preceded by the drums and the musicians, took up his post in the centre of the colour party.

A grenadier sergeant was promoted to second lieutenant there and then. 'Have it done at once!' said Napoleon. The colonel pronounced the sacred words but abstained from embracing the new officer. 'Come, come, colonel! The accolade, the accolade!' the Emperor said sharply. Decorations, promotions, rewards rained down. It could be seen that Napoleon was making a determined effort to distract himself and others from gloomy thoughts.

Moving on to the 95th, he asked the colonel to produce the list of those men who had distinguished themselves in yesterday's battle and the colonel naturally began with the officers. After he had read out six or seven names the Emperor interrupted him, 'How is it, colonel, that your rankers are such cowards?' and personally had the most deserving NCOs and privates step forward from the ranks for promotion or decoration. As I watched this scene I was mesmerised by the fascination Napoleon exerts whenever and on whoever he wishes. But he could not be everywhere.

That very evening looting broke out in the Moscow suburb of Smolensk. This suburb contained warehouses full of leathers and furs – the loss of which we would seriously regret later on. I also saw soldiers throwing heaps of paper roubles into the flames, unaware of their true value.

On the next day, the 21st, the Emperor reviewed Poniatowski's corps and lavished considerable favour upon it. He doubtless wanted to erase any memory of his bitter and malicious reprimand of the Prince earlier in

---

[113] The 127th Line was a regiment recruited in the Hanseatic cities of northern Germany, recently annexed by Metropolitan France; perhaps Napoleon was therefore entitled to ask them to defend 'our' France.

[114] Marshal Louis-Alexandre Berthier (1753–1815) was Napoleon's hard-working and indispensable Chief of Staff.

the campaign, when Poniatowski had asked for an issue of backpay and food. Copies of Napoleon's damaging reply had been secretly circulated throughout the army. There had also been talk of another shameful episode when the Prince and his generals had visited the imperial headquarters just before the seizure of Smolensk. Napoleon had been quite welcoming at first but soon grew impatient with some returns which showed how the corps' effective strength was diminishing. He shouted, 'What the f– has happened to your people?' at General Fischer, Poniatowski's chief of staff. 'Sire, the lack of food, the hard marching, the...' 'Ha! You are always singing me the same old song. Why haven't the other corps left most of their men behind? I know what is behind all this – you are about as tough as Warsaw ballet dancers (or, by some accounts, some other colourful phrase).'

It seems that Poniatowski, once more insulted, was on the point of quitting the army. Even then there were rumours of another episode and it seems that after this review on the 21st, when Napoleon seemed much more satisfied with the Poles, Poniatowski had gone to the Emperor, found him with Davout, and begged him to be allowed to go to Kiev and organise a mass uprising in the old Polish provinces. Napoleon had grown angry and threatened to have him shot if he would not desist from his scheming. All this I had on good authority on the day that it happened, and from reliable sources.

The 22nd was a memorable date for my own military career. Napoleon reviewed his Guards and our division in the Archbishop's Square, which the Russians called *Blonge*. I was one of the officers nominated for promotion. There were fourteen of us in all, and we were asked to step out from the ranks by the colonel. Napoleon stopped in front of me and, as was his habit, drew me towards him by a button on my uniform. He said, 'This officer should have been made a captain in Paris, make him a captain now'. He then continued his inspection and noticed a sergeant who had three chevrons on his sleeve, showing that he had served for twenty years. 'How is it this man has not yet been made an officer?' demanded the Emperor.

'Sire, he can neither read nor write.'

'What does that matter! These poor illiterates often make the best officers. Make him a second lieutenant in the grenadiers. I am sure he was not cowering in the rear at the storming of Saragossa.'

As we filed past the Emperor there was a mix up when one of the majors forgot to give a word of command and his unit almost collided with Napoleon, who was forced to pull sharply on his reins and swerve aside. As he did so, he shouted, 'What the devil are you doing?' but we had not yet heard the full wrath of the imperial temper and the reprimands began to fall in buckets upon the unfortunate officer. 'I would have had you arrested

212

for fourteen days for such unthinkable folly had the Emperor not already corrected you sufficiently,' Chlopicki told him.

After our inspection the Old Guard was reviewed, and I was in a good position to note every detail. Never have I seen such well turned out and imposing soldiers. Our colonel was on the receiving end of a visit from one of these old soldiers and this led to a strange incident which clearly demonstrates the status of these men in the army – a status that even superior officers had to take account of.

It all happened in camp two days before we reached Smolensk. I was with the colonel, Chlusewicz, just as he was about to start shaving. He had a bowl of water on a table at the entrance to his tent. Suddenly, a big white poodle came bounding up, rushed into the tent and then calmly began to lap up all the water. The colonel and myself scarcely had time to realise what was happening when a grenadier of the Old Guard appeared, muttered 'sorry gentlemen' into his moustache and started to put his dog on a lead. The dog leapt to one side to avoid him, knocked over the bowl and spilt all the water. I must add that there was quite a scarcity of water at this particular time.

'Have you ever seen such insolence?' asked the colonel, grabbing the grenadier by the epaulettes and throwing him out of the tent. The grenadier quickly disappeared with his animal.

The colonel thought no more about the incident until, on the next day, we saw the poodle's owner reappear accompanied by a staff officer. They were both in full dress. 'Colonel,' said the officer, 'you have greatly compromised the honour of this honest man, who is greatly esteemed throughout his regiment. I am here in the name of Marshal Berthier to correct this wrong and am convinced that you owe this man a word of apology.'

'It is true,' said the colonel unabashed, 'that I lost my temper and am now sorry for it and would have said so to this brave man had he not disappeared so quickly. I am glad that this visit spares me the trouble of having to seek him out so that I may tell him that I was cross at myself for having mistreated him. Now, grenadier, have we not settled the matter to your satisfaction?' As he said this he took the grenadier by the hand and shook it warmly. The grenadier rather sheepishly murmured that he was fully satisfied with the apology.

The colonel was, deep down, far from satisfied and later told me that he had done all this in good grace to avoid disagreeable consequences for the regiment. Perhaps he was also concerned about his own prospects for promotion or entry into the Guard. Shortly afterwards, in fact after the review in which I was made captain, he was made a major in a Guard Lancer regiment. To celebrate he threw a banquet for his old and new fellow-officers and for other Polish officers. Our first toast was to the reestablishment of Poland from the Wartha to the Dneiper. Then toasts were drunk, often at length, to the health of all who were present whether in the military or civil administration and for success in their respective careers.

Despite the suspicions of the older officers and Napoleon's elusive responses to representatives of the Polish Diet[115] we young officers were still under his spell. It seemed impossible to us that this war, which the Emperor himself had called the Second Polish War at the beginning of the campaign, would not lead, one way or another, to a complete and total restoration of the Polish nation. After all, had not the campaign so far been one of the most glorious exploits of that great captain? If the Russians had managed to avoid being crushed on two occasions that was the fault of Jerome Bonaparte or of Junot. Were we not masters of Smolensk, the citizens of which town had, two centuries before, preferred to die rather than surrender to the besieging Poles? Was it so foolhardy to believe that a decisive victory could be anything other than certain, or that this difficult campaign would end in a blaze of glory at least as great as that of Austerlitz?

---

[115] An eight-man deputation from the Polish Diet – the parliament of the Grand Duchy of Warsaw – arrived to see Napoleon in Vilna on 11 July. It was led by Count Wybicki.

CHAPTER XXXIX

~

QUITTING SMOLENSK – FROM SMOLENSK TO GJATSK – DUST AND
FAMINE – THE SOUND OF THE GUNS – THE SCHWARDINO REDOUBT –
ON THE STAFF – DESAIX AND FABVIER – THE NIGHT BEFORE THE
BATTLE

Claparède's division left Smolensk on 24 August. We crossed over the
battlefield of Valutina, which was still covered in dead bodies, most of
which were in an advanced state of putrefaction. As we made our way
through this scene I found myself shoulder to shoulder with Rakowski, the
old wizard. He said, speaking in French so as not to be understood by the
soldiers, 'Look there, my young friend. We'll all be like that soon enough!'

The march from Smolensk to Gjatsk (24 August–3 September) was one
of the most exhausting I have ever endured. The temperature would swing
dramatically from burning heat to freezing cold. The heat was terrible and
the wind swept up huge billowing clouds of dust that were so thick it was
often impossible to see the great trees on either side of the road. The Holy
Soil of Russia, it seemed, really was rising up against the invaders, just as
the young Russian in Smolensk had promised. The dust was a real torment.
In order to at least protect their eyes the soldiers improvised goggles out of
glass from windows; others marched with their shakos tucked under their
arms and with their heads swathed in handkerchiefs, with openings left
open just enough to see and to breathe; still others made garlands out of
leaves. The army presented a comical appearance, but all signs of this
masquerade would vanish at the slightest shower of rain.

Night was hardly less difficult than day. Our camps were hard to endure.
The water was, on the whole, bad if there was water at all. The soldiers had
been reduced to roasting their meat on ashes; usually it was horse meat, as
the locals had hidden their livestock so far from the columns of march that
it was impossible for us to get our hands on it.

On the 24th the division made camp at Tzarewo-Zaimische, a famous
place in the annals of Polish military history as it was here that Zolkiewski

215

defeated La Gardie's Russo-Swedish force on 4 July 1610. This victory, one of the most decisive the Poles have ever inflicted on the Russians, led to the capture of Moscow, and the dethronement and captivity of the then Czar, Chouiski.[116]

It is true that at that time, when the Poles were laying down the law for the Russians, the Muscovites had been riddled with factions, rather than the other way round.

In 1812 more than one of the descendants of Zolkiewski's companions could be counted in the ranks of the Poles. Perhaps they hoped that the enemy would stop retreating and hold their position so that we could have contested the same ground, but they were going to be disappointed.

Gjatsk is one of the prettiest towns in Russia and also one of the most important militarily. This is largely due to its position on the river of the same name, which is a tributary to the Volga as well as being connected to the Dnieper and the Duna by canals that are navigable even in times of drought. The houses of the town had an air of elegance and prosperity, something quite rare in the Russia of that period. They had two storeys with a porch out front and were painted brilliant white with turquoise cornices. Our stay here was a good one as vegetables were plentiful, something the soldiers had not experienced for some time. In addition we lodged in a well-appointed farmhouse which served as our headquarters. For the first time since the beginning of the campaign, the officers of the 2nd Regiment of the Vistula slept indoors in proper beds.

It was at Gjatsk that we learnt Barclay had been replaced as commander-in-chief of the Russian forces by old Kutuzov, nicknamed 'the runaway of Austerlitz' by the French.[117] We had heard vague reports that Barclay had been chastised for not having defended Smolensk. All in all, this change seemed to augur well for us, but our hopes were quickly dashed. Our hopes were raised to new heights on the 5th by the sound of a cannonade. Napoleon was also keen to finish the matter: each corps was successively urged forwards and we marched shoulder to shoulder with the Guard, hard on the heels of I Corps.

The countryside beyond Gjatsk turned out to be picturesque and hilly. Once, from a vantage point on top of a hill, we caught sight of the French

---

[116] This battle, also known as Klushino, saw the Poles, under Hetman Stanislaw Zolkiewski, defeat the Russians and a Swedish contingent under Jakob de la Gardie (1583–1652). The Poles then took Moscow in August 1610 and ejected Czar Basil (Vasili) Chouiski, the Swedish-backed claimant to the Russian throne. They installed the son of Sigismund III, the king of Poland, in his place and governed the city for two years.

[117] Prince Mikhail Kutuzov (1745–1813) was recalled from fighting the Turks in Bulgaria and became, on 20 August, commander of the Russian armies in the west.

Army and, beyond it, fleeting clouds of cossacks and the enemy masses, which seemed to be concentrating whilst still falling back in retreat.

We could hear the roar of cannon as we marched forwards. After passing through a thick pine forest and climbing the steep slope to Walujewo, still in the wake of I Corps, we saw a majestic sight unfolding beneath our eyes. In front of us, quite close, was a fortified position, the possession of which was being hotly contested by both sides. It was the famous Schwardino Redoubt. It was impossible to see the details of the struggle, but the swarming masses, the bickering of the muskets and roaring boom of the cannons could be clearly heard. Suddenly a shout of triumph went up, carried to us on a stormy wind. The firing grew quieter and at last faded away altogether. Towards eight in the evening we set up our camps not far from the redoubt, in which the body of General Compans was shortly to be buried.[118]

As no rations were issued that evening, I was free to go and visit the redoubt. It was covered in corpses. From it the enemy's huge campfires could be seen, flickering in the distance. There were plenty of them.

Earlier, as we had been marching forwards, I saw the Emperor twice – once on reconnaissance, the other time by his tent. On the following morning I would see him appear and disappear like a shadowy ghost into and out of the thick fog that enveloped the battlefield on the morning of the battle.

At three in the afternoon I was charged with the delivery of a message to Imperial Headquarters and thus managed to see the portrait of the king of Rome which was on display by the imperial tent.[119] The soldiers, especially the veterans, seemed greatly touched by the picture; but the officers were now seriously worried about the outcome of the campaign and seemed as anxious as ever.

I bumped into Captain Desaix, one of the Emperor's orderly officers and an old friend from Spain, where he had been Suchet's aide-de-camp. He pointed out a rather furtive-looking officer, who seemed absolutely exhausted. It was Fabvier, Marmont's aide-de-camp who would later become famous in the Greek struggle for independence.[120] He had ridden flat out from Spain to bring news to Napoleon of the disaster at Salamanca.[121] I first learnt the bad news then but was bound to secrecy and I know of many

---

[118] General Compans was, in fact, only wounded in the arm on the next day.

[119] This portrait of the king of Rome, Napoleon's son, was by Baron François Gérard and had been delivered to Imperial Headquarters by Napoleon's portly Prefect of the Palace, Bausset. The portrait was lost during the retreat from Moscow.

[120] Fabvier distinguished himself the next day by repeatedly leading the 30th Line in assaults on the Grand Redoubt.

[121] Wellington's defeat of Marmont at Salamanca, or Los Apriles to the French, was on 22 July 1812.

officers, some even of high rank, who only became aware of this defeat after the present campaign had drawn to a close.

The lack of food was bitterly felt that night. We dined on grilled corn and horsemeat. The night was wet and cold and many soldiers and officers, soaked to the skin and prey to forebodings, tried in vain to sleep. They would get up and, like lost souls, walk listlessly before the campfires.

CHAPTER XL

BORODINO

Fighting broke out all along the line at around seven in the morning. At first we were posted just in front of the Old Guard, whose plumes and epaulettes showed up blood-red in the early morning light.

It soon became evident that we were standing quite close to where the fighting was fiercest. Cannonballs smashed into the ground before us or passed over our heads. The wind, which was blowing quite strongly into our faces, carried the French shouts of *en avant* intermingled with the Russian *hourrah!* But we could see nothing of the struggle itself.

After a while the wounded began to trickle back from the fighting and they told us that the redoubt closest to us had just been taken.

At around nine o'clock our division advanced, in two columns, about a thousand yards in the direction of Schwardino and came to a halt in a slight depression. Cannonballs were striking the lip of the depression and ricocheting over our heads. Chlopicki, as impassive as he had always been in Spain, moved as far forward as possible to get a view of the enemy's position. Claparède came over to us and gathered the officers of the 2nd Regiment of the Vistula around him in a circle and impressed upon them the need to uphold the good reputation of the regiment.

Meanwhile the struggle raged fiercely, especially in the woods on our right, and it seemed as if the battle might reach us and sweep us away. We could hear the relentless whistle of cannonballs and yet not one man was hit, as the general had deliberately chosen this position to shield his men from needless casualties.

At about ten o'clock one of the Emperor's orderly officers, given the task of guiding us forward, appeared. We moved forward obliquely, heading to the left, and, marching over meadows, crossed a considerable part of the battlefield. On our right a terrible struggle was in progress, to our left we caught sight of long lines of French cavalry in whose ranks the enemy artillery blasted bloody lanes at every moment. We too began to lose men now we were no longer under cover.

We halted again, this time in the shallow valley of the Semenowka. From here we could see nothing of the battle but heard the crackle of muskets and dull thuds of the cannon.

We had walked right over numerous dead men and dead horses for we were approaching that point at which the battle raged most fiercely. Wounded men dragged themselves past us, leaving bloody trails in their wake. We were still sheltered by the lie of the land and we could only see the green dome of Borodino's church, glistening in the sun.

We saw Ouvarov's[122] superbly executed charge skirting around Borodino, an excellent move which might have led to a complete disaster had they not come up against infantry as solid as those of Delzons.[123]

Just then Captain Desaix appeared and paused briefly before us, saying, 'I have just come from the right and your Prince Poniatowski isn't making any progress. The Emperor isn't very pleased with him. Our losses are enormous; the Russians are fighting like madmen.'

At two o'clock we received the order to continue our advance. We crossed a stream, evidently the Semenowka, at a point where the ground had been churned up by the passage of cavalry. But just as we reached the top of the slope on the far side of the valley we were suddenly shrouded in a thick cloud of smoke. At the same time a terrible roar, coming from the mouths of thousands of men, drowned out the noise of the artillery which was now raking our columns. When the smoke cleared, we saw that the Great Redoubt had been taken and that the French cavalry were issuing from it to charge the retreating, but still uncowed, Russians.

We were drawn up behind the redoubt and had evidently been destined to support the main attack or make a supporting one had this one failed. The attack had succeeded, but at what cost! The redoubt and its environs presented a ghastly sight more horrible than anything one could possibly imagine. The earthworks, the ditches and the inside of the redoubt had all disappeared under a mass of the dead and dying piled seven or eight men deep one on top of the other. I shall never forget the sight of a middle-aged staff officer, with a massive head wound, slumped against a Russian howitzer. I saw General Auguste de Caulaincourt,[124] mortally wounded, being carried away in a white cuirassier cloak, stained deep red by his blood. There, in the redoubt, the bodies of infantrymen were scattered amongst

---

[122] Ouvarov commanded the Russian Guard cavalry at Borodino and his attack, supported by Platov, took place around noon and forced a temporary shift in French alignment to bolster their left flank.

[123] Delzons commanded three French line regiments, one light regiment and a Croatian regiment.

[124] General Auguste Caulaincourt (1777–1812) was the younger brother of the Duke of Vicenza, the famous diarist of the 1812 campaign.

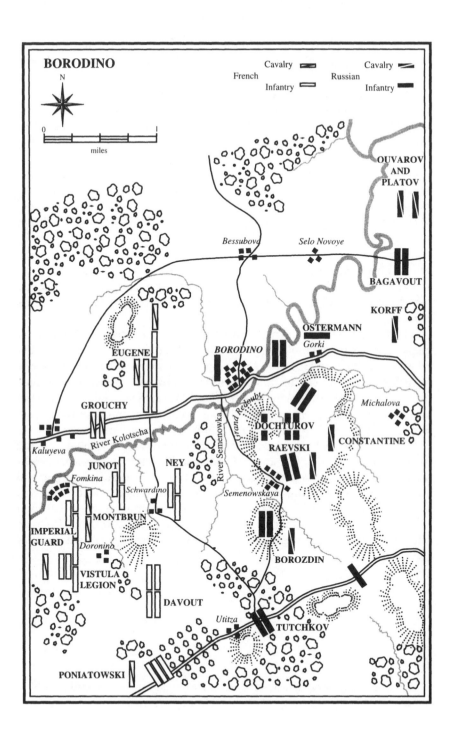

BORODINO

N

0   1
miles

Cavalry   Cavalry
French   Russian
Infantry   Infantry

OUVAROV
AND
PLATOV

Bessubova   Selo Novoye

BAGAVOUT

KORFF

OSTERMANN
Gorki

BORODINO

EUGENE

Michalova

GROUCHY

DOCHTUROV

RAEVSKI   CONSTANTINE

River Kolotscha

Kaluyeva

River Semenowka

Grand Redoubt

JUNOT   NEY

Fomkina

Schwardino

Semenowskaya

MONTBRUN

IMPERIAL
GUARD

Doronino

BOROZDIN

VISTULA
LEGION

DAVOUT

Utitza   TUTCHKOV

PONIATOWSKI

French, Saxon, Westphalian and Polish cuirassiers uniformed in blue and in white. I recognised Captain Jablonski amongst the latter; handsome Jablonski they had called him at Warsaw![125]

This was a crucial moment in the battle and the firing abated a little as if both sides wondered what to do next. After unsuccessfully pursuing the Russians, the French cavalry fell back and the Russian infantry began to advance towards us. They paused or hesitated, perhaps overawed by the sheer scale of the fighting.

It was then that the terrible artillery duel, of which all historians speak, began. The redoubt, which to some extent sheltered us, was torn up by shot and shell. Shots soon began to fall amongst our ranks and our losses began to mount. The soldiers received the order to lie down whilst the officers 'awaited death standing', as Rechowictz put it. He had just finished speaking when we were both splashed by the blood and brains of a sergeant who had had his head blown off by a cannonball just as he had stood up to go and talk to a friend. The horrible stains on my uniform proved impossible to remove and I had them in my sight for the remainder of the campaign as a *memento mori*.

The French batteries, which have always been wrongly marked on all maps I have seen, extended from the Great Redoubt, where we were ourselves positioned, as far as the eye could see. A foot artillery battery close by us had lost every one of its senior officers and was now under the command of a very young-looking junior officer. He seemed to be adapting very well to his new role in the midst of this all too dreadful and horrific carnage which heralded rapid promotion for hundreds of such men.

Suddenly the enemy's ranks showed movement and it seemed as if the Russians now intended to launch a fresh assault despite the massive weight of artillery deployed against them. They came on in superb order and almost reached the redoubt before we counter-attacked, when they fell back, this time for good, after a violent and murderous infantry battle in which my regiment suffered heavily. That day we had a total of 257 men killed or wounded and the majority of these fell during this final phase of the fighting.

---

[125] Ignace Jablonski was a captain in the 14th Cavalry regiment of the Grand Duchy of Warsaw, Poland's only cuirassier regiment.

CHAPTER XLI

We camped where we stood, surrounded by the dead and dying. We were completely without water and firewood but we did find oats, brandy and some other provisions in some of the dead Russians' knapsacks. With some musket butts and splinters from a broken limber we managed to get a fire going and grill our house speciality – horse steaks. In order to make some soup we had to go down and get some water from the Kolotscha, one of the most terrifying experiences of my life.

In the shadows around each of the flickering fires, the agonised and tormented wounded began to gather until they far outnumbered us. They could be seen everywhere like ghostly shadows moving in the half-light, creeping towards the glow of the fire. Some, horrifically mutilated, used the last of their strength to do so. They would suddenly collapse and die, with their imploring eyes fixed on the flames. Others retained some stamina but still seemed more like ghosts than living men. They received as much help as possible from our good surgeons and from the officers and troops them-selves and it was as if our camp had turned into an outdoor hospital.

We kept a sharp lookout that night and were wise to do so. At around two in the morning, a detachment of cossacks swooped out of the night but we received them with a well-nourished fire and they made off as quickly as they had come. Just before dawn the artillery opened up again some distance from us. The morning was clear and the cold sharp. At around nine the Emperor made his appearance. He spent three-quarters of an hour close to us with his eyes fixed on the scene of slaughter. I saw him deep in conversation with one of his staff officers who then went into the redoubt with some of the Guard Chasseurs. They marked out a square and then counted the number of corpses in the square. They repeated this at a number of different points and I understand that using this mathematical technique, they got an approximate idea of the number of victims. Whilst all this was going on, Napoleon's face was quite impassive but he did look a little pale.

We moved forward again that day, coming to a halt at around three in the afternoon and going no further. We made our camp a short distance from the little town of Mojaisk which was still occupied by the Russian rear-guard. Our camp was adjoining that of V Corps' 13th Polish Lancers.[126] The officers of this regiment told us that at one point in the previous day's battle they had followed up a successful attack on cossacks by pushing through some woods to the rear of the Russian army and getting as far as Mojaisk. The charge was led by an officer called Gawroncki and their sudden appearance caused considerable commotion at Russian headquarters.

All this had occurred at around three or four in the afternoon, just as Kniacewicz's[127] and Krasinski's[128] divisions were attacking the enemy frontally. Davout had had the idea of launching the main assault against this wing of the enemy and had hoped to combine his forces with those of Poniatowski and jointly take the offensive. However, he was disappointed and infuriated by the Emperor's constant rejection of this scheme. Another eye-witness, General Tolinski,[129] attached to Poniatowski's staff, had sent his hussars off towards Mojaisk and these had made their way through the same wood and fallen onto the enemy's rearguard. This consisted of a mass of wounded, baggage wagons and fugitives stretching out across a plain. Tolinski, without orders and lacking infantry support, made off with what he could carry and advanced no further. General Toll, a high-ranking officer in the Russian Army, wrote that the Poles had tried to turn the Russian's left but this was of little consequence as they could only bring cavalry into action.

It must be said that V Corps took 2,000 prisoners, more than any of the rest of the army put together and, rightly or wrongly, we were convinced that had the Emperor reinforced Poniatowski by as little as one division, and given him a free hand, he would have managed to take Mojaisk before the close of the day.[130] The Russians, with their lines of retreat thus severed, would, at the very least, have lost most of their guns and baggage. What would have been the consequences of such a victory for the rest of the campaign? None can tell, but surely the effect must have been tremendous

---

[126] Brandt means the 12th regiment, a lancer unit. The 13th was a Hussar regiment.

[127] Charles Kniacewicz (1762–1842) replaced Kamiencki as commander of the 18th Division, V Corps. He later commanded V Corps in the retreat from Moscow.

[128] Isidor Krasinski (1774–1870) commanded the 16th Division, V Corps.

[129] Colonel Joséph Tolinski in fact commanded the Polish 13th Hussars at Borodino.

[130] Poniatowski was actually sent Junot's corps, after some delay, to support the Polish action on the right.

and we must have pushed the Russians right back through Moscow and gained a decisive advantage over them.

As we advanced from Mojaisk to Moscow, we got involved in an attack on a birch wood which dominated the road leading into the village of Krimskoje. A furious battle broke out to our right and the French cavalry were repulsed by the Russians, who were in turn thrust back by our cavalry reserve. This cavalry, in their impetuosity, literally rode over a square of French infantry which had been bypassed by the enemy's attack. As we drew nearer the aforementioned wood we were met by a withering fire. The enemy were well positioned and in considerable numbers; two of our attacks failed successively. General Chlopicki, having exhausted all his patience, led two battalions of Polish infantry into the assault and carried the position. The Russians fell into retreat, but not before they fired a parting volley which brought down 100 men and wounded Chlopicki so seriously that he was *hors de combat* for the rest of the campaign and would never again enter French service. I saw him once more in 1814, when the war was over. Despite being a strict disciplinarian, our soldiers were very upset at his loss. 'Without him,' they would say, 'we would have all been killed in Spain. Now who is going to lead us out of this cursed Russia?'

Thirty men, more or less seriously wounded but with sufficient stamina left to keep on marching, preferred to stay with us at all costs. Seeing one of these unfortunates dragging himself along, I advised him to go and stay in the hospital. He told me that 'by not leaving the regiment I have some chance of saving my skin; if it comes to the worst at least my comrades will bury me. If I go to the hospital I'll be gobbled up by the wolves whether I am dead or alive...'

I almost forgot to mention that at this point we had been without rations for the last three days and we had been living off food found on dead Russians. Frequently our campfires would be blown out by sudden gusts of wind and it was said that this wind was an omen of a terrible winter.

CHAPTER XLII

MOSCOW

On 14 September, at one in the afternoon, Claparède's division formed up outside Moscow's Drogomilov Gate where the Smolensk road enters the city. The King of Naples had entered the city before us with a large body of cavalry which included the regiment of Polish Hussars and one of Prussian Lancers. Up to that point we felt sure that the Russians would not abandon their holy city without one more fight. It seems that they too had held this belief for we found, as we advanced towards the city, that numerous defensive positions had been prepared for our reception.

As we were approaching Moscow, the Emperor had ridden up, dismounted and studied the city through a telescope. Seen from the height that dominates it, Moscow seemed oriental, fantastic even, in appearance. With 500 golden and multicoloured domes shimmering above a sea of rooftops it was a stupendous sight; and yet the French officers seemed troubled. There was consternation that no deputation had come forth to surrender the town. 'They'll be kept waiting,' grumbled one of our old soldiers, 'these Russians would rather emigrate to Siberia than surrender.'

We passed through the city's defences at around two o'clock, following in the wake of the cavalry's vanguard. We entered the suburbs and marched along a wide and unsurfaced street which was flanked on either side by wooden houses, all of which were, very wisely, boarded up.

The rest of the city, from there to the bridge of the Moskva, consisted of similar-looking streets but with larger and more elegant houses, all of which were, again, hermetically sealed. Absolute silence reigned supreme.

Our march was slow and frequently interrupted; so much so that it took us six hours to cover 8,000 yards. Throughout that time we came across just one inhabitant, a gigantic Russian who, as we were filing by, dashed out of one house and made for another over the road. As he crossed the street he knocked into some of our soldiers and an officer who drew his sword. The man, who seemed rather wild, opened his coat and shouted, 'Plunge your steel into this Russian bosom!' As we had been ordered to treat the in-habitants with courtesy we let him be and he disappeared into the house, slamming the door shut behind him. 'If they are all like that,' a sergeant said, 'our troubles have only just begun.'

Every now and then we came across signs of a hurried evacuation and evidence of the passage of troops, such as abandoned wagons of food – the contents of which soon disappeared.

We heard a few cannon shots from the direction of the Kremlin and, occasionally, the sound of distant explosions which sounded exactly like the slamming of doors. The more we penetrated into the heart of the city, the more we came across magnificent and opulent houses complete with gar-dens, greenhouses, fountains and elegant balconies. Most of these seemed so beautiful and yet they were built out of wood; something which we would only learn, to our cost, a few days later. The Kremlin, which we marched past, was just like another and still more beautiful town set within the first.

We finally reached the Semenofski Gate at around eight in the evening and settled down to camp quite close to some windmills. From there we could see the two lines of campfires, those of the Russians and those of our cavalry, clearly marking the position of the front lines.

On the following morning some Polish lancers who had just come through the city informed us that it was being put to the sack. This news was confirmed by some of our men who had been sent in to collect food and had come back well stocked with tea, rum, sugar, wines and precious objects of all kinds. From then on there was no restraining the soldiers. All who weren't actually on duty disappeared. Our kitchens were deserted. Men sent to collect wood or straw, and even men sent out on patrol, never came back.

For the Poles, one of the attractions of joining in the pillaging was the desire to settle old scores. I once saw a lancer urging on a poor Russian, laden with the lancer's booty, with a whip. When I reproached him for this brutality, he grew angry with me and hissed, 'My father and mother were both massacred at Praga.'[131]

Only one man could have kept order in the ranks of the Vistula Legion and he had been absent for some three days now. This reminded me of something that Danusz, from my old voltigeur company, had said when Chlopicki was wounded: 'Now the cat is away, the mice will play!'

The pillaging was the logical consequence of having the troops actually camp within the city, and of the disappearance of any authority which

---

[131] The Praga massacre had taken place in 1794. The Russians, under Suvorov, stormed this suburb of Warsaw and put many of its defenders to the sword as a reprisal for mistreatment of Russian wounded and prisoners.

might have regulated such an occupation. No precautions of any kind had been taken to curb the disorders going on outside the Kremlin. In addition, as with all large towns, there was a huge mass of people from the lower classes prepared to act as guides and assist the invaders in the hope of sharing in the spoils. These circumstances combined to ensure that as they sought out places to live and things to eat and drink, the soldiers broke into a great number of closed and deserted houses and shops.

The pillaging had begun in food shops and those selling wine and spirits, but it rapidly spread to engulf private dwellings, public buildings and churches. In our camp alone there was a vast quantity of silver, enamelled gold, linen, precious gems and furs for the men to sleep on, and these were being brought in on a daily basis. In addition there was a whole mass of objects such as chairs, torches and so on, which the looters were forcing Russians, as drunk as themselves, to carry. Most of the objects were quickly snatched up by dealers, who paid ridiculous prices and appeared out of nowhere. So it was that starvation quickly gave way to excess. Our camps were overflowing with fresh and preserved meats, smoked fish, wine, rum, cognac and so on. Around each fire the men were cooking, eating and, especially, drinking. The arrival of each new consignment of pillaged items was met with loud cheers.

I also saw Russians and Russian wounded being brought in. Most of the unwounded Russians were doubtlessly professional thieves who had lingered on to take their share of the spoil, but there were also, unfortunately, some people who had stayed behind and had been beaten up attempting to protect their property.

This widespread disorder slowly began to diminish as the troops had their fill and saw that the looters were bringing back useless baubles. A monastery close by the city walls had largely been spared due to the fact that our general was quartered there. Even so large inroads were made on the good monks' larders and cellars. One of the monks was roughly handled when he attempted to prevent this abuse and he told me that such sacrilege could only bring us bad luck and that all the priests and monks would now be marching at the head of the Russian troops with crucifixes held high, himself included. I wished him happy hunting and left.

The most serious consequence of the looting was that we were now to reap the full benefits of the disorder we had been sowing ever since crossing the Niemen. When order was finally re-established, there still remained bad characters in each unit who would steal away at night to continue marauding. Others, perhaps still worse, never even rejoined the ranks. Right up to the evacuation of Moscow there were some five or six thousand of this kind, who we knew by the name of 'loners'. These would swell the ranks of marauding bands and these bands reached monstrous proportions during the misfortunes of the retreat. So much so that the marauders ultimately outnumbered men bearing arms.

Much has been said on the causes of the fire which broke out in Moscow. I restrict myself to relating what I actually saw. I was at the time either in our camp or in the mill next to it, from which the whole city could be surveyed. I can vouch that from the evening of the 14th to the night of the 15th of September there were no warnings of that which was to follow. I certainly did not hear the shots supposed, by many writers, to have been signals to the incendiaries to start fires. On the 15th, around noon, we heard an explosion in the south-west of the city. It was one of V Corps' ammunition wagons blowing up. A similar accident occurred later that afternoon on the Kaluga road. There was no question of these explosions being anything other than accidents. They were in the wrong part of the city and the smoke was white – which is certainly not the case when houses are on fire. That evening a series of fires broke out but were easily contained. It was only on the 16th that the real inferno began in the centre of Moscow, fanned by strong, seasonal winds. This conflagration made horrendous progress in but a short space of time. From our vantage point, where all the officers of the division were gathered, the whole city seemed submerged in a sea of flames. The rest is well known.[132]

Much, too, has been made of Napoleon's error in staying in this half-desolated city whilst hoping that his enemies would sue for peace. I have always considered that the Emperor, even in the midst of the ruins, still had time to avert disaster by proclaiming the establishment of Poland and by sending Poniatowski to Minsk. He, combined with Bronikowski's[133] and Dombrowski's[134] divisions, would have obliged the Austrians to act vigorously and frustrate Tormasov[135] and Tchichagov.[136] These troops would then have served to reinforce Napoleon at the Beresina and this alone could have changed the course of the campaign. But Napoleon feared that such actions would forever render Alexander his implacable enemy, as though he was not already.

---

[132] It is generally accepted that the fire broke out on the night of 15–16 September.

[133] Bronikowski's small force was garrisoning Minsk and Dombrowski's division and a cavalry detachment was operating around Mohilev and Minsk in support of the Austrians, on the southern flank of Napoleon's extended lines of communication.

[134] General Dombrowski (1755–1818) had some 5,000 Poles under his command.

[135] Generallieutenant Tormasov (1752–1819) had commanded the 3rd Army of the West and had been engaged in operations against the Austrians and Saxons on Napoleon's southern flank.

[136] Admiral Tchichagov commanded the Russian Army of the Danube. This formation was making its way northwards from present day Romania after war with the Turks had been brought to an end at the Peace of Bucharest.

CHAPTER XLIII

∽

LEAVING MOSCOW – PURSUING THE RUSSIANS – MISSION TO THE
KREMLIN – DANGER IN THE STREETS OF MOSCOW – RETURN TO
THE REGIMENT – MILITARY MANOEUVRES – A DANGEROUS
RECONNAISSANCE – A SKIRMISH – ROSTOPCHINE'S CHÂTEAU – ITS
INSCRIPTION

On the evening of the 16th, Claparède's division received the order to
march to Panki, and shadow the retreating enemy. I remained behind for
a few hours longer so as to 'gather in the stragglers, organise the food
stockpile, put the baggage in order and rejoin the division as soon as
possible'. Carrying out this task took me until midnight. One of the last
pillagers to rejoin the ranks just before we moved out was one of my
voltigeurs, a certain Jedrzyewski, who was very brave under fire but ill-
disciplined. As he was so drunk that he was quite unable to stand, I felt it
necessary to administer a few blows of the cane to sober him up. This
punishment, although prohibited in the French Army, found much favour
among the auxiliaries of the French. I never suspected that, in less than
three months time, this scoundrel would save my life.

We had been marching for quite a while when I received a message from
the colonel suggesting we take a short cut by which I could rejoin the
regiment that bit quicker. Despite being some three miles from Moscow
I could easily read this letter in the light of the fire raging in the city. We
rejoined the regiment the following day. The division moved towards
Riazan, south-east of Moscow, where there was neither sight nor sound of
the enemy. On the 20th we camped at Miaczkovo and crossed the Moskva
the next day. A Russian, bearing a flag of truce, had appeared as early as the
17th and now, on the 21st, another one advanced towards us. Many of my
fellow-officers believed these were signs of an imminent peace, but the
older officers were not the least bit convinced. Up to that point we had only
seen a few cossacks and some armed peasants.

On the 22nd I was charged with carrying some despatches to the
Emperor in the Kremlin. I had to make my way through the still burning

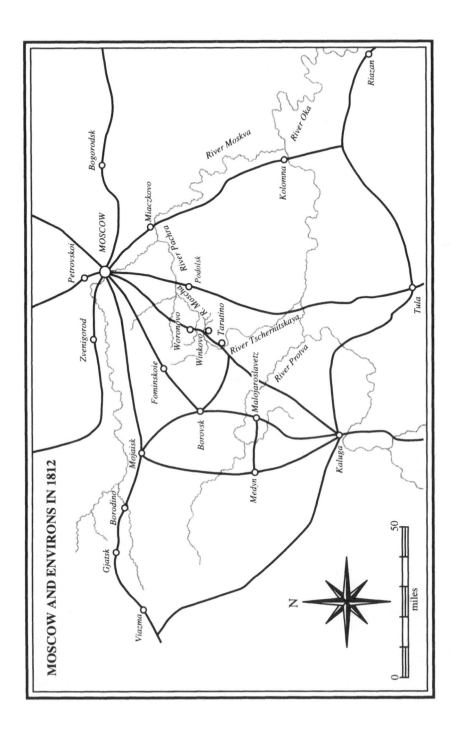

MOSCOW AND ENVIRONS IN 1812

Riazan

River Oka

River Moskva

Kolomna

Bogorodsk

Miaczkovo

River Pachra

MOSCOW

Podolsk

Petrovskoi

R. Moscha

Tarutino

Woronovo

Winkovo

River Tschernitskaya

Zvenigorod

Tula

Fominskoie

River Protva

Malojaroslavetz

Borovsk

Mojaisk

Kaluga

Borodino

Medyn

Gjatsk

Viazma

N

miles

0   50

and smoking city, not without some danger to myself. In a few places the smoke was so black and acrid that it was impossible both to breathe and to see even a few paces ahead. I probably would not have got out of this situation quite so quickly had I not had the good fortune to come across a Russian, who seemed dead drunk, but who, when shown a rouble, revived somewhat and lead me to the square before the Kremlin.

I found the Emperor wearing his habitual clothes reviewing the Old Guard in one of the Kremlin's courtyards just as he might have done at the Tuileries. I was bombarded with questions by the staff, who were astonished that we had been sent to Riazan as they thought we were near Tula to the south of Moscow. Count Monthion[137] interrogated me on all that I had seen and seemed especially interested in whether I considered the armed peasants we had seen to be the nucleus of some 'national uprising'.[138]

Before leaving I partook of some excellent breakfast in a restaurant located just outside the Kremlin. I had some beefsteak with potatoes, a bottle of wine and some coffee, all for the reasonable price of eight francs. The owner told me all about the fire and the looting, which was still going on in some quarters. I have since read about the details of these terrible events in many books. On the way back I again found myself in considerable danger in the smouldering ruins and on several occasions had to force my way, pistol in hand, through drunken gangs of looters.

When I got back, General Claparède, snugly installed in a small country house two miles distant from Moscow, welcomed me with unusual warmth. Inevitably I had to undergo a further interrogation as to the situation in Moscow. My colonel, an intelligent man with gifted foresight, told me of his fears, which would soon be seen as all well justified. He had been attached, since Smolensk, to Imperial Headquarters and had had frequent opportunity to overhear discussions between Berthier, Murat, Duroc,[139] Daru,[140] Narbonne[141] and others who had all tried in vain to prevent this rash march on Moscow. According to him we were now involved in a war

---

[137] Count Bailly de Monthion was the chief of staff at Imperial Headquarters.

[138] The anxiety of the staff at the report of armed peasants was very real. For some time, Murat had been reporting back to Napoleon that he had found the peasants discontented with their Russian masters and talking openly of gaining their freedom – by supporting the French.

[139] General Geraud Duroc (1772–1813), Duke of Frioul, was a close friend of Napoleon's and his Grand Marshal of the Palace. He was killed by a cannonball at Gorlitz in Saxony in May 1813.

[140] Count Pierre Bruno Daru (1767–1829) was a competent administrator and served as Napoleon's *intendant-général*.

[141] General Count Louis de Narbonne (1755–1813) was one of Napoleon's aides-de-camp and reputedly an illegitimate son of Louis XV.

of space and time and in an analogous situation with that of two centuries before when the Poles, in the wake of brilliant victories, had similarly occupied Smolensk and then Moscow. However, the Russians had rallied their forces at Tula and Kaluga, returned to the fight and compelled the Poles to retreat.[142] The colonel was afraid that not only would we have to do the same but that our retreat would also be intercepted, as indeed it was.

We decamped on the 24th and headed in a westerly direction, back into the valley of the Pachra, a tributary of the Moskva. After a long and arduous march we made camp close to a little wood. We spent two days here, pushing out detachments in all directions in an attempt to gain information on the whereabouts of the enemy. The enemy, however, was just as keen to find out where we were and appeared on the evening of the 26th. Russian cavalry detachments gambolled around in front of us and a battery of artillery sent us a few rounds, which we repaid with interest. On the 27th we were on the move at an early hour and soon closed with the enemy, who unmasked a considerable body of cavalry. There followed a series of skirmishes in which artillery played the dominant part. The Russians retreated when they saw we were about to launch a general assault.

We returned to camp at four, close to Czerkovitsa. I was sent out with three companies with orders to lay an ambush as the terrain was wooded and suitable for this kind of surprise.

It was as well we were on the alert as we managed to fall on three regiments of enemy cavalry as they were retreating; these, when they saw how many men I had available, then rallied and came back at us. I had the choice of two possible places to take refuge: either in a wood, which was closer to our camp, consisting of young trees set quite far apart and thus making the wood penetrable even to formed cavalry; or a really dense copse some distance from our camp. I did not hesitate long and we threw ourselves into the copse. I deployed my men in skirmish order and we directed a well maintained fire against the cavalry as they charged at the wood they supposed we had taken refuge in. We brought down some fifteen men. The Russians had charged flat out but now wheeled about and sped off in the opposite direction. This sudden departure made me think that they might have seen something moving near our camp and, a few moments later as we were on the way back, we came across the king of Naples in person at the head of a brigade of cavalry.

---

[142] The Poles, under Zolkiewski, had besieged Smolensk in September 1609. It had fallen to them after a siege of twenty-one months. They went on to capture Moscow and were only ejected in 1612, when the Russian nobles put an end to their factional bickering, united their forces and launched a devastating attack against the Poles and Lithuanians.

We spent another two days in this position, seeking out the bulk of the enemy's forces in vain and, as the soldiers said, in effect wearing ourselves out. We came across plenty of cossacks: they seemed to be multiplying on a daily basis. They never put up a fight against the infantry but stopped our cavalry from foraging and reduced them to inaction by exhausting them.

On the 29th, whilst Poniatowski was gaining an important success at Cyrkovo, we ourselves were involved in a serious vanguard action in which Murat placed himself in great danger. It was already quite late and the cossacks were biting at our heels. The king of Naples wanted to charge them with a body of cavalry. The cossacks fled as most of our cavalry went into the attack. Suddenly they swung about and fell upon Murat, who was close behind them and ahead of his own troops. 'Now, Czar, you won't get away!' they cried, and Murat and his weak escort had to save themselves in flight. Murat, with his own hand, killed many of the pursuers. But two very well-mounted cossacks came on and would have finished him off in this unequal struggle had not a Polish captain, a cousin of our colonel's called Malszewski then serving as Murat's interpreter, fallen on the cossacks, killed one and put the other to flight. The king at once proclaimed him a baron and a member of his order with an annual income of thousands of francs. These were privileges my compatriot would never fully enjoy, as the events of 1815[143] swept away order, title and income!

Claparède's division, held in reserve for the first half of the campaign, now came into its own and passed into the front line. In conjunction with Dufour[144] and Poniatowski's corps, operating around Tula, we achieved more than Murat and Sebastiani[145] ever had.

On 2 October we clashed with the enemy's rearguard, as ever commanded by the 'Russian Murat' – Miloradovitch.[146] As we waited for a bridge to be thrown over the Moscha, Sebastiani rode up and demanded, 'Voltigeurs! Since when have you ever needed a bridge to cross such a stream as this?' So we all threw ourselves into this stream, which came up to our necks and in which one man was even drowned. Thanks to the assistance of some Polish horse artillery, in white cloaks, the enemy were thrown out of the village of Islova-Michalova, which they had fortified, and

---

[143] Murat lost his throne to an Austrian army in 1815. Murat's order was the Royal Order of the Two Sicilies.

[144] General Dufour commanded a brigade in Friant's division of I Corps.

[145] General Horace Sebastiani (1772–1851) commanded a division in the II Reserve Cavalry Corps until the death of General Montbrun at Borodino. He then assumed command of that corps but proved a poor replacement.

[146] General Mikhail Miloradovitch (1770–1835) commanded the Russian advance guard at this time and proved a gallant and enterprising officer.

another position a little further on. As a consequence the Russians fell back behind the town of Woronovo.

Here Rostopchine[147] had his famous country house, which he had burnt down with his own hands. The main part of the building and the out-houses where nothing more than ruins. A single tower, surmounted by a huge effigy of a horse, was all that had escaped the destruction. At what had once been the entrance to the château a huge placard hung bearing the following inscription in French in huge letters: 'I have burnt down my château which cost me a million so that no French dog may lodge there.'

Thousands of people read this inscription, as I did myself, and can vouch that this was the real wording. I can also say that much later I was able to re-read the inscription in the house of a former officer of my regiment, called Madalinski, who had carried off the placard and exhibited it in his own home.

Incidentally, the town of Woronovo also went up in flames.

---

[147] Count Fedor Rostopchine (1763–1826) was governor of Moscow and largely responsible for the fires which burnt the city down. He was also a writer of some note and the author of two comedies and other plays.

235

CHAPTER XLIV

BLOODY, BUT INDECISIVE, BATTLE ON 4 OCTOBER – MURAT AND OUR
REGIMENT – I AM SERIOUSLY WOUNDED – A RUSSIAN VISITING CARD –
TRANSPORTED TO MOSCOW

Throughout the whole of 3 October, we continued our march hard on the
heels of the Russian rearguard. On the evening of the same day we occupied
a village which had not yet been completely evacuated and we took some
baggage and a certain number of sick and wounded. The next morning we
encountered very serious resistance which began after the passage of the
Tschernitskaja. This was the last battle of the campaign I actually fought
in and artillery again played a large part in this well-contested battle, something which revealed more than ever our weakness both in this arm and in
cavalry. Such was the consequence of the terrible condition of our horses,
something Murat himself was well aware of. He was riding past one of our
infantry regiments, which was formed in square because of the presence of
Russian cavalry, when he came over to talk to the major of our second
battalion, a man he was on good terms with, and said, 'It is just like being
in Egypt!'

The infantry always respected Murat because of his bearing and his
outstanding bravery, but the officers of his own arm were very critical of
him, saying: 'He is a good soldier, but he has ruined our cavalry.'

As battle was joined our voltigeurs and those of the 94th Line bravely
dashed across the Tschernitskaja under Russian artillery fire. The enemy
fell back a little to take up better positions from which their artillery, well
placed and numerous, raked us again and again. A battalion of the 94th,
which was taking severe punishment, fell back and became entangled with
one of ours and there was, for a moment, total confusion. Whilst this was
going on I was grazed by some canister which knocked off my shako and
struck me with such force that I fell from my horse. Order was soon restored and the battle raged all along the line with mixed success. Russian
cavalry charges broke against our squares, but when we wanted to advance,

we found that their artillery fire was much too strong for us and had to retreat.

Towards the end of the battle, when it seemed as if we had finally made a breakthrough, Murat appeared and attempted to lead a body of cavalry, which until then had sat idly by, into a charge. His squadrons were decimated by the Russian artillery, and the enemy, seeing the cavalry falter and hoping to capture Murat, launched a vigorous counter-attack. Murat and one of his staff officers had to seek shelter in the square of the nearest infantry regiment – ours. A mass of heavy cavalry bore down on us at the gallop but at around fifty paces suddenly reined in. There followed a moment of terrible silence, broken only by the horses gasping for breath. Then, seeing from our posture that no good would come of charging home, the Russians wheeled about and cantered off in the direction they had come as smartly as on a parade ground.

Murat warmly congratulated the 2nd Regiment of the Vistula Legion on its steadiness which, he said, he would not fail to bring to the attention of the Emperor. He reminded us of the occasion some time later – to be precise in the August of 1813. I was part of a newly formed Polish regiment which had incorporated most of the survivors of the old Vistula Legion[148] who had, like me, sworn to follow the fortunes of France to the last. As we marched out of Dresden, passing under the windows of Murat's residence he recognised our colonel, none other than the old colonel of the 2nd Regiment of the Vistula Legion. He shouted out the order to halt and rushed down to shake the colonel by the hand and then pass through our ranks, happy, so he said, to be among his 'brave brothers in arms' of which, it must be said, there were very few left.

On 4 October 1812 I hoped that I might at last be able to get treatment for the head wound I had received on the previous day's fighting. But fate decided otherwise and the colonel had me take two companies of voltigeurs forward to follow up the Russian cavalry's withdrawal. We were also obliged to throw a detachment of infantry out of a nearby wood they still held. I had the charge sounded and we dashed forwards into the dense thicket. The Russians fell back before us, firing all the time and doing us considerable damage. I got a ball lodged in my ankle and two other officers were seriously wounded. Our regiment alone had lost 268 men killed or wounded in this murderous but indecisive battle.

I was carried with the other wounded to a house in Winkovo. The ball was still in the wound and the surgeons, as they probed into the flesh, could only get fragments of it out. My leg was now terribly swollen. After the

---

[148] This was the two-battalion Vistula Regiment, formed from the debris of the Vistula Legion on 18 June 1813.

operation I fainted but was brought around brusquely by a strange uproar. A cannonball had smashed through the wall and bounced through the room without, thank goodness, having hurt anyone. 'It is a Russian visiting card,' said an officer of the 3rd Vistula Regiment, one of my companions in distress, 'they are always kind enough to announce their visits.'

I was taken to Moscow but the pain had rendered me only semi-conscious and I can scarcely recall anything of our long and difficult progress through the ruined suburbs or of my stay at the Saint-Paul Hospital, where a number of officers were convalescing.[149] I remember the officers leaning on crutches, huddled in the weak rays of autumnal sunshine in an effort to stay warm. I was well tended by a French officer who I myself had saved just a month before and had managed to have brought out alive from the Great Redoubt at Borodino. A good deed is sometimes repaid!

---

[149] The Saint-Paul Hospital was one of three French hospitals established in Moscow. It was evacuated on 22 October and those wounded who had been too ill to follow the retreating army, some 650 men, were abandoned to the Russians.

CHAPTER XLV

THE RETREAT BEGINS – BORODINO IN OCTOBER 1812 – SMOLENSK –
ORSCHA – BORISOV – THE RUSSIANS ATTACK AND CAPTURE THE
BORISOV BRIDGE – THE WOUNDED RETREAT TO BOBR – CHAOS IN BOBR
– OUR STAY AT BOBR – THE IMPERIAL GUARD ARRIVES

I had just undergone another operation in which my wound was again probed for fragments of lead, when news came through that the army was preparing to quit Moscow and that the 400 wounded officers and 12,000 sick and wounded men were to be evacuated with all speed to Smolensk. I was included in the first convoy, a fact to which I probably owe my life.[150]

We left on the 14th. I was in a coach with two other officers of my regiment, one of whom, an officer in my old voltigeur company, had been wounded at the same time as myself. For the first few days of the journey I suffered terribly but the jolting of the carriage evidently shook out the last of the *foreign bodies* and I began to experience a gradual lessening of the pain. In fact I was able to move my toes for the first time.

By the time the convoy reached the field of Borodino I was sufficiently recovered to take note of my surroundings and observe at close hand this cursed place, still covered in corpses. From the heights overlooking the battlefield the huge mounds, which marked the site of the mass graves, looked like an immense flock of giant sheep. The air was cold and a few flakes of that snow which was to prove so fatal to us had already begun to fall and lent an even more depressing tone to the already morbid scene.

The Kolozkoi Abbey, close by the battlefield, was garrisoned by Polish troops who welcomed us as next of kin. The same happened at Viazma, where we bumped into the third battalion of our regiment, a battalion I had

---

[150] General Etienne Nansouty (1768–1815) was assigned as commander of this convoy on 10 October. He himself had been wounded above the knee at Borodino.

helped organise and train at the start of the campaign.[151] The convoy spent a whole day in this town and I took advantage of the halt to practise walking on crutches. I quickly mastered the art.

We continued on for Smolensk, escorted by 300 men of the third battalion under a captain called Wandorf who was a veteran of the Egyptian campaign. He was a short, lively and intelligent man who was also rather plump but fulfilled his duties superbly.

On 4 November at some time in the afternoon we entered Smolensk in the midst of falling snow. In twenty-one days we had travelled 250 miles. Here, too, we came across some of our compatriots who had fought in Spain and who looked after us well.[152] The Poles were billeted in some houses abandoned ever since the French occupation and they procured food by combing the countryside for supplies. However, there were already dangerous signs of insurrection and resistance in the outlying districts.

We had hoped to have been left to recover fully in this town, which seemed to offer excellent winter quarters for the troops returning from Moscow. But this delusion only lasted a few hours and sinister rumours were already circulating. There was talk of the main Russian army marching on Smolensk, via Kaluga. Some talked of our lines of communication having been cut between Smolensk and the Dneiper. Smolensk itself had neither the necessary stocks of food nor arms and munitions to sustain troops over the winter and no measures had been taken for the convoys of wounded which were passing through and were obliged to fend for themselves.

So it became necessary for us to move on, which we did on the 7th, escorted by a battalion of Poles sent off towards Krasnoi to secure our communications and rally stragglers. Some 200 of the wounded and crippled took advantage of the protection they offered and came with us. Wandorf was authorised to accompany us with his unit as far as the Dnieper, as cossacks were known to operate in these parts. We said farewell to this good man on the 9th at Dobruvna. 'My good friends,' he said, 'the Devil will eat us all up in this cursed country. You have the good fortune to be leaving and might still see our homeland. For me, it is all over; pass on my warm wishes to my family at Kalisch and tell them where you saw me last. God be with you, my friends!' Fortunately, Wandorf was no Rakowski and we later saw him safe and sound at Vilna.

At Orscha, which we reached on the 10th, chaos ruled. There were

---

[151] The third battalions of the Vistula Legion had not been sent far into Russia but had remained behind to garrison Smolensk, on account of the conscripts being deemed too young.
[152] The Poles at Smolensk were the 4th Polish Line, part of IX Corps.

rumours of a defeat near Minsk and of the imminent arrival of the Russians. The commandant of the town was General Jomini, so famous for his defection in 1813 and for his military writings.[153] At that time he was out on a reconnaissance and, in his absence, the place had gone to the dogs. As we were informed that all who were capable of marching had been sent on to Borisov, via Toloczyn and Bobr, we decided to follow that road which, even then, was covered with hordes of stragglers. The journey passed without incident until we reached Borisov on the 15th. It was there that the real ordeal began.

We were lodged with a Pole, a veteran of Kosciuszko's armies, who received us as well as he was able. We made our arrangements to continue our journey the next day, but man proposes and God, and sometimes the Devil, disposes!

On the following morning, when we gathered in the market place, there was considerable anxiety as some fugitives had come into the town after their convoy had been attacked on the far side of the Beresina, close to Borisov. They brought news that our communications with Minsk and Vilna had been cut and that there was no way of getting over the Beresina! We were astonished, having thought that the worst of our troubles were behind us.

We stayed rooted to the spot at Borisov for the next very difficult six days, waiting for our fate to be decided. During this enforced halt I exercised daily on my crutches and something told me that I would very soon have to rely on this means of transport. The situation grew more gloomy from one hour to the next. We saw General Bronikowski arrive, whom the Russians had easily kicked out of Minsk, capturing its stores of munitions (a terrible loss).[154] He was followed by General Dombrowski, with his tiny division, entrusted with guarding the Dnieper. The performance of these generals has been heavily censured and it has been said that Bronikowski was better at organising dinners than war and had been well and truly surprised. It has also been said that Dombrowski, who arrived here just twenty-four hours before the enemy, had lost precious time in escorting his wife to Mohilev and I find these accusations repeated in Prodzynski's *Journal*, an eye-witness to the events.

Meanwhile the town was filling up with refugees of all types: the cadres

---

[153] Jomini was not, in fact, governor of Orsha, although he had briefly, and unsuccessfully, served as governor of Vilna. Orsha was governed by the Marquis d'Alorna administering the Mohilev district, and Jomini had only been passing through on a mission from Imperial Headquarters.

[154] Minsk and its massive collection of supplies fell to the Russian general Lambert on 17 November.

of regiments in the process of forming, Lithuanian and Ruthenian emigrants and a clutter of scoundrels who filled the cafés and bars and did nothing but drink and play at cards. The most extreme form of anarchy ruled in this confusion and we were frequently obliged to brandish our pistols in order to preserve our host from unwelcome visits. His house was not in the town itself but on a neighbouring hill which dominated the Beresina. From there we could see the hasty measures taken to defend the Borisov bridge which, to us, seemed most ineffective. We therefore deemed it wise not to wait on the results of the battle but to head back to Bobr. Our concerns proved to be fully justified, as the Russians soon made themselves masters of both the town and of the bridge.[155] We took leave of our host, who we thought we would never see again and a few days later, as we came back to Borisov with the remnants of the army, I saw his house had been devastated and the doors and windows torn off. The owner had gone and, for all I knew, was probably dead.

Our retreat to Bobr had all the qualities of a rout. Isolated stragglers, who at such moments usually ganged together the better to commit evil deeds, exploited the anxiety caused by the sound of cannon coming from the Beresina. They would shout, 'Watch out! Cossacks!' or imitate their cry of '*Hourrah!*' and give the staggering columns of men a shove, and so improve their opportunity to pillage at leisure in the abandoned wagons.

We arrived in Bobr very late and everything was in the most extreme disorder. My two comrades and I managed to get ourselves lodged in a hideous shack only after the most difficult struggle. Our accommodation was very expensive and right on the edge of the town and belonged to a Russian who had once served in the artillery and whose wife was one of the dirtiest women I have ever laid eyes on. The following day I was naïve enough to give the man a tip before he had gone shopping on our behalf and he came back dead drunk, unable to stand, muttering gibberish and without our supplies. As I could now move about relatively easily on my crutches, I volunteered to go and see what I could find, whilst my two fellow officers kept a close guard on our carriage and two horses which would have disappeared in an instant had we not taken such precautions.

It was now that I came across the first signs of the true extent of the calamity that had befallen us. The streets and houses were choked with large numbers of strangely-attired people who had come from the direction of Smolensk and were but one day's march ahead of the Imperial Guard and the Emperor. The necessity of preserving oneself from the bitter cold

---

[155] The Russians under Lambert – who was wounded in the battle – took Borisov on 21 November. The next day, as the French counter-attacked, they burnt the bridge over the Beresina.

easily explained their bizarre dress but what was most shocking was that all these men, the strange vanguard of the *Grande Armée*, were unarmed despite apparently not having suffered from the ill effects of hunger and misery. They gathered round placards which had recently been nailed up and which promised severe punishment for stragglers, but seemed unperturbed by such warnings. Others, having deserted their regiments and severed all links with discipline, had kept their arms but only so that they could pillage at leisure. These marauders were the most dangerous kind.

This utter demoralisation was taking place openly and blatantly in a place where the Emperor was expected to arrive at any minute and was sufficient to demonstrate that the army, to all intents and purposes, no longer existed. I even heard that the Elite Gendarmes had been obliged to use their swords to turf people out of a house the Emperor was to occupy.

I was in the midst of this confusion for some time, seeking news of the army and especially news of Claparède's division. I eventually managed to collar an Imperial Guard officer who informed me that my division was escorting the treasury and trophies and, it seemed, would shortly arrive. I told him that the Russians were now masters of the Borisov bridge over the Beresina – news which came as a considerable surprise to him.

After suffering terribly from the cold the night before and disgusted by our host's shameful antics, we sought out a more comfortable abode the following morning. After searching hard, we stumbled across a stable where many more wounded lay prostrate on the straw amidst thick smoke. However, we were not to be left in peace for long. Some staff officers soon put in an appearance and began clearing out a space for the Prince of Neufchâtel and his suite.[156] This was the cause of some bitter squabbling and the officers were about to threaten to evict the wounded by force if they did not comply. Many of the poor wounded cried out that they would prefer to die and should be killed on the spot rather than be thrown out. Berthier's arrival put an end to all this as he said he would be content to have just one room and a corridor for the duty officers.

Having Berthier as a neighbour was most disagreeable. There were comings and goings all night long which prevented us from getting a wink of sleep. During these long hours of insomnia we exchanged views on the present and on the future, which were, inevitably, of the most serious nature.

I compared our situation to that of our halt here in August when we had marched, in high spirits and full of confidence, under Davout's command.

---

[156] Prince of Neufchâtel was Berthier's official title. Neufchâtel had once been Prussian territory but had been confiscated by Napoleon.

I recalled to mind a quotation from Busset which seemed expressly made to fit our situation: 'What a state to be in!'

On the next day, as we left the stable, we gained some reassurance and confidence when we caught sight of some soldiers still bearing arms and in an unmistakably military posture. The Emperor had arrived and had lodged in the house I and my fellow officers had occupied during our advance in August. It was a modest single-storey building with a porch supported by two wooden columns. Two grenadiers of the Old Guard stood sentry on either side of the door. A picket of some forty of these 'grumblers', more grumbling than ever, were stationed in front of the house. In their tattered uniforms these veterans still preserved the dignity of France and kept true to the prestige of discipline. Their expressions bore the brand of a resolution that would allow them to defy even the greatest of calamities.

CHAPTER XLVI

My Regiment Arrives – We Leave With it – From Bobr to
Studienka – The Crossing of the Beresina

In our terrible situation the arrival of Claparède's division in Bobr on 24
November provided a much needed boost to our flagging morale. Reduced
to less than a thousand bayonets, our soldiers still had a military bearing
worthy of the Old Guard itself. We were reunited in a display of warmth
and fraternal feeling. Captain Lichnowski, who had always been pessimistic
about this campaign, said, 'You never wanted to listen to us. But now see
what has come about. And it is not over yet; in fact, it has only just begun!'
How right he was! He himself was killed just three days later.

Early on the following morning the division set off in the direction of
Borisov and we went with them. The colonels had done all in their power
to look after the wounded and the serious cases had been loaded onto
wagons. The lightly wounded and the officers were having to follow on as
best they could. Our baggage, as with all baggage, was limited to only the
barest essentials.

Despite my as yet unhealed wound, I was delighted to be back amongst
my comrades. I had always been aware that sooner or later I would be
required to march and I had prepared myself as much as possible for the
ordeal. I had brought with me from Moscow a gigantic and superb fur
which, however, was too heavy for an invalid and so I swapped it for a
caftan coat. I swathed my crutches in lambskin and bought a huge piece
of cloth from a soldier to serve as a scarf, to wrap around my neck and
head.

On the evening of the 26th, after a long and difficult march and in
weather which was clear but cold, we came to a halt just outside Borisov.
At ten, when the snow began falling heavily, the order came through to
advance. After passing through Borisov, we stuck close to the banks of the
Beresina and followed it upstream until we reached a village. We halted
there for perhaps fifteen minutes. On the far bank we could see the glare of

245

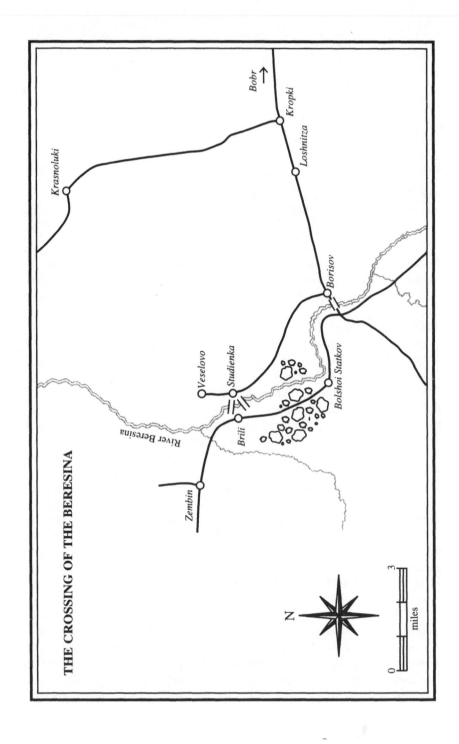

THE CROSSING OF THE BERESINA

Bobr

Kropki

Loshnitza

Krasnoluki

Borisov

Veselovo

Studienka

Bolshoi Statkov

River Beresina

Brili

Zembin

N

miles

0   3

Russian campfires. The snow continued to fall, and we sank into it up to our ankles. We were again ordered to move forwards. Our superior officers had been kept in complete ignorance as to the meaning of these movements and still believed that Napoleon would attempt to repair the Borisov bridge and cross there.

Finally, after stopping and starting our silent march, we arrived, just as dawn was breaking, in a hamlet consisting of some twenty houses and ringed by the amphitheatre of hills which dominate the Beresina. This was the famous village of Studienka. We suddenly caught sight of the two bridges jutting out into that terrible river and this sight, despite our sufferings, caused feelings of the deepest joy and admiration.[157]

We took up a position a short distance from the village. Not long after I saw the Emperor and quite a few of his marshals and generals coming out of a house. Napoleon was deep in discussion with one of them who stood before the Emperor with his hat in his hand. It was the heroic General Eblé.[158] Napoleon's face was as unreadable as ever. He was wearing a grey fur coat which was unbuttoned and revealed his habitual uniform beneath. Murat never allowed circumstances to prevent the wearing of the most outlandish costumes and was today attired in a fur cap surmounted by a huge plume. He came towards us and exchanged a few words with our colonel. A scar on his face from a sabre wound he had received at Aboukir, and which was not normally visible, had been accentuated by the cold and was now rather obvious.[159] 'What do you propose doing with your wounded?' he asked our colonel. 'They will come along as best they can,' replied the colonel. 'Here is the officer who so bravely led the attack on 4 October,' he continued, indicating me as he did so. 'I'll do my best to keep him at my side!'

'It was a brilliant feat of arms,' said the king, 'a brave attack. I shall remember him and will honour him with a decoration when we are through all this.' Naturally, I never received the decoration. The brave and unlucky king of Naples would, from that time on, have too many other preoccupations.

---

[157] It came as a complete surprise to most of the French and the Russians that two bridges had been completed north of Borisov. Napoleon led the Russians to believe that he would force a crossing at Borisov, but then rapidly transferred his available troops onto the west bank of the Beresina before the Russians realised their mistake.

[158] General Jean-Baptiste Eblé (1758–1812) commanded the *Grande Armée*'s bridging train and saved the remnants of that force by the miraculous construction of the two bridges over the Beresina. He died of exhaustion in Germany in late 1812.

[159] Murat was wounded by a sabre cut from the *Seraskier* (Governor) of Roumelia at the battle of Aboukir on 25 July 1799 during Bonaparte's Egyptian campaign.

Berthier and the Viceroy[160] were wearing fur coats. Ney, easily recognisable by his reddish features[161] and lively manner, wore a dark green overcoat. I also recognised Mortier, who stood out from the rest because of his height, Narbonne, with his hair powdered and in a queue just as it would have been at Versailles, Duroc, one of the Emperor's most faithful companions, and many others besides.

Meanwhile, it had stopped snowing, the cold had eased off slightly and it promised to be a fine day. It must have been around ten o'clock when our division, deployed in columns, began to cross the Beresina.

Our carriage was following on behind but was stopped by gendarmes posted by the bridge[162] who told everyone to 'get out as coaches can go no further'. We had to walk, relinquishing our carriage which had served us so well since Smolensk and which we would never see again. The gendarmes, however, had not finished. 'Only combatants can cross,' they told us, blocking our way forwards. 'This is absurd!' I cried, 'you can not confuse wounded with stragglers, damn it!' My eloquent words would probably have been wasted on them had not a superior officer taken our side and have them make us an exception to the rule by insisting that we were 'attached to the regiment that had just crossed'. All the vehicles abandoned on that side of the river fell into the hands of the enemy and this was a savage blow indeed for the wounded.

At this point the Beresina was at least fifty paces wide and was from eight to ten paces deep and bore drifting ice floes along in its current. The planks of the bridge were by no means even and when we crossed some of the planks were already missing, especially as we drew closer to the far bank. There the entire bridge was below the water-level and we had water up to our ankles.

From the point of view of aesthetics, the bridge certainly lacked a great deal. But when one considers under what conditions the bridge was constructed and that it undoubtedly saved the French Army from total catastrophe, and that for each life sacrificed in its construction a thousand lives were saved, then it is obvious that this bridge was the most sublime achievement of the war – perhaps of any war.

---

[160] Eugene de Beauharnais (1781–1824), Viceroy of Italy, commanded IV Corps and, after the departure of Napoleon and Murat, the entire *Grande Armée*.
[161] Ney was nicknamed *Le Rougeant* because of his red hair.
[162] On 22 November a staff officer and fifty gendarmes were given the task of burning superfluous vehicles to release horses for the artillery. Some 25,000 vehicles were either lost or abandoned by the French in Russia.

CHAPTER XLVII

FROM THE BERESINA TO MOLODECZNO

What we had been through was but a small foretaste of what was to come.

My poor comrades of the Vistula Legion were camped in a wood on the right bank of the Beresina, and not very far from the bridges, when they received the order, sometime on the evening of the 27th, to follow Oudinot's Corps.[163] The wounded were told to stay where they were and await further instructions. From then on, until late into the night, we clearly heard the rumble of cannon-fire coming from the other bank. It was the noise of the battle which was deciding the fate of Partouneaux's division[164] after that division made a demonstration towards Borisov in an attempt to gain time to save the rest of the Army.

The next morning we heard a fresh cannonade from two directions at once. On the far bank, Victor[165] kept the Russians under Wittgenstein[166] at bay whilst on our side of the river the vanguard, consisting of a few thousand brave men from Oudinot's, Ney's and Poniatowski's corps, as well as from the Vistula Legion, took on Tchichagov's troops in that bloody but glorious struggle which reopened our escape route to Vilna.

All day long the wind brought the sound of distant cannon, the noise of which resembled trees falling in a forest.

At about noon we saw wounded men drifting back from the fighting and

---

[163] Marshal Nicolas Oudinot (1767–1847) commanded II Corps and it was his men who played a crucial role in fending off Russian attacks on the west bank of the Beresina.

[164] Partouneaux's division of IX Corps was cut off and forced to surrender on the east bank of the Beresina on the night of 26 November. It had taken the wrong road from Borisov and had been overwhelmed by Russian troops.

[165] Marshal Claude Victor-Perrin (1764–1841) commanded IX Corps, the rearguard of the French Army.

[166] Prince Wittgenstein (1769–1843) was of Prussian origin but serving in the Russian army. He captured Partouneaux's division and applied considerable pressure upon Victor's troops on the east bank of the Beresina.

learnt that the struggle was at its height. News was slow in coming and we were prey to all-consuming fears. We were told that Oudinot had been wounded and replaced by Ney. He had reviewed the Vistula Legion and sent it marching past the Emperor into action. The Emperor congratulated it on its good appearance and warlike attitude. Those about to die salute you!

The number of wounded coming back soon increased and they brought back the most sinister of rumours. They told us that most of the Vistula Legion's officers had been killed or wounded. Captain Rakowski, the wizard, was amongst the killed. So his prophecy really had come true. I have told previously of how he had foreseen his death, and handed his possessions over to an officer who was destined to survive the retreat.

Not long after, we saw that very officer, Major Regulski, arrive accompanied by Claparède. Both had been lightly wounded. Their presence here did not bode well for the fate of the rest of the Legion.

The noise of battle continued, but seemed to be growing fainter and fainter. Finally news came to us that a superb cavalry charge had swung the battle our way and victory was ours.[167]

Daylight was almost over when we received the order to march in the direction of Zembin, which we reached some time later. On the way there we passed over a long wooden bridge which had been laid over a vast stretch of marshy ground almost as wide as the Beresina itself. I failed to understand why the Russians had not even attempted to destroy this bridge.

At Zembin we came across fires lit by Davout's troops. The latter had crossed the Beresina the day after we had crossed. Here and there men were gathered around the fires, asleep – forever! We ourselves were just settling down when the cry went up, 'Look out! Here come the stragglers! Let's get going before it is too late!'

Our little column marched on, steadily reducing in numbers. As day approached, it grew colder. We passed a convoy of ammunition wagons onto which badly wounded men had been loaded. They begged us, as we marched past, to put an end to their sufferings.

Onwards, ever onwards. Anguish soon began to turn into despair. We were constantly tripping over officers and men who had fallen to rise no more. The sun was blood red and the cold was unbearable. We stopped at the entrance to a village where there were two fires burning. These were ringed by a crowd of people and we made room for ourselves by pulling out those men who were already dead. I had the good fortune of finding a

---

[167] General Doumerc's 400 cuirassiers destroyed a Russian division in a matter of moments and took 2,000 prisoners.

cooking pot. I melted some snow in it and added a little bread I had in one of my pockets. The resulting broth did me the power of good.

Only when you have undergone such an ordeal as this is it possible to understand the level to which we had been reduced by the overriding consideration of acquiring food. We were as beasts. Whilst we were digesting our meagre meal some soldiers from our regiment appeared and told us that the Legion had been wiped out at the Beresina, which was only too true, and that all the colonels and most of the other officers had been killed. Those men who were still fit and well had formed small bands around the regimental flags.[168]

We stayed where we were for a few hours, beset by the most depressing thoughts, until we made an effort, got up and continued on our way – arriving at Pleszenice quite late, having covered some twenty-five miles in the thirty hours since we had crossed the Beresina.

The town was full of soldiers, the dying and the dead. We were shown the house in which Marshal Oudinot had been wounded the previous evening as he had beaten off a cossack attack. The doors and windows were riddled with bullets.[169]

We spent the night in the town and after a dinner of grilled corn and horsemeat tried to snatch some sleep. But the memory of the terrible things I had seen, the heartfelt loss of my dead friends and bitter anxiety for what the future held in store for us kept sleep well at bay.

At one in the afternoon, in a wind that made our teeth chatter, we set off for Molodeczno guided by the lights of flickering fires found in each village along the way, stumbling along the edges of woods and constantly surrounded by that macabre mixture of the dead and the living. At times the road was marked by a trail of corpses and the calm and serene sky seemed a bitter contrast to the suffering down here below. The cold was getting worse and our small column diminished at every moment.

We caught sight of a steeple at around eight in the morning and the cry went up that it was Molodeczno! At last! But no! It was only Ilia, less than half-way to our intended destination!

Nevertheless, we found some straw in this village to rest on. Most of us were shaking and shivering so much that we found it impossible to sleep. We were obsessed with the idea that if we did fall asleep it would be forever.

---

[168] The regiments of the Vistula Legion, although entitled to carry Eagles, continued to carry standards first presented to the Polish Legions on 30 January 1800. The standard of the 2nd Regiment was carried by Lieutenant Niesceloki (appointed 19 June 1811) throughout the Russian campaign.
[169] Marshal Oudinot was wounded by splinter from a falling beam in a house he and a handful of staff and Italian guards were defending after being surprised at Pleszenice by General Lanskoi's cossacks.

This rest did us much good and we decided not to move on until night fell. We ate a meagre meal which I remember perfectly to this day. We had gruel followed by grilled wheat and a steak of horsemeat, all eaten without salt.

We also made use of this break to adjust our clothing and sort out our effects. We rearranged our bandages, a vital operation, and I wrapped the ragged piece of cloth I had bought at Borisov around my head and shoulders so that it covered my entire face, apart from my eyes. My skin was frozen and brittle from constant exposure. I also remember a good soldier bringing me a piece of leather in which I wrapped my wounded foot and protected it from frostbite.

Most, but not all, of us set out again around midnight. Some men were at the end of their strength and felt they could no longer continue. A voltigeur from my own company, and an excellent soldier, who had received a wound in his forearm, refused to move any further. 'Captain,' he said, 'either today or tomorrow, it is all the same, we'll all perish here!'

As we continued along we would occasionally stumble across half-extinguished campfires and, around these fires, corpses. Some had already been stripped naked but others wore the bizarre costumes described in so many histories of the retreat.

After a few hours' march along this trail of misery some of our group began to slow down and could not keep up. They soon passed out of view. It was impossible to wait for them here in the midst of this harsh terrain and withering cold. Had we done so, every last one of us would have died.

We came across a fire which was still burning brightly and made our camp accordingly. We stayed a long time but none of those who had fallen behind caught up and they have never been seen since.

CHAPTER XLVIII

FROM MOLODECZNO TO OSZMIANA

We reached Molodeczno on the morning of 1 December.[170] It was here that Napoleon, two days later, issued his famous 29th Bulletin.[171] Things seemed less affected than in all the towns we had passed through and I actually saw soldiers carrying their weapons and with a good military bearing. We lodged ourselves in some houses on the Smorgoni side of town and set about dealing with our central concern of subsistence.

I found a German soldier who proved willing, but not very willing, to sell some of his bread ration for the non-negotiable price of two napoleons.[172] With this bread, some fat and a little salt, I was able to make some broth which went down very well.

Some of our soldiers who had made it this far told us some of the harrowing details of the battle fought on 28 November. Many officers, such as Colonel Kousinowski, had worn furs on that day and had been indistinguishable from the Russians. This had led to a terrible mistake when French cuirassiers had fallen upon an infantry melée and sabred friend and foe alike.

The survivors of the Legion had tried to reform but as they had received no orders and their officers had been killed, they had simply tried to survive as best they might. Initially, they had marched together, but, as no rations had been issued, they found it impossible to keep together and were forced to disperse to increase their chances of survival.

---

[170] Brandt was only one day ahead of the French Army's vanguard. It arrived in Molodeczeno at 11 o'clock in the morning of 2 December. Napoleon arrived at 9 o'clock on 4 December.

[171] The 29th Bulletin was written by Napoleon, then lodged in Michel Oginski's château, on 1 December 1812. It finished with the notorious statement that 'His Majesty's health has never been better'.

[172] By the time the army crossed the Beresina the cost of food, according to an Italian officer, was always calculated in gold. He paid one *louis d'or* for a thin cut of pork in Molodeczeno.

We spent the whole of the day and the night at Molodeczno and only set out for Smorgoni on the 3rd. This was a terrible time indeed and we were assailed by a savage blizzard which, fortunately, was of short duration. Had it lasted much longer, we all would have died.

Amidst the wealth of awful sights and scenes I bore witness to in this horrible campaign there is one episode which stands out above all and about which I still cannot think without a shudder. As night fell we reached a village blocked by congestion in the streets. Not far away, however, we caught sight of a fire which still burnt brightly and which was only surrounded by a small number of corpses. The campsite seemed even better as it was shielded from the north wind by a kind of bank, covered over in snow. So the living settled down among the dead and made themselves as comfortable as possible. Those passing by envied our good fortune and some of them even tried to push in amongst us.

The night was calm and passed without incident but as we awoke and made ready to continue our journey the next morning we saw that the snow had been blown off the bank and had revealed thirteen dead soldiers piled one on top of the other and frozen solid. There were Frenchmen, Germans, Italians, Poles; all recognisable from their uniforms and all frozen in different postures and positions. Some had outstretched hands, as though still imploring help from passers by, and had obviously died in convulsive fits. 'They are beckoning us,' remarked one of my companions in misfortune, 'do not worry, we shall be joining you soon.'

A little further on a village had been engulfed in flames and another horrible sight met our eyes. The fire had caught hold in a huge barn in which a large number of unfortunates had been trapped and burnt to cinders. A horrible smoke, which reminded me of Saragossa, hung heavy around the ashes of this charnel house.

As we approached Smorgoni a sealed coach caught up and overtook us. This fast moving vehicle was preceded by a cavalry outrider dressed in green. Just after they had passed by the cavalryman sent a well directed blow with the flat of his sabre against a straggler who obstructed the road. I was told at Smorgoni that the Emperor had been in this coach.

From that point on we began to follow a plan of mine whereby we would steal away from the main road at night and camp as far from the route being followed by the army as possible. That night we found good lodgings with a man who was a famous bear trainer.

It was at least possible to buy the barest essentials at Smorgoni, even though the prices were exorbitant. I managed to buy bread, rice and a little coffee from an elderly Jewess, although she was reluctant to part with her wares. That evening we realised it had been eight days since we had crossed the Beresina – eight terrible days! We decided to spend the night, and get some rest, at Smorgoni and try to make it to Oszmiana for the evening of the following day. But we set off later than I had anticipated and the road proved particularly perilous. Even the most hearty among us began to lose hope. All we managed to do on that particular day was drag ourselves half way to Oszmiana and camp. We came across more dead than ever before on that stretch of the road and, for the first time, the bodies of armed troops. That night the cold was merciless but fortunately we found a fire still blazing brightly and we had enough fuel to keep it going.

At around eleven on the following morning, just as we were about to enter Oszmiana, I witnessed and, indeed, took part in, the ambush and seizure of a food convoy by a starving mob. The convoy was under the command of a young Mecklenburg[173] lieutenant, who did his best to keep us from his wagons but was outnumbered and forced to surrender. I managed to get my hands on a certain quantity of biscuits which helped keep us going and probably saved my life and those of my companions.

As we entered the town proper we once again followed my principle of getting as far away as possible from the mass and pushed on to the far side of town. We were less successful here than we had been at Smorgoni. Everywhere was full or more than full and we had to make do with an outhouse in a garden. We had to build our fire in the garden as there was no chimney in our shelter. We slept on a pile of manure lightly sprinkled with straw.

After crossing the Beresina we had numbered fifty and this had, at one point, risen to seventy. Now there were just twenty-nine of us, including eighteen cripples.

---

[173] Two companies of troops from Mecklenburg-Strelitz, originally part of I Corps, had been left behind in the summer to garrison Vilna as the main body advanced.

CHAPTER XLIX

FROM OSZMIANA TO VILNA

We rose and set off early the next day. But it proved impossible to get as far as our intended destination – Miednicki. We got about half-way there. The cold had never been so intense as it was now and I even began to see men freeze, literally, in their tracks. They would slow down, stagger, as though drunk; and then drop to the ground to rise no more. The road was covered by the corpses of men who had died this way. Many of the bodies had bare feet as shoes were often the first items to be pillaged. Some of the bodies had missing toes; the result of someone tearing off frozen shoes. Sometimes the pillagers did not even wait for their victims to utter their final breath before stripping them.

Next in order of preference were coats. We could not wear enough of them and some men wore three at a time. This was no guarantee of survival and many of these men died nonetheless. Perhaps this was because they were weighed down by coats and blankets and had their feet swathed in sheets which only served to impede their march. Many forgot to cover their noses and ears and these were exposed to the full rigours of the frost. In such cases death was not long in coming.

Miednicki was full of stragglers. We settled down in the open in a garden that was reasonably sheltered by hedges. We used these to feed our fires. It proved impossible to obtain food and if it had not been for my little supply of biscuits from the Oszmiana convoy, we would certainly have died from starvation.

That night (7–8 December) was one of the coldest. The thermometers plummeted and even reached thirty degrees below. We were close to the street and there was such a racket all night long that we could not get a wink of sleep. Some of my wounded companions almost went mad. One of them had not uttered a word since Smorgoni. I told him that we were only eight hours' march from Vilna and asked him if he thought we would make it. He shook his head and kept his eyes fixed on the flames.

Not long after we heard firing and screams of terror. One of my companions, a robust sergeant of the 2nd Regiment of the Vistula called Wasilenka, set off to investigate. We had thought, initially, that it was a false alarm, just as on so many other occasions. But we found out that some cossacks had actually broken into the town and had killed or carried off many of the stragglers.

As we rested here the great mass of stragglers caught up and passed us by and we now found ourselves close to the rearguard.

Wasilenka, a good man, brought back some potatoes he had dug up. 'There is food here if you look for it, but everyone is so demoralised that they are good for nothing,' he said. He also found out, from a reliable source, that the Emperor had indeed abandoned the army to its fate. This led to much consternation and malicious rumour.[174]

We, and many others, set off before dawn. The sky was again suspiciously clear and taunted us with its serenity. The sun was a ball of fire, and yet gave off no heat, and shone through a kind of mist of icicles. These felt like tiny needles, pricking our eyes. Houses, trees, fields were submerged under a blanket of snow.

The march had aggravated my wound and I was in considerable pain and had blisters from constant recourse to crutches.

The footsteps of those who had gone before, hounded by the Russians and their ally the cold, had been covered over by snow and the silence was only broken by the moaning and desperate pleas of those about to succumb to their final agonies. Men died here who might have lived but for lacking one more day of courage.

At about three in the afternoon we at long last caught sight of Vilna. But we found that we could not enter the city proper as the gates were guarded and only troops in formation were allowed to pass through. True, the stores at Orscha and Smolensk had been pillaged but surely the immense quantity of stores at Vilna could have borne such pillage and come off comparatively unscathed. In different circumstances, it might have been a wise precaution; now, on 8 December, it smacked of injustice and cruelty.[175]

Luckily we knew the area well enough to find a hole in the fence, and instead of joining in the throng – a throng which had already claimed

---

[174] Napoleon left the army on 5 December to return to Paris to begin the task of organising a new army and overhauling his government in the wake of the Malet conspiracy.
[175] Roch-Godart, governor of Vilna, and Hogendorp, governor of Lithuania, were completely taken by surprise by the sudden appearance of the wreck of the army. The first stragglers only entered Vilna on the afternoon of 8 December. The order that only troops in formation would be given supplies was not designed to cope with a disaster on this scale.

victims – we slipped around the pressing mass and in about half-an-hour found ourselves inside the town.

Even so, progress was difficult. The streets were full of soldiers, both unarmed and armed, and baggage. Finding lodgings was next to impossible, but I remembered a relative of our colonel who had shown much hospitality when we first passed through the town, and sought him out. I was glad I did so, as our colonel had apparently had the same idea along with some more of my fellow officers such as Gordon, who had been wounded fighting his way into Teruel in 1810 – an episode I have already alluded to.

I had not managed to change my linen for the last eleven days, nor had I changed my clothes or slept in a bed, and now I put some of these things to rights.

Washed, shaved and fortified by some glasses of hot ginger beer, there being no coffee, I slept a deep, deep sleep until dawn and awoke, as they say, a new man.

CHAPTER L

VILNA – PONARI – DESPAIR – CLOSING SCENES

There was a shock awaiting me. Our colonel was the last senior officer remaining to the Vistula Legion. He had carried off the regimental flag and had, since his arrival at Vilna, collected and rearmed some sixty soldiers. These had survived the regiment's destruction at the Beresina and had each been given a little money, issued by Berthier to the colonel for this express purpose.

However, on the evening of 9 December the enemy suddenly appeared and firing broke out. Panic gripped the city and the colonel went off to get orders from Murat. Napoleon had left the army in the hands of the person least capable of replacing him in such circumstances. The colonel found Murat in the Kovno suburb, deep in discussion with Berthier, the Viceroy and the other marshals. Murat told him, 'There is no way we can resist. We have to continue with the retreat. We'll put the army into motion. Try to reach the Niemen and then we'll see...'

This was grave news indeed for myself and the other wounded. Everyone made ready to depart. The colonel at first thought to leave the wounded at Vilna but we protested that this would be as good as sentencing us to death.

It was perhaps now, in this final phase of the retreat, that we ran the greatest risks.

We left Vilna in sledges and the night was calm. Never before have such scenes of confusion been illuminated by so beautiful a moon. It was as cold as ever. The road was almost blocked by a writhing mass of cannon, wagons, coaches, sledges, and armed and unarmed soldiers.

Suddenly this mass ground to a halt. The traffic had come up against the slippery and impassable slope of Ponari and vehicles could not progress any further. This was one of the saddest incidents in the entire campaign. In the confusion we had the idea of making off across open country to the left and working our way round the hill that way. Progress was slow, especially for myself and my fellow-officer, Gorzcynski, who had also been wounded in the battle of 4 October. We soon found that we had to get out and walk, abandoning the sledge. Our unwounded companions, Garlicki and Wandorf, took us onto their backs and carried us some distance. But this could not be kept up for long, and we had to make our way as best we could on foot.

We had despaired of making it before we finally caught sight of the main road. We had almost been exhausted by crossing streams, climbing hills and negotiating all the varied obstacles the countryside can produce. But our ordeal was not yet over!

It was just after dawn when we rejoined the confused column of fleeing men. Firing could be heard from Vilna. Suddenly, the cry of 'Cossacks!' went up. The crowd stampeded, seized by terror, and hurled itself forwards. Gorzcynski and I were separated from our companions in the crush. It transpired that this was a false alarm, raised by marauders keen to get their hands on the abandoned wagons.

We were borne along in the direction the crowd was taking and were knocked, trampled, crushed and punched at various times, until my friend finally turned to me and said that he had not the strength to go on.

We collapsed on a small mound which gave us a good view of the surrounding area. We now thought it was all over with us.

The main column seemed like a huge black snake, sliding its way through the snow. From the direction of Vilna, the sound of cannon still came to us. Soon the unarmed mass passed by and were followed by a small band of armed troops. Once they too had passed, my companion turned to me and said, 'Well, I am not going one step further, here I stay'.

'Well, we'll see what happens,' I said, 'but we must not separate.'

I was depressed that we had made so much effort and made so little progress. I contemplated turning back to Vilna and seeing what fate had in store for us there.

The last of the procession had filed by and looked at us in the same way we had studied so many other unfortunates – indifferently. We were alone at the mercy of the Russians and of the cold, which we could feel gnawing at our bones. Suddenly, as we still gazed at Vilna, our attention was caught by a black spot which grew larger and larger. Soon we could make out two horses. 'Cossacks!' said Gorzcynski, and I thought the same.

However, what we took to be cavalry turned out to be two horses harnessed to a sledge. Then I was suddenly overcome when I saw that the sledge was being driven by Jedrzyewski, the soldier from my own company whom I had punished in Moscow but who, despite this, was still fond of me.

As soon as he caught sight of us, he reined in and shouted: 'Good God! What are you doing here? Get on board quick! The cossacks will be here in ten minutes!' He helped us on and drove the horses on with a crack of the whip.

We soon came up to the main column, through which our driver dextrously negotiated his way. We were weeping for joy in the back and my friend turned to me and said, 'God works in mysterious ways!'

That scoundrel, Jedrzyewski, had done wonderfully well, for not only had he saved us, but he had even managed to lay his hands on some food. He revived us with some bread and some brandy.

At around eleven in the morning, we swept into Irvie, which was full of stragglers. 'We should not linger here,' said our saviour, 'they'll make off with our horses in no time and then where will we be. We'll only be safe with our regiment.'

On the far side of the next village we came to we had the tremendous good fortune of finding our regiment camped around a house, and this time I realised we had been well and truly saved!

Appendices

APPENDIX A

Ambushed by Spanish Guerrillas, May 1810

An Account by Captain Mrozinski
of the 1st Regiment of the Vistula Legion

We had hardly left Gratallops when we came under musketry fire. Soon, bands of armed men could be seen gathering on the slopes to our right and their fire enfiladed the road along which we would have to pass. It became apparent that we would have to flush them out of their position and to this effect we clambered up the slope and charged the enemy. However, when we reached the plateau, we realised that these troops had been but the vanguard of a detachment of from five to six hundred men issuing out of Povoleda. These troops were already in range. Some of our men deployed and took up a defensive position to cover the retreat of the rest. The enemy advanced to the attack; our troops pushed them back with the bayonet whilst the rest clambered up the mountain.

The enemy, confident of success with overwhelming numbers, pressed its attacks without interruption. They sent some troops out on our right to harry us whilst sending their main body against our left. They attacked three times in quick succession and each time were bravely repulsed. Even so, the Spanish sharpshooters and armed peasants had pretty much surrounded us and we had suffered more than seventy casualties – that is, more than half of our force. Captain Dulceron, of the 115th Line, and Lieutenant Barthaire of the same regiment, and Lieutenant Suchodolski of the 1st Regiment of the Vistula Legion, were amongst the wounded. We thought Lieutenant Leclerc of the 1st Regiment of the Vistula Legion had been killed, but we later learnt that he had advanced too far on the right, got cut off, wounded and made prisoner.

Night put an end to the combat. It would have been impossible to continue the retreat on account of having no means to transport the wounded. Our mules had been lost even before we left the main road. In addition all the roads to Mora had been cut by the guerrillas, who were increasing in numbers by the minute.

I do not know the name of the guerrilla chief whose bands we fought; but I have subsequently heard that *el Cura de la Palma* was in their ranks and Colonel Villamil was their commander.

That night we sheltered in a hermitage; we made loopholes in the walls with our bayonets and we barricaded the doors. Our men were utterly exhausted. There was a little rainwater in a trough but this was not even sufficient for the wounded. I had to ration it strictly to guard this limited resource. The officers, most of whom were wounded, took charge of the different parts of the hermitage.

Having seen to our defence, we thought of how we might alert the garrison at Mora as to our plight. In our ranks were five Spanish soldiers, in King Joseph's service, from the company based at Mora. I had hoped one of these men would have volunteered to go. I told them, 'Should we be obliged to surrender we French and Poles would become prisoners of war. You, on the other hand, can only expect a cruel death. You know the region and the language and it will be easy for you to get to Mora; you have to do it – for your own sakes' at least.' They replied that it would be impossible to get through the guerrillas' lines and that if fate decreed they were to be massacred they would prefer that to be later rather than sooner. Any possibility of getting word to Kousinowski seemed to be rapidly disappearing. The locals we had taken hostage from Gratallops had all escaped during the battle except for three who we had managed to drag with us to the hermitage. I had them kneel before the altar and had them swear on the cross that they would go to Mora. I thought that my little talk on the enormity of the crime of perjury had touched their religious sentiments not a little, and so I sent them off at half-hour intervals, in three separate directions. Not one of them reached Mora.

The Spanish troops had been considerably augmented during the night: fifty cavalry were based on the Mora road; their infantry surrounded us; their posts were pushed forward and reached almost to our walls. In order to preserve ammunition I had forbidden firing except in the case of an attack. We turned away an emissary who had ridden forward with a trumpet. The Spanish had been busy gathering wood and straw and were now stacking it up against the walls of the hermitage with the intention of burning us all to cinders. We sent a few men up onto the roof to fire at the enemy – they wounded a few of the guerrillas and drove the rest off. Two more emissaries came forward and were turned away in the same style.

That evening, we were desperate and we doubted that we would ever be relieved. Help should have arrived that morning. We thought hard about cutting our way through the enemy lines that night and taking with us those wounded who were able to keep up. Suddenly, however, we caught sight of a body of troops marching down the Mora road – it was Colonel Dupeyroux with the 115th Line. The Spanish fell back in retreat before them and our troops leapt over the walls to give chase. The 115th greeted us with extreme joy; the soldiers offered us wine and food and the officers gave us their horses and mules to carry our wounded. Colonel Dupeyroux accompanied us to Falcet.

The evening before, the commandant at Falcet had heard firing from the direction of Gratallops and had despatched a spy. He had come back and given a full report into what had happened. The commandant sent word to Kousinowski at Mora. As it happened, the 115th were just then passing through Mora en route for Reuss. Kousinowski informed Dupeyroux of our situation. Dupeyroux, without wasting any time, set off for Gratallops. As all was quiet and the sound of firing had died away, he thought things were all over with us and it was only when he stumbled upon the Spanish astride the Mora road that he realised we were still defending ourselves – although by then almost out of ammunition.

Captain Mrozinski
1st Regiment of the Vistula Legion

APPENDIX B

Table of Strengths of the
Vistula Legion Regiments, 1808–13

	1st Regiment	2nd Regiment	3rd Regiment
1 August 1808	1,391	1,236	1,324
15 May 1809	1,039	880	964
1 August 1809	1,073	861	1,086
1 December 1809	1,520	1,463	1,561
15 March 1810	1,641	1,824	1,637
14 May 1810	1,527	1,586	1,802
1 August 1810	1,621	1,604	1,840
27 June 1811	2,187	1,975	2,025
1 October 1811	1,863	1,129	1,750
15 July 1812	1,338	1,284	1,272
15 August 1812	1,068	912	1,018
30 January 1813	152	151	154
15 April 1813	187	154	175

APPENDIX C

Officer Casualties of the Vistula Legion, 1808–14

Based on Martinien's list, expanded, corrected and revised
from Polish sources.

FIRST SIEGE OF SARAGOSSA,
15 JUNE – 14 AUGUST 1808
Killed
Hemmerich, Captain,
  1st Regiment. 15 July.
Zawadski, Lieutenant,
  1st Regiment. 1 August.
Szott, Major,
  3rd Regiment. 2 July.
Geite, Lieutenant,
  3rd Regiment. 1 August.
Suraski, Lieutenant,
  1st Lancers. 15 June.
Wounded
Chlopicki, Colonel,
  1st Regiment. 4 August.
Burakouski, Captain,
  1st Regiment. 4 August.
Godlewski, Captain,
  1st Regiment. 4 August.
Karnowski, Captain,
  1st Regiment. 5 August.
Wysocki, Captain,
  1st Regiment. 4 August.
Borakowski, Lieutenant,
  1st Regiment. 4 August.
Borowski, Lieutenant, 1st
  Regiment. 5 August.

Kocurko, Lieutenant,
  1st Regiment. 4 August.
Wagrowski, Lieutenant,
  1st Regiment. 1 July.
Kilisz, Surgeon,
  1st Regiment. 4 August.
Bielenski, Major,
  2nd Regiment. 4 August.
Regulski, Major,
  2nd Regiment. 4 August.
Gariski, Captain,
  2nd Regiment. 5 August.
Zawitowski, Captain,
  2nd Regiment. 4 August.
Bobieski, Lieutenant,
  2nd Regiment. 4 August.
Dluski, Lieutenant,
  2nd Regiment. 5 August.
Lewiecki, Lieutenant,
  2nd Regiment. 5 August.
Surmacki, Lieutenant,
  2nd Regiment. 4 August.
Osieski, Captain,
  3rd Regiment. 5 August.
Ciesliski, Lieutenant,
  3rd Regiment. 4 August.
Krajewski, Lieutenant,
  3rd Regiment. 4 August.

Lipinski, Lieutenant,
3rd Regiment. 5 August.
Ponkowski, Lieutenant,
3rd Regiment. 5 August.
Skorupski, Lieutenant,
3rd Regiment. 4 August.
Zubricki, Lieutenant,
3rd Regiment. 5 August.
Konopka, Colonel,
1st Lancers. 4 August.
Tanski, Captain,
1st Lancers. 4 August.
Blonski, Lieutenant,
1st Lancers. 4 August.
Darowski, Lieutenant,
1st Lancers. 4 August.
Leduchowski, Lieutenant,
1st Lancers. 4 August.

TUDELA, 23 NOVEMBER 1808
Wounded
Kousinowski, Colonel,
2nd Regiment.
Mazdryzykowski, Captain,
2nd Regiment.
Paciorkowski, Lieutenant,
2nd Regiment.
Skarzynski, Captain,
1st Lancers.

**SECOND SIEGE OF SARAGOSSA,
12 DECEMBER 1808 –
20 FEBRUARY 1809**
Killed
Egersdorf, Captain,
1st Regiment. Wounded
23 February, died 25 February.
Karwozewski, Captain,
1st Regiment. Wounded
27 January, died 1 February.
Kielczewski, Captain,
1st Regiment. Wounded

2 February, died 30 June.
Nagrodski, Captain,
1st Regiment. 27 January.
Wronski, Captain,
1st Regiment. 15 December.
Dabkowski, Lieutenant,
1st Regiment. Wounded
2 February, died 30 June.
Skaradowski, Lieutenant,
1st Regiment. 5 January.
Slawoszewski, Lieutenant,
1st Regiment. Wounded
27 January, died 1 February.
Matkowski, Captain,
2nd Regiment. Wounded
20 February, died 1 April.
Bielenski, Major,
3rd Regiment. 6 February.
Wiszniewski, Lieutenant,
3rd Regiment. Wounded
20 February, died 28 February
Wounded
Fialkowski, Captain,
1st Regiment. 10 February.
Murzinowski, Lieutenant,
1st Regiment. 27 January.
Kilisz, Surgeon,
1st Regiment. 27 January.
Beyer, Major,
2nd Regiment. 27 January.
Bobieski, Lieutenant,
2nd Regiment. 27 January.
Malinowski, Lieutenant,
2nd Regiment. 27 January.
Ratkowski, Lieutenant,
2nd Regiment. 27 January.
Ciwinski, Lieutenant,
3rd Regiment. 20 February.
Glinski, Lieutenant,
3rd Regiment. 21 February.
Karwoski, Lieutenant,
3rd Regiment. 21 February.

Krajewski, Lieutenant,
  3rd Regiment. 20 February.
Zinliewicz, Lieutenant,
  3rd Regiment. 10 January.

In addition a number of officers
are mentioned as killed or
wounded at Saragossa by Fieffé,
but are not listed by Martinien:

Bachans, Budziatowski, Dembicki,
  Dostaniak, Dragowski,
  Holubowicz, Ivan, Jakowiaz,
  Kardasziewski, Kawiatak,
  Koszciesza, Kubazewski,
  Macinski, Murzynowski,
  Nowadski, Nowarski, Perlik,
  Rykowski, Suchodolski,
  Sukowiez, Szinarenko, Szitak,
  Waykow, Zadezak.

PASSAGE OF THE CINCA,
16–19 MAY 1809
Wounded
Laszewski, Captain,
  2nd Regiment. 19 May.

ALCAÑIZ, 23 MAY 1809
Wounded
Fondzielski, Major,
  1st Regiment.
Czarneck, Lieutenant,
  1st Regiment.
Wezyk, Captain,
  3rd Regiment.
Karwoski, Lieutenant,
  3rd Regiment.
Zubricki, Lieutenant,
  3rd Regiment.

MARIA, 15 JUNE 1809
Wounded
Kocurko, Lieutenant,
  1st Regiment.

BELCHITE, 18 JUNE 1809
Wounded
Smargewski, Lieutenant,
  1st Regiment.

SIEGE OF LERIDA,
29 APRIL – 13 MAY 1810
Killed
Mazewski, Captain,
  3rd Regiment. 7 May.

SIEGE OF TORTOSA,
16 DECEMBER 1810 –
2 JANUARY 1811
Killed
Boll, Captain,
  2nd Regiment. 18 July.
Solnicki, Captain,
  2nd Regiment. 4 August.
Falkouski, Lieutenant,
  2nd Regiment. 13 July.
Rzempulowski, Lieutenant,
  2nd Regiment. Wounded
  4 August, died 30 December.
Sierakowski, Lieutenant,
  3rd Regiment. 8 November.
Sobieski, Lieutenant,
  3rd Regiment. 9 July.
Wounded
Mazdrzykowski, Captain,
  2nd Regiment. 3 August.

FUENTE SANDE,
12 NOVEMBER 1810
Killed
Zarski, Lieutenant,
  1st Regiment.

Wounded
Plater, Lieutenant,
  1st Regiment.
Ustricki, Lieutenant,
  1st Regiment.

SIEGE OF TARRAGONA, 5 MAY – 29 JUNE 1811
Killed
Rezenski, Lieutenant,
  3rd Regiment. 5 May.
Wounded
Dombrowski, Captain,
  1st Regiment. 16 June.

SAGUNTO, 25 OCTOBER 1811
Wounded
Mieroslawski, Major,
  1st Regiment.
Loski, Lieutenant,
  1st Regiment.
Orda, Lieutenant,
  1st Regiment

SIEGE OF VALENCIA, 3 NOVEMBER 1811 – 8 JANUARY 1812
Killed
Isajewicz, Lieutenant,
  1st Regiment. 7 January.
Karwoski, Lieutenant,
  3rd Regiment. Wounded
  7 January, died 10 January.
Wounded
Dombrowski, Captain,
  1st Regiment. 4 January.
Dabrowski, Lieutenant,
  1st Regiment. 7 January.
Zilenkowicz, Lieutenant,
  2nd Regiment. 2 January.

IN SPAIN, AGAINST GUERRILLAS
Killed
Stutmann, Lieutenant,
  1st Regiment. 30 June 1809
  (in Aragon).
Winski, Lieutenant,
  1st Regiment. 1 July 1809
  (near Pamplona).
Kolecki, Lieutenant,
  2nd Regiment. 26 September
  1810 (at Orpisa).
Laskaris, Captain,
  3rd Regiment. 2 September
  1808 (near Saragossa).
Berger, Lieutenant,
  3rd Regiment. 18 November
  1810 (killed by 'brigands').
Oranowski, Lieutenant,
  3rd Regiment. 6 November 1811
  (near Valencia).
Warzewski, Lieutenant,
  3rd Regiment. 15 May 1812
  (near Pamplona).
Wounded
Bialobzycki, Captain,
  1st Regiment. 10 March 1810
  (near Alventosa).
Cieslicki, Lieutenant,
  1st Regiment. 21 December
  1809 (in Navarre).
Leclerc, Lieutenant,
  1st Regiment. 18 May 1811
  (Gratallops).
Suchodolski, Lieutenant,
  1st Regiment. 18 May 1811
  (Gratallops).
Suchodolski, Lieutenant,
  1st Regiment. 20 May 1811
  (Falcet).
Weys, Lieutenant,
  1st Regiment. 30 March 1810
  (near Alcaniz).

Zawitowski, Captain,
2nd Regiment. 2 December
1810 (in Navarre).
Brandt, Lieutenant,
2nd Regiment. 16 February
1810 (at Villel).
Gordon, Lieutenant,
2nd Regiment. 8 March 1810
(at Teruel).
Krakowski, Lieutenant,
2nd Regiment. 27 July 1809
(near Pamplona).
Milewski, Lieutenant,
2nd Regiment. 11 February
1811 (at Azuara).
Glinski, Lieutenant,
3rd Regiment. 30 June 1809
(near Saragossa).
Komorek, Lieutenant,
3rd Regiment. 17 January 1810
(on patrol in Aragon).
Lipinski, Lieutenant,
3rd Regiment. 5 May 1810
(at Tarracon).
Nowicki, Lieutenant,
3rd Regiment. 30 April 1809
(in Aragon).
Rzewuski, Lieutenant,
3rd Regiment. 15 May 1810
(at Aiguillon).
Walowicz, Lieutenant,
3rd Regiment. 16 June 1809
(at Salmonia).
Walowicz, Lieutenant,
3rd Regiment. 20 January 1810
(at Almunia).
Walowicz, Lieutenant,
3rd Regiment. 3 June 1810
(at Epila).

MOJAISK, 10 SEPTEMBER 1812
Killed
Skoryski, Lieutenant,
2nd Regiment.
Wounded
Zimmer, Captain,
1st Regiment.

WORONOVO (2–4 OCTOBER 1812) AND WINKOVO (18 OCTOBER 1812)
Killed
Murzinowski, Captain,
1st Regiment. 4 October.
Kraiewski, Lieutenant,
1st Regiment. 4 October.
Zeilinger, Surgeon,
1st Regiment. 2 October.
Degourdin, Lieutenant,
2nd Regiment. 18 October.
Jablonski, Lieutenant,
2nd Regiment. 18 October.
Wounded
Brandt, Captain,
2nd Regiment. 4 October.
Gorzcynski, Captain,
2nd Regiment. 4 October.
Kozlowski, Captain,
2nd Regiment. 4 October.
Rechowicz, Captain,
2nd Regiment. 4 October.
Leveque, Lieutenant,
2nd Regiment. 18 October.

KRASNOI, 17–18 NOVEMBER 1812
Killed
Fondzielski, Colonel,
3rd Regiment. Wounded,
died 5 February 1813.
Lebrun, Captain,
3rd Regiment.

Krajewski, Lieutenant,
3rd Regiment.
Kuezewski, Lieutenant,
3rd Regiment. Wounded,
died 7 January 1813.
Skorapski, Lieutenant,
3rd Regiment.
Wounded
Leszeyenski, Captain,
3rd Regiment.
Luczycki, Captain,
3rd Regiment.
Pagoroski, Captain,
3rd Regiment.
Wezyk, Captain,
3rd Regiment.
Ciszewski, Lieutenant,
3rd Regiment.
Dombrowski, Lieutenant,
3rd Regiment.
Rutkowski, Lieutenant,
3rd Regiment.
Serocynski, Lieutenant,
3rd Regiment.
Tysiwiczz, Lieutenant,
3rd Regiment.
Walowicz, Lieutenant,
3rd Regiment.
Witkowski, Lieutenant,
3rd Regiment.
Geiger, Surgeon,
3rd Regiment.

BERESINA, 28 NOVEMBER 1812
Killed
Kousinowski, Colonel,
1st Regiment. Wounded,
then 'disappeared'.
Loski, Captain,
1st Regiment.
Kuniecki, Lieutenant,
1st Regiment.

Dobrzyki, Captain,
2nd Regiment.
Lichnowski, Captain,
2nd Regiment.
Rakowski, Captain,
2nd Regiment.
Starwolski, Captain,
2nd Regiment.
Zignowski, Captain,
2nd Regiment.
Ratkowski, Lieutenant,
2nd Regiment.
Kitz, Surgeon,
3rd Regiment.
Wounded
Mieroslawski, Major,
1st Regiment.
Bardzinski, Captain,
1st Regiment.
Czarnecki, Captain,
1st Regiment.
Kozlowski, Captain,
1st Regiment.
Plater, Captain,
1st Regiment.
Varinot, Captain,
1st Regiment.
Zmierski, Captain,
1st Regiment.
Zymer, Captain,
1st Regiment.
Borakowski, Lieutenant,
1st Regiment.
Czarnek, Lieutenant,
1st Regiment.
Derengowski, Lieutenant,
1st Regiment.
Etchandy, Lieutenant,
1st Regiment.
Gourmetz, Lieutenant,
1st Regiment.
Kluczewski, Lieutenant,

1st Regiment.
Koczurek, Lieutenant (standard-
bearer), 1st Regiment.
Kopyczinski, Lieutenant,
1st Regiment.
Merle, Lieutenant,
1st Regiment.
Niechcielski, Lieutenant,
1st Regiment.
Piontkowski, Lieutenant,
1st Regiment.
Ragoski, Lieutenant,
1st Regiment.
Sliwinski, Lieutenant,
1st Regiment.
Ziemecki, Lieutenant,
1st Regiment.
Zolders, Surgeon,
1st Regiment.
Regulski, Major,
2nd Regiment.
Kozlowski, Captain,
2nd Regiment.
Rechowicz, Captain,
2nd Regiment.
Szelinski, Captain,
2nd Regiment.
Bierynski, Lieutenant,
2nd Regiment.
Dobrzynski, Lieutenant,
2nd Regiment.
Karpiz, Lieutenant,
2nd Regiment.
Madalinski, Lieutenant,
2nd Regiment.
Marzewski, Lieutenant,
2nd Regiment.
McAuliff, Lieutenant,
2nd Regiment.
Pomarnicki, Lieutenant,
2nd Regiment.
Radziszewski, Lieutenant,

2nd Regiment.
Robert, Lieutenant,
2nd Regiment.
Wieckowski, Lieutenant,
2nd Regiment.
Zorawski, Lieutenant,
2nd Regiment.
Broszkowski, Major,
3rd Regiment.

NEAR VILNA, DECEMBER 1812
Killed
Slarowslski, Captain,
2nd Regiment. Wounded 12
December, died 7 January 1813.
Wounded
Fondrouge, Lieutenant,
1st Regiment. 10 December.
Voznicki, Lieutenant,
1st Regiment. 11 December.
Pomarnicki, Lieutenant,
2nd Regiment. 10 December.
Glaszer, Lieutenant,
3rd Regiment. 9 December.
Kulezycki, Lieutenant,
3rd Regiment. 9 December.
Radzibor, Lieutenant,
3rd Regiment. 9 December.
Seroczewski, Lieutenant,
3rd Regiment. 9 December.
Strzalkowski, Lieutenant,
3rd Regiment. 3 December.

Casualties of the Vistula Regiment, 1813–1814

FREYBERG, 18 SEPTEMBER 1813
Killed
Paprocki, Captain.

Wounded
Rybinski, Major.
Braun, Lieutenant.

LEIPZIG, 18–19 OCTOBER 1813
Killed
Malezewski, Colonel.
Wounded
Krasicki, Major.
Regulski, Major.
Brandt, Captain.
Kimiowski, Captain.
Palinski, Captain.
Pogaiski, Captain.
Svoboda, Captain.
Celner, Lieutenant.
Kannowski, Lieutenant.
Karwoski, Lieutenant.
Kondracki, Lieutenant.
Mozecko, Lieutenant.
Niewodowski, Lieutenant.
Rogola, Lieutenant.
Vallesbrun, Lieutenant.
Wewiorowski, Lieutenant.

SOISSONS, MARCH 1814
Killed
N., Captain.
Wounded
Kosinski, Colonel.
Wawrowski, Captain.
N., Lieutenant.
N., Lieutenant.

ARCIS-SUR-AUBE, 20 MARCH 1814
Killed
Swierczakiewicz, Lieutenant.
  Wounded, died 19 April.
Wounded
Koslowski, Captain.

SKIRMISHES IN 1814
Killed
Zelitz, Lieutenant.
  Wounded 24 March,
  died 16 April.

BIBLIOGRAPHY

Alexander, Don. *Rod of Iron: French Counter-Insurgency Policy in Aragon during the Peninsular War*. Wilmington, Scholarly Resources, 1985.

Belmas, Jacques Vital. *Journaux des siéges faits ou soutenus par les Français dans la péninsule, de 1807 à 1814*. Paris, Firmin-Didot, 1836–7, 4 vols and atlas. (Volume II for Saragossa.)

Bigarré, General Auguste Julien. *Mémoires du général Bigarré, aide de camp du roi Joseph 1775–1813*. Paris, Kolb, 1893.

Brandt, Heinrich von. *The Two Minas and the Spanish Guerrillas*. 'Translated by a General Officer', London, J. Murray, 1825.

Britten Austin, Paul. *1812: The March on Moscow*. London, Greenhill Books, 1993.
— *1812: Napoleon in Moscow*. London, Greenhill Books,1995.
— *1812: The Great Retreat*. London, Greenhill Books, 1996.

Brett-James, Antony. *1812: Eyewitness Accounts of Napoleon's Defeat in Russia*. London, Macmillan, 1966.

Caulaincourt, Armand de. *Mémoires du général Caulaincourt*. Paris, Plon, 1933, 3 vols.

Chelminski, Jan, and Malibran, A. *L'Armée du Duchie du Varsovie*. Paris, Leroy, 1913.

Chlapowski, Désiré. *Mémoires sur les guerres de Napoleon, 1806–1813*. Paris, Plan-Nourrit, 1908. (Translated as *Memoirs of a Polish Lancer*. Chicago, Emperor's Press, 1992.)

Chodzko, Leonard: *Histoire des Légions Polonaises en Italie*. Paris, Barbezat, 1829.

Coignet, Jean-Roch. *The Note-Books of Captain Coignet*. London, Peter Davis 1928. (Reprinted London, Greenhill Books, 1998.)

Duffy, Christopher. *Borodino and the War of 1812*. London, Seely, 1972.

Fieffé, Eugene. *Histoire des troupes étrangères au service de France depuis leur origine jusqu'a nos jours, et de tous les régiments levés dans les pays conquis sous la Première République et l'Empire*. Paris, Dumaine, 1854.

Foy, Maximilien Sébastien. *Histoire de la guerre de la Péninsule*. Paris, Baudouin, 1827, 4 vols.

Gonneville, Aymar Olivier le Harivel de. *Recollections of Colonel Gonneville*. London, Hurst and Blackett, 1876. (Reprinted Newcastle, Worley Publications, 1995.)

Grabowski, Josef. *Mémoires Militaires*. Paris, Plan-Nourrit, 1907.

Johnston, Robert. *Travels Through the Russian Empire and Country of Poland*. London, J. Murray, 1815.

Lejeune, Baron Louis François. *Mémoires du General Lejeune*. Paris, Firmin-Didot, 1896, 2 vols. (Translated as *The Memoirs of Baron Lejeune*, London, Longmans, Green, 1897.)
— *Siéges de Saragosse*. Paris, Firmin-Didot, 1840.

Mina, Don Francisco Espoz y. *A Short Extract from the Life of General Mina*. London, Taylor and Hessey, 1825.

Oman, Sir Charles. *History of the Peninsular War*. Oxford, 1902–30, 7 vols. (Reprinted London, Greenhill Books, 1995–97.)

Pachonski, Paul, and Wilson, Reuel. *Poland's Caribbean Tragedy: A Study of Polish Legions in the Haitian War of Independence, 1802–3*. New York, Boulder, 1986.

Palafox y Melzi, José. *Autobiografia*. Madrid, Taurus, 1966.

Przyborowski, Walery. *Polacy W Hiszpanii*. Warsaw, Gebethner i Wolff, 1888.

Rogniat, General Joseph. *Relations des siéges de Saragosse et de Tortose par les Français, dans la Dernière Guerre d'Espagne*. Paris, Magimel, 1814.

Rudorff, Raymond. *War to the Death: The Sieges of Saragossa, 1808–1809*. London, Hamish Hamilton, 1974.

Senén de Coñtreras, Juan. *Relation of the Siege of Tarragona, and the Storming and Capture of that City by the French in June, 1811*. London, Booth, 1813.

Six, Georges. *Les Généraux de la Révolution et de l'Empire*. Paris, Bordas, 1947.

Smith, Digby. *The Greenhill Napoleonic Wars Data Book*. London, Greenhill Books, 1998.

Suchet, Marshal Louis Gabriel. *Mémoires du Marechal Suchet, Duc d'Albufera, sur ses Campagnes en Espagne, depuis 1808 jusqu'en 1814*. Paris, Bossange, 1828, 2 vols and atlas.

Szymanowski, General Josef. *Mémoires du General Szymanowski*. Paris, Charles-Lavauzelle, 1900.

Tone, John L. *The Fatal Knot: The Guerrilla War in Navarre and the Defeat of Napoleon*. Chapel Hill, University of North Carolina Press, 1994.

Turno, General Charles. *Souvenirs d'un officier polonais*. Paris, Revue des Etudes Napoleoniennes 33, 1931.

Vaughan, Charles Richard. *Narrative of the Siege of Zaragoza*. London, Ridgway, 1809.

Zalusky, Joseph-Henri. *Souvenirs du général comte Zalusky*. Paris, Carnet de la Sabretache, 1897. (Reprinted Paris, Librairie Teissedre, 1998.)

INDEX